TOP FEDERAL TAX ISSUES FOR 2012
CPE COURSE

CCH Editorial Staff Publication

a Wolters Kluwer business

Contributors

Technical Reviewer...................................... George G. Jones, J.D., LL.M
Contributing Editors....................................Anne E. Bowker, JD, LL.M
Brant Goldwyn, J.D.
Adam R. Levine, J.D., LL.M
Jennifer J. Rodibaugh, J.D.
Leo V. Roinila, JD, LL.M
Raymond G. Suelzer Jr., J.D., LL.M
Kenneth L. Swanson, J.D., LL.M
George L. Yaksick, Jr., J.D.
Production Coordinator .... Gabriel E. Santana
Design/Layout...Laila Gaidulis
Production ....Lynn J. Brown

This publication is designed to provide accurate and authoritative information in regard to the subject matter covered. It is sold with the understanding that the publisher is not engaged in rendering legal, accounting, or other professional service. If legal advice or other expert assistance is required, the services of a competent professional person should be sought.

ISBN 978-0-8080-2739-3

No claim is made to original government works; however, within this Product or Publication, the following are subject to CCH's copyright: (1) the gathering, compilation, and arrangement of such government materials; (2) the magnetic translation and digital conversion of data, if applicable; (3) the historical, statutory and other notes and references; and (4) the commentary and other materials.

MIX
Paper from
responsible sources
FSC® C101537

TOP FEDERAL TAX ISSUES FOR 2012 CPE COURSE

Introduction

Each year, a handful of tax issues typically require special attention by tax practitioners. The reasons vary, from a particularly complicated new provision in the Internal Revenue Code, to a planning technique opened up by a new regulation or ruling, or the availability of a significant tax benefit with a short window of opportunity. Sometimes a developing business need creates a new set of tax problems, or pressure exerted by Congress or the Administration puts more heat on some taxpayers while giving others more slack. All these share in creating a unique mix that in turn creates special opportunities and pitfalls in the coming year and beyond. The past year has seen more than its share of these developing issues.

CCH's *Top Federal Tax Issues for 2012 CPE Course* identifies those recent events that have developed into the current "hot" issues of the day. These tax issues have been selected as particularly relevant to tax practice in 2012. They have been selected not only because of their impact on return preparation during the 2011 tax season but also because of the important role they play in developing effective tax strategies for 2012 and beyond. Some issues are outgrowths of several years of developments; others have burst onto the tax scene unexpectedly. Among the latter are issues directly related to the recent economic downturn and tax legislation designed to assist in a recovery. Some have been emphasized in IRS publications and notices; others are just being noticed by the IRS.

This course is designed to help reassure the tax practitioner that he or she is not missing out on advising clients about a hot, new tax opportunity; or that a brewing controversy does not blindside their practice. In addition to issue identification, this course provides the basic information needed for the tax practitioner to implement a plan that addresses the particular opportunities and pitfalls presented by any one of those issues. Among the topics examined in the *Top Federal Tax Issues for 2012 CPE Course* are:

- New and Expiring Tax Provisions: Planning for Changing Rates, Deductions and Credits
- Health Care Reform and Closely Held Businesses
- Expensing and Bonus Depreciation: Dealing with Sunsets
- Information Reporting: Increasing Demands
- New IRS Requirements for Return Preparers
- Electronic Filing: Current Rules and Future Challenges
- Navigating IRS Collection: New Standards and Procedures
- Exempt Organizations: More Transparency, More Rules

Throughout the course you will find Study Questions to help you test your knowledge, and comments that are vital to understanding a particular strategy or idea. Answers to the Study Questions with feedback on both correct and incorrect responses are provided in a special section beginning on page 9.1.

To assist you in your later reference and research, a detailed topical index has been included for this course beginning on page 10.1.

This course is divided into three Modules. Take your time and review all course Modules. When you feel confident that you thoroughly understand the material, turn to the CPE Quizzer. Complete one, or all, Module Quizzers for continuing professional education credit. Further information is provided in the CPE Quizzer instructions on page 11.1.

October 2011

COURSE OBJECTIVES

This course was prepared to provide the participant with an overview of specific tax issues that impact 2011 tax return preparation and tax planning in 2012. These are the issues that "everyone is talking about;" each impacts a significant number of taxpayers in significant ways.

Upon course completion, you will be able to:

- Identify the legislation that enacted the tax incentives set to expire in 2011 and 2012;
- Prepare for the expiration of various tax breaks in 2011 and 2012;
- Identify the requirements for new and grandfathered health coverage plans;
- Describe the new taxes being imposed on higher-income taxpayers;
- Determine the basic rules for the small employer healthcare coverage tax credit;
- Identify the types of property that quality for bonus depreciation;
- Compute safe harbor luxury car depreciation on passenger cars eligible for a 100 percent rate;
- Differentiate similarities and differences between bonus depreciation and the Section 179 allowance;
- Understand the rationale behind Congress and the IRS' ongoing efforts to expand information reporting, both at home and abroad;
- Articulate the obligations placed upon many banks and other financial institutions by the payment card processing rules;
- Understand the mandatory Preparer Tax Identification Number (PTIN) rules;
- Understand the final Circular 230 Regulations;
- Identify which paid return preparers are exempt from competency testing and continuing education;
- Explain the IRS's e-file mandate;
- Describe the mandatory e-file requirements for tax return preparers and the consequences of not complying;
- Describe the methods and tools the IRS employs to collect unpaid taxes;
- Identify options that are available to taxpayers with outstanding tax liabilities;
- Identify and explain the various required elements to be contained in a written community health needs assessment; and
- Determine whether specific activities of credit unions constitute the conduct of unrelated business subject to tax.

CCH'S PLEDGE TO QUALITY

Thank you for choosing this CCH Continuing Education product. We will continue to produce high quality products that challenge your intellect and give you the best option for your Continuing Education requirements. Should you have a concern about this or any other CCH CPE product, please call our Customer Service Department at 1-800-248-3248.

NEW ONLINE GRADING gives you immediate 24/7 grading with instant results and no Express Grading Fee.

The **CCH Testing Center** website gives you and others in your firm easy, free access to CCH print courses and allows you to complete your CPE exams online for immediate results. Plus, the **My Courses** feature provides convenient storage for your CPE course certificates and completed exams.

Go to **CCHGroup.com/TestingCenter** to complete your Quizzer online.

One **complimentary copy** of this course is provided with certain CCH Federal Taxation publications. Additional copies of this course may be ordered for $39.00 each by calling 1-800-248-3248 (ask for product 0-4457-500).

TOP FEDERAL TAX ISSUES FOR 2012 CPE COURSE

Contents

MODULE 2: COMPLIANCE-DIRECTED CHANGES

4 Information Reporting: Increasing Demands

5 New IRS Requirements for Return Preparers

6 Electronic Filing: Current Rules and Future Challenges

MODULE 3: CHANGING CIRCUMSTANCES

7 Navigating IRS Collection: New Standards and Procedures

8 **Exempt Organizations: More Transparency, More Rules**

MODULE 1: LEGISLATION-DRIVEN CHANGES — CHAPTER 1

New and Expiring Tax Provisions: Planning for Changing Rates, Deductions and Credits

Taxes and uncertainty seem to go hand in glove no matter what the period or economic forecast. Although businesses and investors call for certainty in the tax law so they can plan for the long
term with a more predictable outcome, they are glad to accept tax breaks at anytime. Add to such a moving target the ability of Congress to raise or lower taxes retroactively to the start of a calendar year, or provide tax breaks or increases through a time-delayed or phased-in implementation, and unpredictability increases.

This chapter cannot provide the proverbial crystal ball in which the future of tax law may be seen; rather, it is designed to help lay out what provisions are due to expire under the tax code either at the end of 2011 or 2012. It also lays out the possibilities now being considered or soon up for debate in Washington with respect to extending or modifying some of them.

LEARNING OBJECTIVES

Upon completion of this chapter you will be able to:

- Identify the legislation that enacted the tax incentives set to expire in 2011 and 2012;
- Prepare for the expiration of various tax breaks in 2011 and 2012;
- Evaluate how the changes in tax credits will affect tax returns starting in 2012; and
- Analyze the current and future effects of health care reform on tax-payers' income and deductions.

INTRODUCTION

This chapter outlines several variables now in play: the sunsetting of the Bush tax cuts after 2012, the sunsetting of a variety of recent stimulus tax benefits—some in 2011 and others in 2012; the fate of the next round of extenders legislation now covering more than a dozen expiring provisions, and recent deficit-reduction recommendations that are likely to continue to shape the tax legislative landscape. With the review offered by this chapter, taxpayers can do some contingency planning that may prevent them from being completely blindsided over the next year or two.

EXPIRING PROVISIONS OF THE 2010 TAX RELIEF ACT

The *Tax Relief, Unemployment Insurance Reauthorization, and Job Creation Act of 2010* (2010 Tax Relief Act), signed into law on December 17, 2010, extended the tax benefits found in more than 400 Internal Revenue Code subsections created in the Bush-era *Economic Growth and Tax Relief Reconciliation Act of 2001* (EGTRRA) and *Jobs and Growth Tax Relief Reconciliation Act of 2003* (JGTRRA). In most cases, the 2010 Tax Relief Act extended the benefits for two years. More than 50 provisions, however (some of which are popular business preferences), are set to expire at the end of 2011. These provisions expiring at the end of 2011 were often—but not always—the result of a two-year extension that first ran retroactively back to January 1, 2010, before moving forward two years, through December 31, 2011.

Additional confusion may result from more than a dozen provisions that had been considered part of the everyday tax landscape but expired either in 2010 or earlier. Examples include the homebuyer credit, the 65 percent COBRA subsidy for health insurance, the exclusion of unemployment compensation from taxable income, the above-the-line alternative real estate tax deduction, the making work pay credit, and an enhanced startup deduction to name a few.

Finally, with December 31, 2012, approaching, tax planners must also take into account the possibility that at least a sizeable number of the remaining extended EGTRRA provisions will sunset as well.

Most notably among an extensive list of enhanced provisions sunsetting at the end of *2011* are:

- 100 percent bonus depreciation;
- Code Sec. 179 expensing;
- Small gain business stock exclusion;
- Higher exemption amounts for taxpayers subject to the AMT; and
- Numerous business tax "extenders."

Important provisions set to expire at the end of *2012,* unless Congress acts, include:

- Reversion of individual income tax rates to 2001 levels;
- Favorable tax rate on capital gains income;
- Availability of itemized deductions without the "Pease" limit;
- Preferential treatment of the estate tax ; and
- The increased phaseout range of the earned income credit.

Each of these sunsetting provisions, both for 2011 and for 2012, is discussed in this chapter, below.

STUDY QUESTIONS

---

1. Deductions and credits now expiring after either 2010 or 2011 for individual taxpayers include all of the following *except:*

a. Higher exemption caps for the alternative minimum tax

b. Itemized tax deductions available without the Pease limit

c. The exclusion of unemployment compensation from taxable income

---

EXPIRING AT THE END OF 2011

Individuals-Facing 2011 Expiring Provisions

For most individuals, the immediate impact of the 2010 Tax Relief Act was also a provision that lasts only one year and expires at the end of 2011: a reduction in the payroll tax. Nevertheless, other provisions important to individuals that sunset at the end of 2011 also were triggered by passage of the 2010 Tax Relief Act. Some, such as the higher alternative minimum tax exemption, are effective only for 2011; others, such as the option to itemize state and local sales taxes, extend for a two-year period that started on January 1, 2010, and ends after December 31, 2011.

Payroll Tax Cut

For the 2011 tax year only, Sec. 601 of the 2010 Tax Relief Act created a tax cut for more than 155 million workers by reducing the employee-share of the OASDI portion of Social Security taxes from 6.2 percent to 4.2 percent for wages earned up to the taxable wage base of $106,800. As scheduled, the payroll tax holiday period ends on December 31, 2011.

President Obama, however, recently proposed in his *American Jobs Act* a measure by which the employee share of OASDI taxes would fall from 6.2 percent to 3.1 percent for calendar year 2012 (known as the "payroll tax holiday period"). His proposals would also extend OASDI relief to employers for increasing the number of employees or hiring certain veterans and certain other individuals. The employee-side payroll tax cut proposed for 2012 places the GOP-controlled House in a quandary because many GOP lawmakers have pledged not to raise taxes. Allowing the 2011 employee-side payroll tax rate cut to expire would effectively raise taxes.

Alternative Minimum Tax Imposed on Individuals

The 2010 Tax Relief Act provided an AMT "patch" intended to prevent the AMT from encroaching on middle-income taxpayers by providing higher exemption amounts and other targeted relief for 2010 and 2011. Without this patch, which had expired at the end of 2009, an estimated 21 million additional households would have been subject to the AMT.

The 2010 Tax Relief Act increased the AMT exemption amounts for 2010 to $47,450 for individual taxpayers and $72,450 for married taxpayers filing jointly and surviving spouses. For 2011 the statutory amounts are, respectively $48,450 and $74,450. However, for the 2012 tax year and beyond, the exemption amounts will decrease to $33,750 for unmarried individuals and $45,000 for jointly filing married couples and surviving spouses, unless Congress acts again on an extension of higher exemption amounts.

Transit Benefits

Code Sec. 132(a) provides that qualified transport benefits may be excluded from a taxpayer's gross income. These benefits may be realized as a tax-free fringe benefit offered by employers or as pretax benefit when paid for by the employee. The 2009 Recovery Act provided for parity among employer-provided transit benefits, raising the monthly maximum exclusion for transit passes to $230 (the same amount excludable for parking) for March 2009 through the end of 2010. The 2010 Tax Relief Act extended this parity for one year, through December 31, 2011, after which time the maximum tax-free benefits for transit passes will be $120, adjusted for inflation. Those inflation-adjusted amounts for 2012 as projected will be $240 per month for qualified parking and $125 per month for transit passes and van pooling.

Mortgage Insurance Premiums

Under the tax code provisions through 2011, taxpayers may deduct certain premiums paid for qualified mortgage insurance during the tax year in connection with acquisition indebtedness on a qualified residence. Using that deduction, a taxpayer may itemize the cost of mortgage insurance on a qualified personal residence. The deduction is phased out ratably by 10 percent for each $1,000 by which the taxpayer's AGI exceeds $100,000. Thus, the deduction is unavailable for a taxpayer with an AGI in excess of $110,000. The 2010 Tax Relief Act extended the deduction through December 31, 2011, subject to some limitations, but no further.

Adoption Credit

The 2010 Tax Relief Act extended the adoption credit as specified under the original EGTRRA until December 31, 2012. However, the provisions of the June 2010 *Protection and Affordable Care Act,* which enhanced the adoption credit to $13,170 and made it refundable for the 2011 tax year, are not extended. The adoption credit available during the 2012 tax year, as adjusted for inflation, will therefore be $12,650.

STUDY QUESTIONS

---

2. The 2010 Tax Relief Act "patched" the alternative minimum tax exemption by:

  a. Raising the exemption for 2010 and again for 2011, but letting those amounts sunset for 2012

  b. Raising the exemption for 2010, leaving it unchanged for 2011, and lowering it in 2012

  c. Leaving the exemptions the same for 2010 and 2011, and increasing it for 2012

3. The adoption credit will change for 2012 by:

  a. Increasing by $550

  b. Decreasing by $520

  c. Being sunsetted after 2011

Individual Tax "Extenders"

The 2010 Tax Relief Act extended a number of tax breaks directed toward individuals that have been commonly called "extenders." All of the following extenders had been extended at least once before passage of the 2010 Tax Relief Act.

Deduction of state and local general sales taxes. The 2010 Tax Relief Act extended through December 31, 2011, the election to take an itemized deduction for state and local general sales taxes in lieu of the itemized deduction permitted for state and local income taxes.

Above-the-line deduction for qualified tuition and related expenses. The 2010 Tax Relief Act extended for the above-the-line tax deduction for qualified education expenses through December 31, 2011. The deduction is capped at $4,000 for individual taxpayers whose adjusted gross income is $65,000 or less and married joint filers whose income is no more than $130,000. For individual taxpayers whose AGI is between $65,000 and $80,000 and married joint filers whose AGI is between $130,000 and $160,000, the deduction is capped at $2,000.

Residential energy property credit. The 2010 Tax Relief Act extended with modifications the residential energy property credit under Code Section 25C for one year, with respect to qualifying property placed in service in 2011. Effective for property placed in service after December 31, 2010, an individual is entitled to a credit against tax in an amount equal to (subject to specified caps):

- 10 percent of the amount paid or incurred for qualified energy efficiency improvements (building envelope components) installed during the tax year, and
- The amount of residential energy property expenditures paid or incurred during the tax year.

The maximum credit allowable is $500 over the lifetime of the taxpayer. The $500 amount must be reduced by the aggregate amount of previously allowed credits the taxpayer received in 2006, 2007, 2009, and 2010 (the maximum aggregate credit for 2006 and 2007 was $500 and $1,500 for 2009 and 2010).

Further, the maximum amount of the residential energy property credit that may be allocated to exterior windows and skylights is $200. With regard to other residential energy property expenditures, the following credit dollar limitations apply to property placed in service in 2011:

- $50 for any advanced main air circulating fan;
- $150 for any qualified natural gas, propane, or oil furnace or hot water boiler; and
- $300 for any item of energy-efficient building property.

Classroom expenses. The 2010 Tax Relief Act extended for two years (through 2011) the $250 above-the-line tax deduction for teachers and other school professionals for expenses paid or incurred for books, supplies (other than nonathletic supplies for courses of instruction in health or physical education), computer equipment (including related software and service), other equipment, and supplementary materials used by the educator in the classroom. The $250 cap is limited to expenses incurred during the calendar tax year, irrespective of the period measured in a school year. Although the $250 maximum deduction was enacted in recognition of the out-of-pocket expenses incurred by many teachers, they must nevertheless substantiate their expenses and show that they were not reimbursed.

Extension of tax-free distributions from individual retirement plans for charitable purposes. The 2010 Tax Relief Act extended for two years (retroactively through 2011) the provision that permits tax-free distributions to charity from an individual retirement account (IRA) of up to $100,000 per taxpayer, per taxable year. This benefit is primarily directed toward retirees who no longer would otherwise itemize deductions, including charitable contributions. The 2010 Tax Relief Act also allows individuals making such charitable transfers during January of 2011 to elect to treat them as if made during 2010 instead of in 2011.

Extension of provision encouraging contributions of capital gain real property for conservation purposes. The 2010 Tax Relief Act extended for two years (through 2011) the increased contribution limits and carryforward period for contributions of appreciated real property (including partial interests in real property) for conservation purposes.

STUDY QUESTIONS

---

4. Which tax incentive for charitable contributions does **not** expire after 2011?

   a. Tax deductions for donations of noncash items to charity

   b. Longer carryforward periods and increased limits for contributing real property for conservation purposes

   c. Tax-free distributions from IRAs for charities

BUSINESSES FACING 2011 EXPIRING PROVISIONS

The 2010 Tax Relief Act carried forward, and in many cases enhanced, a handful of important tax provisions directed toward giving businesses certain immediate tax breaks to jumpstart economic growth. In all, these provisions represented more than $200 billion in revenue costs that Congress at the time did not want to see increased further by extending these provisions beyond 2011.

Bonus Depreciation

The 2010 Tax Relief Act increased the bonus rate for qualifying assets acquired after September 8, 2010, and placed in service through December 31, 2011, from 50 to 100 percent. The bonus rate is scheduled to drop to 50 percent for assets placed in service in 2012. No bonus depreciation is scheduled after 2012, although the provision has been routinely extended throughout the Obama Administration. The latest proposed extension, through 2012 at the 100 percent rate, was made in the President's *American Jobs Act* recommendations to Congress in September 2011.

Currently, bonus depreciation (an extra deduction offered in addition to the maximum allowable Section 179 expensing limits and standard first-year depreciation or in their place in the case of bonus depreciation at the 100 percent rate) permits businesses to write off up to 100 percent of the cost of depreciable property acquired in the same year. However, that deduction may only be claimed on qualifying property that satisfies "acquisition date" and "placed-in-service date" requirements. An asset is placed in service on the date that it is in a condition or state of readiness for a specifically assigned function in a trade or business on a regular, ongoing basis. The placed-in-service deadlines for the 50 percent and 100 percent rates are extended one year for property with a "longer production period."

Especially relevant to year-end planning, the rules for determining the acquisition date of an asset are different for the 50 percent and 100 percent rates. For purposes of the 50 percent rate, an asset is considered to be acquired on the date that the taxpayer takes physical possession or control of the property (or under a written contract before January 1, 2013). In contrast, 100 percent rate property is considered acquired when its cost is paid for by a cash-basis taxpayer or incurred by an accrual-basis taxpayer. An accrual-basis taxpayer generally incurs the cost of property when the property is "provided," which is usually when it is delivered. A taxpayer, however, is also permitted to treat property as "provided" when title to the property passes. In making the choice, the taxpayer should remember that the elected treatment constitutes a method of accounting that must be used consistently in the future and cannot be changed without IRS consent.

Code Sec. 179 Expensing

Code Sec. 179 currently allows a business expense deduction for taxpayers (other than estates, trusts, or certain noncorporate lessors) who elect to treat the cost of qualifying property as an expense rather than a capital expenditure. The current levels introduced during the Bush Administration and extended by the 2010 Tax Relief Act allow for a $500,000 deduction, which is reduced dollar-for-dollar by every dollar over the $2 million investment limitation. After December 31, 2011, however, the temporary extension of the higher limits is scheduled to expire, and for the 2012 tax year, levels will drop to $125,000/$500,000, although both will be indexed for inflation. Also extended through 2012 only is the treatment of off-the-shelf computer software as property allowed to be considered Code Sec. 179 property.

COMMENT

Congress has repeatedly increased the dollar and investment limits under Code Sec. 179 to encourage business spending. The 2010 *Small Business Jobs Act* increased the Code Sec. 179 dollar and investment limits to $500,000 and $2 million, respectively, for tax years beginning in 2010 and 2011. The 2010 Tax Relief Act, however, provided for a $125,000 dollar limit and a $500,000 investment limit (both indexed for inflation) for tax years beginning in 2012. For the tax year beginning in 2012, the Code Sec. 179 expensing limit will be $139,000 and the cost-of-equipment limit set at $560,000. For 2013, the limits are scheduled to drop to a $25,000/$200,000 level, unless Congress intervenes.

Code Sec. 1250 Expensing

For tax years beginning in 2010 and 2011, up to $250,000 of qualified lease-hold improvement property, qualified restaurant property, and qualified retail improvement property also have been expensable and subject to the Code Sec. 179 limitations. This is an exception to the rule that generally only tangible property subject to the modified accelerated cost recovery system (MACRS) that is Section 1245 property may be expensed under Section 179. Unlike other section property, however, the amount of a carryforward of a Section 179 deduction that is attributable to qualified real property may not be carried forward to a tax year that begins after 2011. Expensing of qualified real property at any level ends at the end of 2011 unless extended by Congress.

Small Business Stock

The 100 percent exclusion from gain income from a sale of small business stock expires after December 31, 2011. Congress initially intended Code Sec. 1202 to encourage entrepreneurial investment by providing a permanent 50 percent exclusion for qualifying gains. In other words, noncorporate taxpayers could exclude 50 percent of the gain from the sale of certain small business stock acquired at original issue and held for more than five years. For stock acquired after February 17, 2009, and on or before September 27, 2010, Congress increased exclusion first to 75 percent in the midst of the economic downturn. Then in the subsequent 2010 *Small Business Jobs Act,* in order to assist small businesses even further, it increased the exclusion to 100 percent for stock acquired after September 27, 2010 and before January 1, 2011, with the AMT preference item also eliminated. The 2010 Tax Relief Act extended the 100 percent exclusion for one more year, for stock acquired before January 1, 2012.

Qualifying small business stock is common stock issued by a C corporation whose gross assets do not exceed $50 million (including the proceeds received from the issuance of the stock) and who meets a specific active business requirement. The amount of gain eligible for the exclusion is limited to the greater of 10 times the taxpayer's basis in the stock or $10 million of gain from stock in that corporation. The provision extended the 100 percent exclusion of the gain from the sale of qualifying small business stock that is acquired before January 1, 2012, and held for more than five years.

Research and Development Tax Credit

The 2010 Tax Relief Act extended the Code Sec. 41 research tax credit available to businesses that spend on incremental qualified research through December 31, 2011. As the credit had expired on December 31, 2009, the Tax Relief Act applied it retroactively to expenses incurred in 2010, as well as through 2011.

> **COMMENT**
>
> Congress has extended the Code Sec. 41 research credit 14 times since its first introduction in the *Economic Recovery Tax Act of 1981,* and it currently enjoys bipartisan support.

Work Opportunity Tax Credit

The work opportunity tax credit (WOTC) aims to encourage the hiring of individuals from targeted groups by giving employers a credit of up to 40 percent of the employee's first-year wages or $6,000, whichever is the lesser amount. (For qualified veterans, the cap is $12,000; for qualified summer youth employees, the cap is $3,000.) When the employee is a long-term family assistance (LTFA) recipient, the WOTC is a percentage of first and second year wages, up to $10,000 per employee. The 2010 Tax Relief Act extended the WOTC for most individuals who begin employment after August 31, 2011, and before January 1, 2012.

STUDY QUESTIONS

5. The acquisition date for the 100 percent bonus depreciation rate applies when cash-basis taxpayers pay for the property or accrual-basis tax-payers incur the cost of property as it is provided. ***True or False?***

6. Unless Congress creates an extender for Code Sec. 1250 expensing for qualified real property:

    a. Will decrease to 50 percent of 2011 allowances

    b. Ends for any level after 2011

    c. Will revert to the same MACRS rules as Section 1245 property

Business Tax Extenders

Each year or two, a group of business-related provisions collectively called "extenders" come up for renewal before Congress. The latest group of these extenders is due to sunset after December 31, 2011, unless extended by Congress.

Fifteen-year recovery period for qualified leasehold improvements. The sunset of provisions allowing accelerated depreciation for qualified restaurant building improvements and retail improvements acquired before January 1, 2012, will cause such properties to be subject to the longer 39-year period for nonresidential real estate.

Extension of special expensing rules for U.S. film and television productions. The 2010 Tax Relief Act extended through December 31, 2011, the provision that allows film and television producers to expense the first $15 million of production costs incurred in the United States ($20 million if the costs are incurred in economically depressed areas in the United States).

Extension of expensing of environmental remediation costs. The 2010 Tax Relief Act extended through December 31, 2011, the provision that allows for the expensing of costs associated with cleaning up hazardous sites.

Extension of railroad track maintenance credit. The 2010 Tax Relief Act extended the railroad track maintenance credit for 50 percent of the qualified railroad track maintenance expenditures paid or incurred through January 1, 2012.

Mine rescue team training credit. The 2010 Tax Relief Act extended until December 31, 2011, the 20 percent credit (or $10,000, whichever is lesser) for training of qualified mine rescue team employees.

Seven-year motor sports entertainment costs recovery. Extension of seven-year straight-line cost recovery period for motorsports entertainment complexes. The 2010 Tax Relief Act extended through December 31, 2011, the special seven-year cost recovery period for property used for land improvement and support facilities at motorsports entertainment complexes.

Extension of enhanced charitable deduction for contributions of food inventory. The 2010 Tax Relief Act extended through December 31, 2011, the provision allowing businesses to claim an enhanced deduction for the contribution of food inventory.

Extension of enhanced charitable deduction for contributions of book inventories to public schools. The 2010 Tax Relief Act extended through December 31, 2011, a credit to C corporations that contribute qualified book inventory to public schools providing elementary or secondary education.

Extension of enhanced charitable deduction for corporate contributions of computer equipment for educational purposes. The 2010 Tax Relief Act extended through 2011 the provision that encourages businesses to contribute computer equipment and software to elementary, secondary, and postsecondary schools by allowing an enhanced deduction for such contributions.

...ial rule for S corporations making charitable contri-
...rty. The 2010 Tax Relief Act extended through 2011 the
...ing S corporation shareholders to take into account their
...of charitable deductions even if such deductions would exceed
...holders' adjusted basis in the S corporation.

New ...arkets tax credit. Congress intended the new markets tax credit
(NMTC) program to encourage private investment in businesses located
in low-income communities. The tax credit provides 5 to 6 cents per dollar that private investors contribute to qualified businesses. The 2010 Tax
Relief Act extended the new markets tax credit through December 31,
2011, capping the annual amount of qualified equity investments to $3.5
billion each year.

Differential wage credit. Eligible small business employers that pay differential wages can claim a credit equal to 20 percent of up to $20,000 of
differential pay made to an employee during the tax year. Differential wages
are payments to employees for periods that they are called to active duty
with the U.S. uniformed services (for more than 30 days) that represent
all or part of the wages that they would have otherwise received from the
employer. This credit will not be available for differential wages paid after
December 31, 2011.

Indian reservation employment credit. The 2010 Tax Relief Act extended
through December 31, 2011, the business tax credit for employers of qualified employees that work and live on or near an Indian reservation. The
amount credited to the taxpayer is limited to $20,000 per qualified employee
or 20 percent of the excess of wages and health insurance costs paid in the
current year over the amount paid in 1993, whichever is lesser.

Accelerated depreciation for business property on an Indian reserva-
tion. The 2010 Tax Relief Act extended through December 31, 2011,
the placed-in-service date for the special depreciation recovery period
for qualified Indian reservation property. In general, *qualified Indian
reservation property* is property used predominantly in the active conduct
of a trade or business within an Indian reservation, which is not used
outside the reservation on a regular basis and was not acquired from a
related person.

Deduction allowable with respect to income attributable to domestic
production activities in Puerto Rico. The 2010 Tax Relief Act extended
through December 31, 2011, the provision extending the section 199
domestic production activities deduction to activities in Puerto Rico.

Extension of special tax treatment of certain pay
exempt organizations. The 2010 Tax Relief Act exte
(through 2011) the special rules for interest, rents, roya
received by a tax-exempt entity from a controlled entity.

Treatment of certain dividends of regulated investme
(RICs). The 2010 Tax Relief Act extended a provision allo　　　　.IC,
under certain circumstances, to designate all or a portion of a dividend as
an "interest-related dividend," by written notice mailed to its shareholders
not later than 60 days after the close of its taxable year. In addition, an
interest-related dividend received by a foreign person generally is exempt
from U.S. gross-basis tax under Code Secs. 871(a), 881, 1441 and 1442.
The proposal extended the treatment of interest-related dividends and
short-term capital gain dividends received by a RIC to taxable years of the
RIC beginning before January 1, 2012.

Treatment of RIC investments as "qualified investment entities" under
FIRPTA. The 2010 Tax Relief Act extended the inclusion of a RIC within
the definition of a *qualified investment entity* under Code Sec. 897 through
December 31, 2011.

Active financing exception. The 2010 Tax Relief Act extended through
2011 the active financing exception from Subpart F of the tax code.

Look-through treatment of payments between related controlled foreign
corporations. The 2010 Tax Relief Act extended through 2011 the current law look-through treatment of payments between related controlled
foreign corporations.

Empowerment zones. The 2010 Tax Relief Act extended through 2011 the
designation of certain economically depressed census tracts as empowerment
zones. Businesses and individual residents within empowerment zones are
eligible for special tax incentives.

District of Columbia Enterprise Zone. The 2010 Tax Relief Act extended
through 2011 the designation of certain economically depressed census
tracts within the District of Columbia as the District of Columbia Enterprise Zone. Businesses and individual residents within this enterprise
zone are eligible for special tax incentives. The 2010 Tax Relief Act also
extended through 2011 the $5,000 first-time homebuyer credit for the
District of Columbia.

...ness Energy Extenders

The 2010 Tax Relief Act also temporarily extended a number of energy tax incentives targeted to businesses, with most scheduled to sunset after December 31, 2011, unless extended again by Congress.

Biodiesel and renewable diesel. The 2010 Tax Relief Act extended through December 31, 2011 the Sec. 40A tax credits, including one for $1 per gallon of biodiesel fuel that the taxpayer used in the production of a qualified biodiesel mixture. The Section as extended also provides a $0.10 credit per gallon of qualified agri-biodiesel produced by a small manufacturer.

Refined coal. The 2010 Tax Relief Act extended the credit available to qualifying refined coal facilities placed in service before January 1, 2012.

Energy-efficient new homes credit. The 2010 Tax Relief Act extended the credit available to eligible contractors who construct and sell a qualified new energy efficient residence before January 1, 2012.

Alternative fuels credit. The 2010 Tax Relief Act extended the $0.50 per gallon alternative fuel tax credit through December 31, 2011.

Special rule for sales of electric transmission property. The 2010 Tax Relief Act extended through 2011 the deferral of gain on sales of transmission property by vertically integrated electric utilities to FERC-approved independent transmission companies.

Special rule for marginal wells. The 2010 Tax Relief Act extended through 2011 the suspension on the taxable income limit for purposes of depleting a marginal oil or gas well. Section 1603. The 2010 Tax Relief Act also extended for one year the start-of-construction deadline for the cash grant in lieu of tax credit program, established in Section 1603 of the American Recovery and Reinvestment Act.

Ethanol. The 2010 Tax Relief Act extended through 2011 the per-gallon tax credits and outlay payments for ethanol. The 2010 Tax Relief Act also extended through 2011 the existing 14.27 cents per liter (54 cents per gallon) tariff on imported ethanol and the related 5.99 cents per liter (22.67 cents per gallon) tariff on ethyl tertiary-butyl ether (ETBE).

Energy-efficient appliances. The 2010 Tax Relief Act extended through 2011 and modifies standards for the Section 45M credit for US-based manufacture of energy-efficient clothes washers, dishwashers, and refrigerators.

Alternative vehicle refueling property. The 2010 Tax Relief Act extended through 2011 the 30% investment tax credit for alternative vehicle refueling property.

STUDY QUESTIONS

---

7. Charitable deductions extended through 2011 for businesses include all of the following **except:**

    a. Corporate contributions of computer equipment for educational purposes

    b. Increased deductions of cash donations to Code Sec. 527 organizations

    c. Enhanced charitable deduction for contributions of food inventory

8. The 2010 Tax Relief Act extended through 2011 the inclusion of a regulated investment company (RIC) as a *qualified investment entity* under Code Sec. 897. ***True or False?***

EXPIRING AT THE END OF 2012

Provisions expiring at the end of 2012 are primarily the direct consequence of the sunsetting of the so-called Bush-era tax cuts, as extended through 2012 by the 2010 Tax Relief Act. The Tax Relief Act of 2010 extends lower marginal individual income tax rates, marriage penalty relief, lower capital gains tax rates, as well as more that 50 other tax benefits put into place pursuant to the *Economic Growth and Tax Relief Reconciliation Act of 2001* (EGTRRA) and the *Jobs and Growth Tax Relief Reconciliation Act of 2003* (JGTRRA). In order to comply with budget requirements, the provisions in EGTRRA were subject to a sunset provision. Pursuant to the sunset provision, the changes made by EGTRRA would no longer have applied after December 31, 2010. The provisions contained in JGTRRA, which primarily addressed lower capital gains and dividends rates, were subject to similar sunset rules.

Individual Income Tax Rates

The individual income tax rates of the EGTRRA, extended by the 2010 Tax Relief Act, are 10, 15, 25, 28, 33, and 35 percent. If they are allowed to expire on December 31, 2012, the rates will revert to their higher 2001 levels of 15, 28, 31, and 39.6 percent. In both his FY 2012 proposal and his deficit reduction plan, however, President Obama supports extension of the cuts in all but the highest two tax brackets, which he defines as starting at $250,000 for joint filers and $200,000 for others. Republican leadership continues to resist any proposal short of a blanket, across-the-board permanent extension of the Bush-era rates to all income levels.

Capital Gains/Dividends

Qualified capital gains and dividends are currently taxed at a maximum of 15 percent (taxpayers in the 10 and 15 percent brackets pay 0 percent).

When the two-year extension from the 2010 Tax Relief Act expires on December 31, 2012, this treatment is scheduled to end. Without further action on Capitol Hill, the maximum rate on net capital gain is scheduled to rise to 20 percent in 2013 (10 percent for taxpayers in the 15 percent bracket). The rate on qualified dividends will be taxed as regular income, meaning it can be subject to a maximum tax rate of 39.6 percent.

Reinstated "Pease" Limit on Itemized Deductions

If the Bush tax cuts extended by the 2010 Tax Relief Act expire on December 31, 2012, then starting in 2013 the so-called "Pease" limitation on itemized deductions will return in full force. So, too, would a similar limitation on personal exemptions. The limitation on itemized deductions at its original 2001 level, which was gradually reduced and finally repealed for the 2010 tax year, calls for the subtraction from the dollar amount of itemized deductions of 3 percent of whatever adjusted gross income (AGI) exceeds the statutory threshold.

As it now stands, for tax years beginning after December 31, 2012, the amount of otherwise allowable itemized deductions will be reduced for higher-income taxpayers whose AGI exceeds the threshold amount. The threshold amount of $100,000 for most taxpayers was set by statute when Code Sec. 68 was originally enacted in 1991, and is adjusted annually for inflation. If it went into effect in 2012, those amounts would be $173,650.

Under the itemized deduction (Pease) limitation, taxpayers with AGI exceeding the threshold amount must reduce their otherwise allowable itemized deductions by the lesser of:

- 3 percent of the amount of the taxpayer's AGI in excess of $100,000, as adjusted for inflation, or
- 80 percent of the itemized deductions otherwise allowable for the tax year.

> **COMMENT**
>
> President Obama's recent deficit reduction plan proposes a 28 percent cap on itemized deductions claimed by higher income taxpayers. Higher income taxpayers are defined as single filers who make $200,000 or more and married couples filing jointly with incomes of $250,000 or more.

Personal Exemption Phaseout

The 2010 Tax Relief Acts extended the repeal of the PEP through December 2012. The phaseout will reduce the total amount of exemptions that may be claimed by 2 percent for each $2,500 or portion thereof by which the taxpayer's AGI exceeds the applicable threshold.

Similar to the Pease limitation, when the phaseout of the personal exemption returns for tax years beginning in 2013 (after the EGTRRA sunset occurs at the end of 2012), the deduction for personal exemptions will be reduced or even eliminated for certain high-income taxpayers. If a taxpayer's AGI exceeds the appropriate threshold amount (based on filing status), the exemption amount will be reduced by 2 percent for each $2,500, or fraction thereof, by which the AGI exceeds the threshold amount. In the case of a married individual filing separately, the exemption will be reduced by 2 percent for each $1,250 or fraction thereof by which AGI exceeds the threshold amount.

The deduction for personal exemptions will be fully eliminated when AGI exceeds the threshold amount by more than $122,500 ($61,250 in the case of a married individual filing separately). It takes 50 2-percent reductions to achieve a 100-percent reduction. Because 49 2-percent reductions would result from an excess of $122,500 (49 × $2,500 = $122,500), any excess above that amount would be a fraction of a $2,500 amount and create the fiftieth 2-percent reduction.

Marriage Penalty Relief

The EGTRRA provisions designed to mitigate the so-called marriage penalty are set to expire on December 31, 2012. The provisions extended the basic standard deduction for joint married filers to double the single filer's standard deduction. In addition, EGTRRA expanded the size of the 15 percent tax bracket for married couples filing a joint return.

Dependent Care Credit

The dependent care credit allows a taxpayer a credit for an applicable percentage of child care expenses for children younger than age 13 and disabled dependents. EGTRRA increased the maximum amount of expenses eligible for the dependent care credit from $2,400 to $3,000 for one child and from $4,800 for two or more children to $6,000. EGTRRA also raised the maximum credit from 30 to 35 percent of qualifying expenses and provided for a reduction in the credit, but not below 20 percent, by one percentage point for each $2,000, or fraction thereof, of AGI above a $15,000 threshold. The 2010 Tax Relief Act extended these provisions through December 31, 2012.

Employer-Provided Child Care

Under EGTRRA as extended by the 2010 Tax Relief Act, certain employers that provided child care facilities are eligible for a tax credit equal to 25 percent of qualified expenses for employee child care plus an amount equal to 10 percent of qualified expenses for child care resource and referral services. The credit is subject to a $150,000 annual cap on qualified costs. The 2010 Tax Relief Act extended the credit for two years, through December 31, 2012 only.

American Opportunity Tax Credit

The 2009 Recovery Act enhanced the hope education credit, renamed the American opportunity tax credit (AOTC), for 2009 and 2010. The 2010 Tax Relief Act extended the AOTC for two years, through December 31, 2012. Also extended are income limitations (the AOTC begins to phase out for single individuals with modified AGI of $80,000 ($160,000 for married couples filing jointly) and completely phases out for single individuals with modified AGI of $90,000 ($180,000 for married couples filing jointly).

Child Tax Credit

Generally, taxpayers with incomes below certain threshold amounts may claim the child tax credit to reduce federal income tax for each qualifying child younger than age 17. The EGTRRA increased the credit from $500 to $1,000. The EGTRRA also expanded refundability. The amount that may be claimed as a refund was 15 percent of earnings above $10,000. The *American Recovery and Reinvestment Act of 2009* provided that earnings above $3,000 would count toward refundability for 2009 and 2010. This proposal also generally extended the current child tax credit for an additional two years, through December 31, 2012.

Earned Income Tax Credit

Under current law, working families with two or more children currently qualify for an earned income tax credit equal to 40 percent of the family's first $12,570 of earned income. The *American Recovery and Reinvestment Act of 2009* increased the earned income tax credit to 45 percent of the family's first $12,570 of earned income for families with three or more children and increased the beginning point of the phase-out range for all married couples filing a joint return (regardless of the number of children). The 2010 Tax Relief Act extended these provisions through December 31, 2012.

Educational Assistance Exclusion

EGTRRA allowed employees to exclude up to $5,250 in employer-provided education assistance annually from income and employment taxes. Employers in turn may deduct up to $5,250 annually for qualified education expenses paid on behalf of an employee. Any additional amounts must be treated as wages by both the employee and the employee. This treatment was scheduled to expire after 2010. The 2010 Tax Relief Act extended these provisions for two years, through December 31, 2012.

> **COMMENT**
>
> If the education is in the form of job-related training or enhancement directly related to the business operations, and the education does not qualify the employee to work in a new trade or business, the costs may be considered a business expense.

Student Loan Interest Deduction Phaseout

EGTRRA eliminated a 60-month rule for the $2,500 above-the-line student loan interest deduction and expanded the modified AGI range for phaseout. The 2010 Tax Relief Act extended the enhancements for two years, through December 31, 2012.

If the EGTRRA changes sunset, for tax years beginning after December 31, 2012, the deduction begins to phase out for taxpayers whose modified AGI exceeds an inflation-adjusted $40,000 ($60,000 for joint returns), and phases out to zero at a modified AGI of $55,000 ($75,000 for joint returns). Those numbers are down from $50,000 ($100,000 for joint returns with a zero phaseout at modified AGI of $65,000 ($130,000 for joint returns)). Additionally, for tax years beginning after December 31, 2012, education loan interest will be deductible only if paid during the first 60 months, whether or not consecutive, that interest payments are required. The 60-month period is determined by treating any loan and all of its refinancings as one loan. This means that a taxpayer will not be able to obtain a longer period of deductions by consolidating loans and changing payment schedules.

Coverdell Education Savings Accounts

EGTRRA increased the maximum contribution amount to a Coverdell Education Savings Account (ESA) from $500 to $2,000 and, among other things, made elementary and secondary school expenses, in addition to postsecondary school expenses, qualified expenses. These enhancements were scheduled to sunset after 2010. The 2010 Tax Relief Act extended them for two years, through December 31, 2012.

Scholarships

Under EGTRRA, the National Health Service Corps Scholarship Program and the Armed Forces Scholarship Program are qualified scholarships for exclusion from income purposes. Because of EGTRRA's sunset rules, these scholarships were scheduled to be included in a recipient's income after 2010. The 2010 Tax Relief Act extended the income exclusion for these scholarships for two years, through December 31, 2012.

Disaster Incentives

The 2010 Tax Relief Act extended a number of targeted disaster relief areas with provisions set to expire at the end of 2011 or 2012:

Extension of tax incentives for the New York Liberty Zone. The 2010 Tax Relief Act extended through 2011 the time for issuing New York Liberty Zone bonds effective for bonds issued after December 31, 2009.

Extension of increased rehabilitation credit for historic structures in the Gulf Opportunity Zone. The 2010 Tax Relief Act extended through 2011 the increased rehabilitation credit for qualified expenditures in the Gulf Opportunity Zone. The *Gulf Opportunity Zone Act of 2005* increased the rehabilitation credit from 10 percent to 13 percent of qualified expenditures for any qualified rehabilitated building other than a certified historic structure, and from 20 percent to 26 percent of qualified expenditures for any certified historic structure.

One-year extension of Gulf Opportunity Zone low-income housing placed-in-service date. The *Gulf Opportunity Zone Act of 2005* provided an additional allocation of low-income housing tax credits to the Gulf Opportunity Zone in an amount equal to the product of $18 multiplied by the portion of the State population that is in the Gulf Opportunity Zone. The additional allocations were made in calendar years 2006, 2007, and 2008, and required that the properties be placed in service before January 1, 2011. The 2010 Tax Relief Act extended that placed-in-service date for one year (through 2011).

Extension of tax-exempt bonds for the Gulf Opportunity Zone. Under current law, bonds were authorized to help rebuild areas devastated by Hurricane Katrina and must be issued by December 31, 2010. The amendment provides one additional year to use these bonds, through December 31, 2011.

Temporary depreciation allowance for Gulf Opportunity Zone property. The 2010 Tax Relief Act extended for two years, through 2011, an additional depreciation deduction claimed by businesses equal to 50 percent of the cost of new property investments made in the Gulf Opportunity Zone. The provision makes expenditures in 2011 eligible provided the property is placed in service by December 31, 2011.

FEDERAL ESTATE TAX

EGTRRA gradually reduced over a period of years and then abolished the federal estate tax for decedents dying in 2010. The pre-EGTRRA estate tax (with a maximum tax rate of 55 percent and a $1 million applicable exclusion amount), however, was scheduled to be revived after 2010. Additional EGTRRA changes affected the gift and generation-skipping transfer (GST) tax.

The 2010 Tax Relief Act revived the estate tax for decedents dying after December 31, 2009, but at a significantly higher applicable exclusion amount and lower tax rate than had been scheduled under EGTRRA. The maximum estate tax rate is 35 percent with an applicable exclusion amount of $5 million. This new estate tax regime, however, is itself temporary and is scheduled to sunset on December 31, 2012, after which a pre-2001 regime of only a $1 million exclusion and a top rate of 55 percent would apply.

Reinstatement of the estate tax for 2010, however, is subject to one exception. The executor of the estate of a decedent who died after December 31, 2009, and before January 1, 2011 (i.e., a decedent who died in 2010), may elect to apply the Internal Revenue Code as if the reinstatement of the estate tax by the Tax Relief Act of 2010 had not occurred. This election, however, comes at a price that the executor must weigh carefully: the carryover basis rules that had been scheduled to apply in 2010 under EGTRRA would be triggered. Under the election, subject to certain minimum amounts, the heir receive property with a basis equal to that held by the decedent rather than at the customary "stepped-up" basis set at death of date value. This election is not available in 2011 or 2012.

COMMENT

In 2009, the maximum federal estate tax rate was 45 percent and the exemption level was $3.5 million. For 2010, 2011, and 2012, the estate tax rate is 35 percent and the unified estate and gift tax exclusion is $5 million for 2010 and 2011 and an inflation-adjusted $5.120 million projected for 2012.

For 2009, the gift tax lifetime exclusion was $1 million. It is uncertain whether the president's deficit reduction plan would unify the exclusion at $3.5 million for both estate and gift tax purposes. For 2012, a donor's inflation-adjusted annual gift tax exemption amount per donee is projected to be $13,000 ($26,000 for split gifts), the same level it has been since 2009. No proposal has been made to change that regime.

Generation-skipping transfer tax (GST). The 2010 Tax Relief Act provides a $5 million exemption amount for 2010 (equal to the applicable exclusion amount for estate tax purposes) ,with a GST tax rate of zero percent for 2010. For transfers made after 2010, the GST tax rate would be equal to the highest estate and gift tax rate in effect for the year (35 percent for

2011 and 2012). The 2010 Tax Relief Act also extended certain technical provisions under EGTRRA affecting the GST tax.

THE HEALTH CARE ACT: IMMEDIATE AND POST-2012 IMPACT

Long-term tax planners must also take into account certain health care reform provisions. Passage of the *Health Care and Education Reconciliation Act of 2010* (P.L. 111-152) (Reconciliation Act) by Congress on March 25, 2010 completed a massive overhaul of the nation's health insurance and health delivery systems. The Reconciliation Act amends the *Patient Protection and Affordable Care Act of 2010* (P.L. 111-148), which President Obama signed on March 23, 2010. Combined, the two new laws include more than $400 billion in revenue raisers and new taxes on employers and individuals.

President Obama's signature on the Reconciliation Act signaled an end to the legislative process of health care reform (at least for the immediate future) and set in motion the regulatory process as the IRS and many other federal agencies gear up to implement health care reform. The IRS is responsible for overseeing a significant part of health care reform, such as the administration of additional taxes and penalties on individuals and employers, determinations of various exemptions from those taxes, and oversight of new information reporting requirements.

The health care reform package (the Patient Protection Act as amended by the Reconciliation Act) does not mandate employer-provided coverage, but it includes "play or pay language." The health care reform package also imposes a penalty on nonexempt individuals who fail to carry minimum essential coverage. On the revenue side, the health care package includes an additional Medicare tax on wages and self-employment income of higher income taxpayers, a new Medicare contribution tax on net investment income, and a delayed excise tax on high-dollar insurance plans, among its $437 billion in new taxes, fees, and penalties.

Small Business Tax Credit

Beginning in 2010, the health care reform package provided a temporary, sliding-scale small employer tax credit to help offset the cost of employer-provided coverage. Generally, a *qualified small employer* is one with no more than 25 employees, each with average annual wages of no more than $50,000. The qualified small employer must contribute at least one-half of the cost of health insurance premiums for coverage of its participating employees.

In 2010 through 2013, qualified small employers may qualify for a tax credit for up to 35 percent of their contribution toward the employee's health insurance premium. After 2013, small employers that purchase coverage through an insurance exchange may qualify for a credit for two years of up to 50 percent of their contribution. Salary reduction contributions are not counted.

Small employers with 10 or fewer employees, whose average annual wages are less than $25,000 per person, would be eligible for the full credit. The credit is reduced for small employers with 11 to 25 employees and average annual wages of $26,000 to $50,000. The wage amounts are indexed for inflation.

Qualified small tax-exempt employers would be eligible for a reduced credit.

Cafeteria plans. The health care reform package relaxes the cafeteria plan rules to encourage more small employers to offer tax-free benefits to employees, including those related to health insurance coverage. It does so by carving out a safe harbor from the nondiscrimination requirements for cafeteria plans for qualified small employers.

Medicare Payroll Surtax

Starting in 2013, the health care reform package broadens the Medicare tax base for higher-income taxpayers by:

- Imposing an additional Hospital Insurance (HI) tax rate of 0.9 percent on earned income in excess of $200,000 for individuals and $250,000 for married couples filing jointly; and
- Imposing a 3.8-percent "unearned income Medicare contributions" tax on higher-income taxpayers.

The 3.8-percent unearned income Medicare contributions tax is imposed on the lesser of:

- Net investment income; or
- The excess of modified adjusted gross income (AGI) over the threshold amount
  - $200,000 for single individuals or heads of households,
  - $250,000 for married couples filing a joint return and surviving spouses, and
  - $125,000 for married couples filing separate returns).

When the 3.8-percent surtax is added to the 0.9-percent tax also imposed by the health care reform package on higher-income taxpayers, $210.2 billion is estimated to be raised over the 2013 to 2019 period. Neither the $200,000 nor $250,000 amount is indexed for inflation.

Modified AGI is adjusted gross income increased by the amount excluded from income as foreign earned income less deductions attributable to such income.

Net investment income includes interest, dividends, royalties, rents, gain from disposing of property from a passive activity, and income earned from a trade or business that is a passive activity. In determining net investment income, investment income is reduced by deductions properly allowable to that income. Net investment income does not include distributions from qualified retirement plans, including pensions and certain retirement accounts. For example, income from individual retirement accounts (IRAs), 401(a) money purchase plans, and 403(b) and 457(b) plans would be exempt.

EXAMPLE

Alice and Bob Matthews, a married couple who file a joint return, collectively earn $270,000 in wages and have $80,000 of net investment income in 2013. Their modified AGI is $350,000. For 2013, the couple will incur a 3.8 percent unearned income Medicare contribution tax on the lesser of their: $80,000 of net investment income or $100,000 of modified AGI in excess of the $250,000 threshold for married taxpayers filing jointly. Thus, Alice and Bob will incur a $3,040 (3.8 percent × $80,000) unearned income Medicare contribution tax in 2013.

EXAMPLE

In 2013, Richard Josephson, a single taxpayer, receives no wages or self-employment income. He does, however, earn $3.2 million in net investment income from a stock and bond portfolio that is not part of a qualified employee benefit plan. This is the total amount of Richard's modified AGI for 2013. Richard will incur a 3.8 percent unearned income Medicare contribution tax on the lesser of his: $3.2 million net investment income, or $3 million modified AGI in excess of the $200,000 threshold amount for a single taxpayer. Thus, Richard will incur a $114,000 (3.8 percent × $3 million) unearned income Medicare contribution tax in 2013.

Estates and trusts. Estates and trusts will also pay a 3.8 percent unearned income Medicare contribution tax on the lesser of

- Their undistributed net investment income for the tax year; or
- Any excess of their adjusted gross income over the dollar amount at which the highest tax bracket for estates and trusts begins for the tax year (currently at $11,200, but subject to inflation adjustment each year).

Charitable remainder and other tax-exempt trusts are excluded.

Medical Expense Deduction

The health care reform package raises the threshold for the itemized medical expense deduction from 7.5 percent of AGI to 10 percent of AGI for regular income tax purposes effective for tax years beginning after December 31, 2012. However, individuals ages 65 and older (and their spouses) will be temporarily exempt from the increase. The exemption for seniors applies to tax years beginning after December 31, 2012, and before January 1, 2017.

The health care reform package made no adjustment to the allowable medical expense deduction for purposes of computing alternative minimum tax (AMT) liability. For now, the AGI floor for AMT purposes remains at 10 percent.

FSAs and HSAs

The health care reform package modifies the definitions of qualified medical expenses for health FSAs, HSAs, and HRAs to conform them to the definition used for the medical expense itemized deduction beginning in 2011. Thus, over-the-counter medicines are excluded unless prescribed by a health care professional. The health care package also caps health FSA contributions at $2,500 per year after 2012, which is indexed annually for inflation after 2013.

The health care reform package also increases the additional tax on non-qualified distributions from HSAs from 10 percent to 20 percent and from Archer MSAs from 15 to 20 percent beginning in 2011.

To prevent an end-run around the new FSA restrictions using cafeteria plan rules, the health care reform package provides that, if a benefit is available under a cafeteria plan through employer provided contributions to a health FSA, the benefit will not be treated as a qualified benefit unless the cafeteria plan provides that an employee may not elect for any taxable year to have salary reduction contributions in excess of $2,500 made to the arrangement.

Medicare Part D

Starting in 2013, the health care reform package eliminates the deduction for the subsidy for employers that maintain prescription drug coverage for retirees who are eligible for Medicare Part D.

Tax on High-Cost Insurance

Beginning in 2018, the health care reform package is scheduled to impose a 40-percent nondeductible excise tax on insurance companies or plan administrators for any health insurance plan with an annual premium in excess of an inflation-adjusted $10,200 for individuals and an inflation-adjusted $27,500 for families. The health care reform package provides higher premium levels for employees in certain high-risk professions: $11,850 for individual coverage and $30,950 for family coverage. Non-Medicare retirees ages 55 and older are also eligible for the higher thresholds.

Congress delayed application of the excise tax from 2013 until 2018 to give plans "time to implement and realize the cost savings of reform." Because of this delay, however, the final health care reform package eliminates the three-year transition relief that had been available in the Patient Protection Act for coverage in 17 high-cost states.

Undoubtedly, the delay also was engineered to remove some of the immediate criticism of the bill from front-page headlines. Although a rollback of these provisions by another Congress is possible, repealing legislation is a much more difficult process than passage and, therefore, prudent planning for the time being ought to consider the law as its is now written.

An insurer would be free to pass along the excise tax to consumers in the form of higher premiums as an alternative to, or in combination with, finding cost-cutting opportunities.

Cost of living adjustments. The threshold amounts for 2018 are indexed using the Consumer Price Index for All Urban Consumers (CPI-U). For 2019 only, an additional one percent is added to the cost of living adjustment. Thereafter, the amounts will be adjusted only using the base CPI-U.

The health care reform package excludes completely the value of stand-alone dental and vision plan coverage from determining the excise tax thresholds. Fixed indemnity health coverage purchased by the employee with after-tax dollars is also excluded. The health care reform package also provides adjustments to the thresholds to account for plans that carry a higher premium cost because of the participants' age or gender.

Market Sector Fees

Although the health care reform package imposes annual nondeductible fees on pharmaceutical manufacturers, importers, and health insurance providers, certain companies are exempt.

The health care reform package removes an annual fee that would have been imposed on medical device manufacturers. However, as a tradeoff, the health care reform package adds an excise tax of 2.3 percent on medical device sales. Certain medical devices routinely purchased by consumers, such as eyeglasses and hearing aids, are exempt from the excise tax.

STUDY QUESTIONS

> **9.** Because of the personal exemption phaseout's return in 2013, the deduction is eliminated for higher-income taxpayers whose annual gross income exceeds:
>
> **a.** $100,000
> **b.** $122,500
> **c.** $250,000

---

10. The generation-skipping transfer tax rate for transfers made in 2011 and 2012 is scheduled to be:

   a. 28 percent

   b. 35 percent

   c. 40 percent

CONCLUSION

Congress has created a complex moving target of temporary tax provisions for taxpayers to follow when trying to plan for both the present and the immediate future. The driving force behind creating this uncertainty is the cost to the government of the many tax breaks that are now in play. To lower the overall cost, Congress has latched onto making tax provisions either temporary or, in the case of some health care reform taxes, time delayed. A current snapshot of temporary provisions falls into no fewer than four baskets:

- Tax provisions that ended in 2010 and should now be forgotten;
- Tax provisions that will sunset at the end of 2011 (primarily as the result of temporary provisions within the 2010 Tax Relief Act);
- Tax provisions that will sunset at the end of 2012 (primarily as the result of the "temporary" 10-year tax breaks that end with 2012 after being extended another two years by the 2010 Tax Relief Act); and
- Tax provisions, principally in the form of tax increases related the 2010 Health Care Reform Acts that become effective on a rolling basis between 2013 and 2018.

Congress also has the ability to change these sunsets and effective dates by the simple act of passing further tax legislation...the proverbial "moving the goal post." Nevertheless, it is tax advisor's task to work within these boundaries. Keeping close score of existing and proposed temporary tax provisions can only help in meeting that challenge.

Health Care Reform and Closely Held Businesses

Health care reform consists of two laws: the *Patient Protection and Affordable Care Act of 2010* (PPACA), P.L. 111-148, as amended by the *Health Care and Education Reconciliation Act of 2010* (HCERA), P.L. 111-152. The new laws contain more than $400 billion in estimated revenue raisers and new taxes on employers and individuals, new fees on insurers and health-related industries, and significant nontax mandates for health insurance coverage. The IRS will play a significant role in overseeing health care reform, administering additional taxes, determining exemptions from those taxes, and overseeing new information reporting requirements.

LEARNING OBJECTIVES

Upon completion of this chapter you will be able to:

- Identify the requirements for new and grandfathered health coverage plans;
- Describe the new taxes being imposed on higher-income taxpayers;
- Determine the basic rules for the small employer healthcare coverage tax credit;
- Explain the difference between the employer mandate and the individual mandate;
- Describe the state-established health care exchanges;
- Apply the rules for the premium tax credit; and
- Explore other aspects of the health care reform law that affects employers and businesses.

INTRODUCTION

This course explores the comprehensive health care reform package enacted in March 2010 and its impact on employers and closely held businesses. This new law establishes requirements for health insurance coverage provided by insurance companies and employers. The new law expands health insurance coverage to millions of Americans who currently lack coverage by imposing coverage mandates on employers and individuals. These coverage mandates will significantly affect closely held businesses, including those operating as C corporations, S corporations, partnerships, limited liability companies, and sole proprietorships.

Some claim that health costs will rise substantially as the result of the new law; the administration says that is not the case. At the same time, the law provides credits for small employers who provide health insurance and for low- and middle-income individuals who obtain health insurance through a state "exchange." To fund health care reform, the law imposes new taxes on higher-income individuals and on a variety of industries and services.

Because of the law's new, far-reaching requirements, some people that oppose the law have filed lawsuits claiming that the law (or at least its individual mandate) is unconstitutional. Despite the uncertainty created by this litigation, the IRS and other federal agencies must provide guidance to promote the effective administration of health care reform. The provisions of the package will be defined mainly in the regulations. Because of the Supreme Court's *Mayo Foundation* (2011-1 USTC ¶50,143) decision, courts will be inclined to give great deference to the IRS's regulations.

Not all of the law's requirements apply immediately. Some requirements took effect in 2010; others will not take effect until 2013 or 2014; and some requirements are deferred until 2018. This chapter looks at many of the developments generated by the new law and some of the potential consequences on employers, employees, and other individuals. Owners of closely held businesses generally operate on a smaller cash cushion than larger businesses and therefore must be more accurate in immediately assessing the impact that the new requirements will have on their businesses.

NEW REQUIREMENTS FOR EMPLOYER-SPONSORED PLANS

Employers do not have to provide health insurance for their employees, but many choose to do so. This is a costly benefit expense, but under traditional employment practices, one that is considered necessary. Employers pay a portion of the premiums charged for individual and family coverage under group health plans covering their employees.

Plans that were in existence on March 23, 2010, when PPACA became law, are *grandfathered plans* with respect to the employer. This status carries over to new employees and their families that enroll after March 23, 2010.

COMMENT

Grandfathered status is significant. President Obama promised that individuals could keep their current coverage. This continuity applies to plans that are grandfathered. For the most part, this status is determined at the employer level, not the employee level. A grandfathered plan is not covered by new discrimination requirements; thus, its coverage can favor highly paid employees. Self-insured plans cannot be grandfathered.

PPACA added extensive new requirements to group health insurance plans. Some of these requirements apply to all plans, whether grandfathered or new. Other requirements only apply to new plans. In general, fewer requirements apply to grandfathered plans; thus, employers with grandfathered plans will generally want to keep them. (Of course, a plan can lose its grandfathered status if it makes certain changes.) Some requirements started to apply in 2010, generally on September 23, 2010, the date six months after PPACA's enactment. Other requirements do not apply until later years.

Regardless of the details, these requirements will cause plan costs paid by employers to increase; how much is unclear and remains to be seen. The Obama Administration has said that costs should not increase by more than 1 to 2 percent. Many insurance companies have a different view, saying that costs may increase substantially, by even as much as 10 percent. The government is projecting that expanded health insurance coverage will reduce costs and the federal government deficit, but commentators are skeptical. Much of the cost impact depends on new taxes that will be borne by employers and higher-income individuals.

Plan Requirements

What are some of these new requirements? For all plans, including grand-fathered plans, they include the following requirements that take effect for plan years beginning on or after September 23, 2010:

- No limits on lifetime benefits;
- Plans cannot rescind an individual's participation in the plan except for fraud or intentional misrepresentation;
- Children who are not themselves eligible for employer-sponsored coverage can be covered up to age 26 on the parent's policy (family coverage), even if the children no longer qualify as dependents under the tax code;
- Preexisting condition exclusions are not allowed for covered individuals younger than age 19;
- Annual limits on benefits are modified for essential benefits.

Beginning March 23, 2012, all health insurers and group plans, including grandfathered plans, must provide a "plain English" summary of benefits and coverage (SBC). Issuers and plans failing to provide the required information will be subject to an excise tax.

COMMENT

Beginning on January 1, 2014, the SBC must include a statement whether the plan's coverage meets PPACA's minimum essential coverage requirements.

> **NOTE**
>
> Nondiscrimination rules do not apply to grandfathered plans. This can benefit closely held businesses that want to provide better (more expensive) coverage to owner-employees and other highly compensated individuals.

New plans. For new plans and for other plans that are not grandfathered, the following requirements also apply to plan years beginning on or after September 23, 2010:

- Plans cannot impose cost-sharing for preventive services;
- No discrimination based on salary;
- Requirements for internal appeals and external review of the insurer's coverage decisions (to be provided by insurers, not employers);
- Emergency services must be provided at in-network cost-sharing level, with no prior authorization; and
- Specialized primary care physicians—parents must be able to pick a pediatrician as primary caregiver for their children, and women must be able to choose an OB-GYN as their primary caregiver.

Nondiscrimination requirements. The IRS has announced that the discrimination rules will not take effect until it issues regulations. But in general, insured plans will be required not to discriminate, based on the concepts of Code Sec. 105(h) (which governs self-insured plans and payments to highly compensated employees). The new regulations will apply to all types of employers, not just corporations. There is a significant penalty—$100 per day per affected participant. The tax is an excise tax and is not deductible. It appears that affected participants are employees who are not "highly compensated" (the top 25 percent of compensation). Thus, the amount of the tax is based on the "bottom" 75 percent of employees.

"Small" employers can meet the nondiscrimination rules by establishing a new SIMPLE cafeteria plan. This option is available only for businesses with 100 or fewer employees (counting employees working for related employers) during either of the preceding two years. If the number of employees increases and exceeds 100, the employer can still maintain the plan until the employer has more than 200 employees.

> **COMMENT**
>
> This plan can provide an easier method for employers to meet the nondiscrimination rules without worrying about the contributions and benefits provided for health insurance.

The SIMPLE cafeteria plan can offer a medical reimbursement plan and/or dependent care assistance. Employers are required to make a contribution equal to either 2 percent of the employee's compensation, or a 200 percent match of employee contributions up to 6 percent of the employee's compensation. The plan must cover employees with at least 1,000 hours of service in the preceding year. However, employees with less than one year of service, as well as nonresident aliens, do not have to be covered.

COMMENT

Owners of C corporations can be covered as employees; owners of other closely held businesses (2 percent shareholders of S corporations, partners, members of a limited liability company) may not qualify.

Loss of grandfather status. Costs of grandfathered plans for employers may be less than costs of new and nongrandfathered plans. However, plans are at risk of losing their grandfather status. The following changes in a health insurance plan could terminate grandfather status:

- Eliminating or significantly cutting coverage and benefits;
- Increasing coinsurance charges, such as the percentage of a hospital bill;
- Significantly raising copayment charges;
- Significantly raising deductibles; or
- Lowering employer contributions by more than 5 percent.

Not all changes terminate grandfather status. The following changes would not cause loss of grandfather status:

- Voluntary changes to increase benefits or to adopt health care reform requirements;
- Increasing a copayment by less than $5 increased by medical inflation; and
- Good faith changes made to comply with health care reform grandfather requirements prior to June 14, 2010.

Initially, the government said in regulations that a change in insurance company would terminate grandfather status. It later removed this rule, but only prospectively, as of November 15, 2010. Thus, during the period June 14, 2010 through November 14, 2010, a plan could not change insurers without losing its grandfather status.

> **COMMENT**
>
> For changes before June 14, 2010, there were no regulations, so plans can argue that they made a good faith effort to comply and that changing insurers should not be a problem.

STUDY QUESTIONS

1. A grandfathered health plan:

   a. Allows individuals to keep their current coverage

   b. Does not allow parents to keep their children covered

   c. Cannot favor highly paid employees with better coverage

2. Generally, employers who establish a SIMPLE cafeteria plan must cover:

   a. Employees from their date of hire

   b. Employees who worked with the employer for at least 1,000 hours during the previous year

   c. Nonresident alien employees as well as U.S. citizens

Other Provisions

2010 changes. An important benefit for employers took effect in 2010: the small employer health care tax credit, based on a percentage of the employer's health care costs paid for its employees. This credit is intended to help offset some of the cost increases to small employers triggered by other PPACA requirements.

PPACA requires employers to report the value of health insurance provided to their employees—another compliance cost. But the IRS also delayed this requirement: first until the 2012 calendar year; then, indefinitely, for an employer who was required to file fewer than 250 Forms W-2 for the preceding year.

2014 changes. Other important provisions take effect in 2014. Many concern the individual mandate and the related employer mandate. The latter requires "applicable large employers" to offer health insurance to their employees or pay a penalty. To help individuals and employers with these requirements, the law mandates that states establish *health care exchanges* to give individuals and small businesses a place to shop for health insurance. In addition, lower- and middle-income individuals and families will be entitled to a *health insurance premium tax credit* to apply toward the cost of insurance. Medicaid eligibility will increase to 133 percent of the federal poverty level. Larger employers will be required to auto-enroll their employees into health plans, while allowing them to opt out of coverage.

2018 changes. Finally, in 2018, a 40 percent excise tax will be imposed on insurance companies (and presumably passed on to their customers) that offer high-cost health plans ("Cadillac plans"). A *Cadillac plan* includes employee-only coverage that costs $10,200 or more for the year, and family coverage that costs $27,500 or more. These amounts will be indexed in 2019 and beyond. The cost of standalone coverage (dental or vision), cancer coverage, and certain other benefits are not counted.

Uncertainty Breeding Litigation

While employers try to figure out how to comply and how to pay the costs of compliance, some states and private groups are challenging the law itself. A number of cases have been litigated in federal district courts and in the U.S. courts of appeal.

Most challenges are aimed at the individual mandate, which requires individuals to obtain health insurance beginning in 2014, or else pay a fine. The mandate requires that individuals ensure, for each month, that the individual and his or her dependents are covered by health insurance that provides minimum essential coverage.

PLANNING POINTER

The health care law is making watershed changes in how health care is handled by closely held businesses. For example, the individual mandate is bound to affect compensation packages for key employees, and possibly for rank-and-file employees.

Courts of appeal. The lawsuits allege that the individual mandate exceeds Congress's power to regulate activity under the U.S. Constitution's Commerce Clause. At least one appeals court—the 11th Circuit, based in Atlanta—concluded that the individual mandate is unconstitutional, because it seeks to regulate commerce by compelling individuals to enter into commerce (*State of Florida v. U.S. Department of Health and Human Services*, 2011-2 USTC Par. 50,573). The court said that under the government's argument, there is literally no individual decision that does not have an economic impact and affect interstate commerce, giving the federal government unlimited license to regulate activities. However, the court did uphold the rest of the law. Another appeals court—the Sixth Circuit, based in Cincinnati—upheld the mandate itself and the overall law (*Thomas More Law Center v. Obama,* 2011-2 USTC Par. 50,473).

Interstate commerce issues. In some cases, the government has argued that that the law stands as a whole, and is based on the overall impact of health care decisions on interstate commerce. If the individual mandate is overturned, the statute would fail, the government has said. However, now that some courts have shown a willingness to throw out the individual mandate, this issue of "severability" of the statute has taken a different turn, with the government no longer emphasizing the interrelationship of different parts of the statute. Some cases against the federal government have been dismissed on grounds of standing; other cases have recognized the standing of parties to bring a lawsuit.

U.S. Supreme Court. From the beginning, many commentators have said that the Supreme Court will have to decide the validity of this law. Federal courts of appeal will be anxious to pass the issue on for review. With a split in the courts of appeal, the High Court has a convenient basis for taking jurisdiction of the issue. Many expect the court to take the case in its 2011–2012 term (beginning October 2011), with a decision coming in 2012 (by June 2012). This would result in a decision before the 2012 presidential election. Some analysts see four liberal judges upholding the law, three conservative judges rejecting the law, and Chief Justice Roberts and Justice Anthony Kennedy having wildcard positions.

STUDY QUESTIONS

3. Starting in 2018, insurance companies will be subject to a 40 percent excise tax if they offer:
   a. Major medical coverage
   b. Cadillac plans
   c. Reports to employees of the value of their health insurance

4. Litigation about the individual mandate for health care under the reform package often centers on the:
   a. Due Process Clause of the U.S. Constitution
   b. Commerce Clause of the U.S. Constitution
   c. First Amendment of the U.S. Constitution

NEW TAXES

The health care package imposes substantial new taxes on higher-income taxpayers, estates, and trusts. The taxes take effect in 2013 and include a 3.8 percent "unearned income Medicare contributions" tax and a 0.9 percent additional hospital insurance tax on earned income. These taxes will apply to owners of passthrough entities as well as other high-income individuals.

PLANNING POINTER

Commentators indicate that choice of entity decisions will not be strongly affected, because the new taxes primarily increase the tendencies that are already present: the taxes may have less impact on passthrough entities than C corporations; S corporations may be more beneficial than partnerships. But there will be an impact on spending and compensation choices for closely held businesses.

The 3.8 Percent Tax

The 3.8 percent unearned income tax is imposed on the lesser of:
- Net investment income; or
- The excess of modified adjusted gross income (AGI) over the threshold amounts
  - $200,000 for single individuals or heads of household,
  - $250,000 for joint filers and surviving spouses, and
  - $125,000 for married couples filing separate returns.

EXAMPLE

Teresa Sanchez has modified AGI of $225,000 and net investment income of $50,000. The tax applies to the lesser of her net investment income ($50,000), or modified AGI ($225,000) reduced by the threshold for a single person ($200,000), or $25,000. Thus, her tax is 3.8 percent of $25,000, or $950. The tax does not apply to the entire $50,000 of net investment income.

EXAMPLE

Robert and Cindy Collins file a joint return. They have $300,000 in wages and $75,000 in net investment income. The tax applies to the lesser of net investment income ($75,000) or modified AGI ($375,000) reduced by the applicable threshold ($250,000), or $125,000. Their tax is 3.8 percent of $75,000, or $2,850.

COMMENT

None of these amounts is adjusted for inflation. The tax revenues are estimated to raise $210 billion during the period 2013–2019. If the Bush tax cuts expire for higher-income individuals, the highest income tax rate will become 39.6 percent plus 3.8 percent, or a total of 43.4 percent.

Net investment income. *Net investment income* includes:

- Interest, dividends, royalties, and rents, unless derived in the ordinary course of a trade or business;
- Gains from property used in a passive activity; and
- Income earned from a trade or business that is a passive activity.

Investment income is reduced by allowable deductions allocated to the income.

COMMENT

Ordinarily, passive activity income is useful because it can offset passive activity losses, which otherwise would not be deductible. Under the new law, passive activity income will trigger the 3.8 percent tax.

COMMENT

If an interest in a partnership or S corp is sold, net investment income only includes net gain attributable to property held by the entity that is not used in an active trade or business.

Net investment income does not include:

- Distributions from qualified retirement plans and individual retirement accounts;
- Tax-exempt interest; or
- Excluded gain from the sale of a principal residence (but does include taxable gain).

In addition, the tax does not apply to nonresident aliens.

PLANNING POINTER

Insurance and deferred annuities will become more appealing, as well as tax-exempt bonds. Owners of closely held corporations may want to pay more salary and fewer dividends to avoid the 3.8 percent tax. The 3.8 percent tax will be significant to closely-held C corporations; the tax is an extra charge on corporate income distributed as dividends. S corporations avoid this: the tax does not apply to day-to-day income or to income from the sale of the business. For partnerships, the results are mixed. There will be an increase in the self-employment tax, but a continued flowthrough of profits from a business.

The threshold amount includes income from an IRA, even though IRA income is not net investment income.

> **PLANNING POINTER**
>
> Roth conversions may become more appealing, because distributions from a Roth account are not income and will not enter into the calculation of the threshold amount.

Estates and trusts. Estates and trusts pay the 3.8 percent tax on the lesser of undistributed net investment income, or the excess of adjusted gross income over the dollar amount at which the highest income tax bracket begins, adjusted for inflation ($11,350 for 2011 and $11.650 for 2012). Thus, trusts may be less beneficial for income-splitting with children. However, charitable remainder trusts and other tax-exempt trusts are excluded from the tax.

The 0.9 Percent Tax

The 0.9 percent hospital insurance (HI) tax applies to wages and self-employment income that exceeds a threshold. The earned income threshold is:

- $200,000 for single individuals;
- $250,000 for joint filers; and
- $125,000 for married taxpayers filing separately.

In the case of a joint return, the 0.9 percent tax is imposed on the combined wages of the taxpayer and the taxpayer's spouse.

The *Federal Insurance Contributions Act* already imposes a 1.45 percent HI tax on both employers and employees with respect to the employee's wages, a total tax of 2.9 percent. Unlike Social Security taxes, which apply to a specified wage base (capped at $106,800 for 2011), the HI tax is not capped and applies to all wages.

Self-employed taxpayers. Self-employed individuals pay both the employer and employee portions of the 2.9 percent tax, but those taxpayers are entitled to a business deduction for one-half of their self-employment tax liability to determine adjusted gross income. However, this deduction does not apply to the 0.9 percent tax.

Withholding. An employer is required to withhold the 0.9 percent tax if the employee receives more than $200,000 in wages from a single employer. The employer does not have to determine wages earned by the spouse or by the same employee for another employer. Thus, an employee could meet the wage threshold ($200,000) without the tax being withheld. In that case, the employee is responsible for paying the tax.

PLANNING POINTER

It will be necessary to plan for and compute this additional tax when preparing an individual's tax return. Withholding and/or estimated tax payments may need to be adjusted. These considerations may also apply to the 3.8 percent tax on unearned income.

Result: Avoiding current income. The additional tax on high earners, plus the potential rollback of the Bush tax cuts, will encourage many small business owners to look for methods of avoiding current income, such as increased retirement plan savings, consideration of Subchapter S status, or becoming limited liability companies.

S corporations may become more desirable, because proper planning can shift taxable earnings subject to the 0.9 percent tax to certain S corporation income that is not subject to the tax. If the owner materially participates in the S corp's business, profits reported to the owner on Schedule K-1 will be income but will not be subject to the self-employment tax, whereas profits reported by a partnership or LLC on Schedule K-1 may still be treated as wages and be subject to the tax. Taxpayers may also want to consider borrowing by the entities to generate interest deductions against business income.

COMMENT

Owner-employees of S corporations must take a reasonable salary, but this is a subjective test that is not easily enforced. Owners can limit their salary and then take higher corporate distributions that are not subject to the 0.9 percent tax.

SMALL EMPLOYER TAX CREDIT

The health care laws provide a temporary tax credit to help small employers offset the cost of employer-provided health coverage. The credit is set at 35 percent of health insurance premiums through 2013 (25 percent for tax-exempt employers), and increases to 50 percent in 2014 and 2015 (35 percent for tax-exempt). After 2013, the credit applies only to health insurance purchased through a state-established insurance exchange. For earlier years, the employer has the option of offering the insurance through an exchange. The credit expires after 2015, although it is possible it could be extended.

PLANNING POINTER

Each state must establish an American Health Benefit Exchange and a Small Business Health Options Program (SHOP Exchange) by January 1, 2014, to provide qualified individuals and qualified small business employers with access to qualified health exchanges.

Qualifying for the credit. The maximum percentage is available for the smallest employers, with 10 or fewer employees and average annual wages of $25,000 or less. The employer must pay a uniform percentage of premiums, equal to at least one-half of the cost of health insurance premiums for its participating employees (determined for single coverage). Salary reduction contributions, health reimbursement arrangements, and health savings accounts are not counted. The credit phases out as the number of employees rises to 25 and as average annual wages increase to $50,000. The wage amounts are indexed for inflation after 2013.

> **COMMENT**
>
> The phaseout is equal to 6.67 percent for each full-time equivalent employee in excess of 10, and is four percent for each $1,000 of wages in excess of $25,000.

Because the credit is temporary, some think it will not have much of an impact on hiring and the decision to provide health insurance. When the law was enacted, the Obama Administration estimated that up to 4 million small businesses may be eligible for the credit, although some of those may not offer any health insurance coverage.

The number of employees is the number of "full-time equivalent employees," determined by dividing total hours of compensated service by 2,080 (52 weeks × 40 hours/week). Owners are not taken into account, including self-employed individuals, partners, 2 percent shareholders of S corporations, and 5 percent owners of C corporations. Dependents and most relatives of owners are also excluded.

> **COMMENT**
>
> Thus, the number of FTE employees is not increased by owner/employees and does not increase the phaseout. On the other hand, premiums paid for owners' health insurance are not counted toward the total premiums paid for employees (and eligible for the credit).

Revisiting the small employer status. An employer determines its status as a small employer each year. An estate or trust must apportion the credit between itself and its beneficiaries based on the income allocated to each. For tax-exempt employers, the credit offsets, and is limited to, the amount of the organization's payroll taxes. The deduction for employer-paid premiums is reduced by the credit amount. The credit is part of the general business credit; therefore, it can be carried back 1 year and carried forward 20 years.

Companies treated as a single employer under Code Sec. 414(b) are also aggregated and treated as a single employer, when applying the credit. The IRS can issue rules to prevent the use of multiple entities to qualify for the credit and avoid the phaseout rules.

The credit may not be claimed on "excessive" premiums. Premiums eligible for the credit cannot exceed the average premium for the small group market in the ratings area (generally the state) in which the employee enrolls for coverage. The IRS provides information about average premiums.

STUDY QUESTIONS

5. Because it will trigger the 3.8 percent tax on net investment income and higher AGI income starting in 2013, passive activity income will become less attractive. **True or False?**

6. The small employer tax credit is part of and subject to the carryover periods of the:

    a. Work opportunity credit

    b. General business credit

    c. Empowerment zone and renewal community employment credit

EMPLOYER MANDATE

The health care law does not, in so many words, require employers to provide health insurance coverage for their employees. However, beginning in 2014, an "applicable large employer" (50 or more employees or full-time equivalents) will owe a penalty—termed an "assessable payment"—if it does not offer its full-time employees (and their dependents) an employer-sponsored plan that provides "minimum essential coverage." This is the *employer mandate.* The penalty applies for any month in which one or more full-time employees has enrolled in a qualified health plan through a state-established exchange, *and* the employee qualifies for a premium tax credit or cost-sharing reduction.

COMMENT

The credit or reduction is generally available to lower- and middle-income employees that are not offered affordable minimum essential coverage.

Penalties

$2,000 penalty. This "all-employee" penalty amounts to $2,000 per year per employee, but is imposed per month. The penalty is 1/12 of $2,000, or $166.67 per month, times the number of full-time employees for the month. The number of full-time employees is reduced by 30 when calculating the penalty. The payment is nondeductible and can be substantial; some have called it "draconian."

> **EXAMPLE**
>
> In 2014, Penn Corporation fails to offer minimum essential coverage. Ten of its employees receive a premium tax credit for enrolling in a health insurance plan offered by a state exchange. Penn has 90 full-time employees. Therefore, for each of 60 of its employees, it owes $166.67 a month. This equals $10,000 a month or $120,000 for the year.

$3,000 penalty. Alternatively, there is a $3,000 annual ($250 per month) penalty or "assessable payment" on an employer that offers minimum essential coverage to its full-time employees, if any employee with household income below 400 percent of the federal poverty level instead chooses to obtain insurance through a state-established exchange. The employer pays the penalty based on the actual number of employees who purchase insurance through the exchange. The $3,000 payment is also nondeductible. The amount of this penalty cannot exceed the $2,000 per employee penalty for a failure to offer coverage.

> **COMMENT**
>
> Some view the $3,000 penalty as applying under the same circumstances as the $2,000 penalty, with the employer liable for the lower amount. Others view the penalties as different, depending on whether the employer offers adequate coverage.

An IRS list of "open" issues that need guidance identified the following:

- Will an applicable large employer be subject to the "all-employee" penalty, even if the employer fails to provide minimum essential coverage to only one of its full-time employees or their dependents? The IRS has indicated that this penalty will not apply if the employer provides coverage to "substantially all" of its employees, but how much is "substantially all"?
- Will employers be subject to a $40,000 penalty just because they hire a 50th employee and become an applicable large employer?
- Will an employer who provides minimum essential coverage to all of its employees still be subject to the penalty because a related employer does not? Does the employer providing coverage serve to increase the penalty for another taxable employer?

Impact. Many have questioned whether the $2,000 per employee penalty could apply to an employer that offers coverage to some, but not all, of its employees. What if the employer misclassifies an employee as an independent contractor and does not offer coverage to that individual? Although the application of the alternative penalties would seem to depend on the availability of minimum essential coverage, the legislative history itself suggests that the $2,000 per employee penalty may apply if a single employee is not covered. Whatever the number is, whether one employee, or less than "substantially all" employees, there will be a cliff effect. At some point, not covering one additional employee will trigger the penalty.

COMMENT

Commentators state that if the employer is not providing minimum essential coverage or better, the penalty puts tremendous pressure on the employer to offer that coverage. Some employers may choose to cancel coverage, but if the employer wants to provide coverage, it will need to offer at least minimum essential coverage. Another concern is that with all the new requirements for employer-provided coverage, a plan that lacks one requirement will inadvertently fail to provide minimum essential coverage. Employers will also have to be comfortable that they meet the "substantially all" test for covering all employees.

Because the $2,000 penalty only applies to employers with at least 50 full-time employees, employers nearing the 50-employee threshold may be reluctant to hire that 50th employee if their health coverage does not satisfy the requirements. The numbers requirement also puts a premium on using independent contractors and on properly classifying workers. Suppose an employer has 49 full-time (equivalent) employees and hires one more employee. The employer can be liable for the penalty. If the employer treats the individual as an independent contractor, the employer would seem to be in the clear, but what if the individual is later reclassified as an employee? Would the IRS retroactively assert the penalty?

COMMENT

Under a safe harbor, affordability is based on income at the beginning of the year. If coverage was not affordable, and the employee's income increases during the year, the coverage will still not be affordable, so that the employee will not lose eligibility for a premium credit. The IRS has indicated it will issue guidance providing that an employer will not be subject to a penalty if the employer in fact provides affordable coverage, even though an Exchange determined the coverage was unaffordable, based on an earlier estimate of household income.

The $3,000 employee-by-employee penalty applies for each employee who purchases coverage through the exchange and receives a credit, if the employer-sponsored coverage is "unaffordable." Coverage is unaffordable if the premium costs more than 9.5 percent of the employee's household income, or if the share of benefits paid by the plan is less than 60 percent.

COMMENT

Enrollment in Medicaid does not require the employer to pay a penalty.

EXAMPLE

In 2014, Jersey Corporation offers coverage to its 100 full-time employees. Ten employees enroll in a plan through a state exchange and receive a tax credit. Jersey owes $250/month times 10 employees, a total of $2,500 per month or $30,000 for the year. Jersey has 100 full-time employees, so the penalty is capped at (100 – 30) × $2,000/year, or $140,000 per year. Since the assessable penalty is less than the cap, Jersey owes $30,000 for the year. This is assessed on a monthly basis.

Another concern is that employers must offer coverage to dependents, as well as full-time employees. Dependents can include not only children but parents and other relatives who live in the same house. The need to provide this additional coverage will drive up costs to the employer (and the employee).

COMMENT

Another concern is the tension between an employee's right to privacy and the employer's need to accurately assess its employer mandate penalty. What if an employer questions whether a particular individual is a dependent?

Some commentators have claimed that an employer's annual health care costs are likely to be much greater than the penalties that would apply for failing to provide adequate coverage. Will some employers stop offering insurance? It is possible. Commentators suggest that employers and employees could both come out ahead if the employer saves substantial dollars and shares some of the savings with employees as additional compensation, after accounting for the penalty. This assumes that the employees would qualify for government credits or cost-sharing and would not be hurt by the lapse in employer coverage.

> **COMMENT**
>
> If an employer suspended coverage for its employees, it presumably would have to suspend coverage for any owner-employees, or risk penalties for maintaining a discriminatory health plan. Penalties would be imposed as an excise tax of $100 per day per "affected employee."

Determining the Size of Employers

In determining the employer's size, the aggregation rules in Code Secs. 414(b), (c), (m) and (o) treat multiple employers as a single employer. This includes partnerships, corporations, and proprietorships under common control. Thus, two or more commonly controlled businesses may be treated as one business, with the employer mandate rules applying to both (or all) companies.

An applicable large employer is based on the number of *full-time employees*, defined as:

- Any employee who averages at least 30 hours at work per week;
- An employee who works 130 hours a month; and
- Seasonal employees (who work up to 120 days) can be excluded, but part-time employees are counted. Their hours are aggregated and divided by 120 to determine full-time equivalent employees.

Owner-employees are excluded.

> **COMMENT**
>
> This contrasts with the small employer tax credit for health insurance costs, which is based on employees working 40 hours per week.

> **COMMENT**
>
> For new employers, the 50-employee threshold is determined based on the "average number of employees that it is reasonably expected such employer will employ." This "reasonable expectations" test may complicate planning for startup companies.

Minimum Essential Coverage

Plans that provide minimum essential coverage include:

- Government-sponsored programs, such as Medicare, Medicaid, the Children's Health Insurance Program (CHIP), and veterans' health care;
- An eligible employer-sponsored plan; or

- An eligible individual market plan—the market for insurance coverage offered to individuals not in connection with a group health plan.

Minimum essential coverage does not include coverage that consists of excepted benefits. Excepted benefits are coverage for:
- Accident or disability income insurance;
- Liability insurance;
- Automobile medical payment insurance;
- On-site medical clinics;
- Limited vision or dental benefits in a separate policy;
- Long-term, nursing home, or home health care; and
- Coverage for a specified disease or illness.

An *employer plan* is a group health plan or group health insurance coverage offered through the small or large group market within a state. It includes grandfathered plans. The large group market generally consists of employers with more than 100 employees; the small group market is for employers with 100 employees or fewer. Each state can reduce this threshold to 50 employees through 2016. Employers that grow beyond the size limit can remain eligible for the smaller market. The plan must meet the respective PPACA requirements for grandfathered or nongrandfathered plans.

> **COMMENT**
>
> Loss of grandfathered status will result in more requirements for employer-provided health insurance and will result in increased costs for more employers. Changes in coverage (e.g., elimination of benefits to diagnose or treat a particular condition) or cost (e.g. an increase in co-pays or the percentage of costs covered by the plan), or a decrease in the employer contribution rate by more than 5 percent, may terminate grandfather status. There also are questions about the treatment of self-insured plans, although typically these are maintained by larger employers.

State Health Care Exchanges

State health care exchanges (American Health Benefit Exchanges) must be established in each state by 2014. An exchange must make qualified health plans available to qualified individuals and qualified employers (those having 100 or fewer employees). An exchange cannot make available a plan that is not qualified.

A plan offered through an exchange must offer an essential health benefits package that includes specific categories of benefits; meets certain cost-sharing standards; and provides certain levels of coverage. The exchanges will have four levels of "essential benefits coverage" available to participants:

- Bronze—benefits that are actuarially equivalent to 60 percent of the full actuarial value of the benefits provided under the plan;
- Silver—70 percent;
- Gold—80 percent; and
- Platinum—90 percent.

Exchanges are supposed to facilitate the comparison and purchase of qualified health plans by small employers and individuals. Exchanges must:

- Implement procedures for certifying plans as qualified health plans;
- Provide standardized comparative information on health plans;
- Assign a rating to each qualified plan offered through the Exchange;
- Establish a calculator to determine the actual cost of coverage after applying the premium assistance tax credit or any cost-sharing reduction;
- Provide the IRS with the name and Social Security number of each individual who was an employee but was determined to be eligible for the premium assistance tax credit; and
- Provide employers with the names of its employees who ceased coverage under a qualified health plan.

COMMENT

The penalties and the premium tax credit depend on employees using the exchanges to obtain their health insurance coverage. The law encourages employees to go to the exchanges.

STUDY QUESTIONS

---

7. Minimum essential coverage includes plans such as:

   a. Eligible employer-sponsored plans

   b. Disability insurance

   c. Long-term insurance

8. The deadline for establishing American Health Benefit Exchanges (state health care exchanges) is:

   a. 2014

   b. 2013

   c. 2012

THE INDIVIDUAL MANDATE

Terms of the Mandate

The individual mandate becomes effective in 2014. A penalty is imposed on individuals who fail to obtain minimum essential health coverage for themselves and their dependents. The penalty is imposed monthly and is equal to 1/12 of the greater of a flat dollar amount or the applicable percentage of household income. It is imposed irrespective of whether the individual is an employee, independent contractor, or otherwise self-employed.

Penalty for Those Not Having Minimum Essential Health Coverage

The amount of the penalty is tied to the tax year:

- For 2014, the penalty is the greater of $95 or 1 percent of income;
- For 2015, the greater of $325 or 2 percent of income;
- For 2016, the greater of $695 or 2.5 percent of income; and
- The $695 amount is indexed for inflation after 2016, with each adjustment rounded down to the lowest multiple of $50.

For a family of four with income of $89,400 (four times the FPL), the penalty would be $894 for 2014 (1 percent of income); $1,788 for 2015 (2 percent of income); and $2,235 for 2016 (2.5 percent of income).

> **COMMENT**
>
> Household income includes adjusted gross income plus tax-exempt interest for the taxpayer, spouse (if filing a joint return), and dependents whose taxable incomes exceed their filing threshold for the year.

> **COMMENT**
>
> The government is trying to impose a significant enough penalty to encourage everyone to buy health insurance. This goes hand-in-hand with guaranteed eligibility for health care. An individual who discovers that he or she has a health problem can still get coverage. The mandate is designed to prevent employees from jumping in and out of coverage, so that the healthiest individuals cannot cherry-pick their timing. However, the penalties are not huge. A penalty that amounts to approximately $2,200 is not much compared to family coverage that could cost over $10,000. Plus the penalty will be difficult to collect. The IRS itself asks whether it can only collect the penalty by offsetting a refund.

The flat dollar amount is the sum of the penalty for each person in the household who lacks minimum essential health coverage whom the taxpayer is required to insure (spouse and dependents). However, the total penalty cannot exceed the lesser of three times the flat dollar amount (e.g., $285 for 2014; $2085 for 2016), or the *national* average premium for qualified health coverage offered through an exchange at the bronze level of coverage. For individuals younger than age 18, the applicable flat dollar amount is one-half of the specified amounts.

COMMENT

An individual who is divorced might ordinarily want to claim the dependency deduction for a child. However, the increase in the potential individual mandate penalty for dependents may discourage such arrangements, so that the individual will not be obligated to obtain health insurance for the child. Parents may not want to provide more than one-half of the individual's support for the calendar year.

Exemptions. A number of exemptions from the individual mandate will apply:

- A significant exemption applies to an individual whose "required contribution" would exceed 8 percent of household income ("unaffordable coverage");
- Individuals with incomes below the federal income tax filing thresholds are also exempt;
- Other exemptions apply to people with religious objections, undocumented aliens, individuals suffering hardship, individuals outside the United States, and dependents (because the person claiming the dependency exemption is liable); and
- Persons enduring short lapses of coverage (less than three months) are also exempt.

COMMENT

There are no corresponding exceptions for employers under the employer mandate.

In determining whether coverage is affordable, household income is based on the most recent tax year for which information is available. Household income is increased by any portion of the required contribution made through a salary reduction agreement and excluded from the individual's gross income.

Impact of required participation. Because the FPL for a family of four is $22,350 for 2011, the required contribution for a family at the poverty line is 8 percent of that amount, or $1,788. The filing thresholds for individuals for 2010 were:

- $9,350 (single);
- $12,050 (head of household);
- $18,700 (joint or surviving spouse); and
- $3,650 (married filing separately).

Required contribution. If the individual can purchase coverage through an employer-sponsored plan, the required contribution is the employee's share of the annual premium paid for self-only coverage. Otherwise, the required contribution is the annual premium for the lowest cost bronze plan available in the individual market through the state exchange, in the rating area in which the individual resides, reduced by the individual's premium assistance credit as if the individual were covered by an exchange-offered health plan.

Employer concerns. The individual mandate is a major source of uncertainty for employers. First, much of the litigation challenging the health care law is focused on the individual mandate. As stated earlier, some courts have upheld the entire law, including the individual mandate; other courts have thrown out the individual mandate as an unconstitutional extension of Congress's power to regulate interstate commerce, while upholding other aspects of the law.

Another uncertain aspect of the individual mandate is its potential impact on employer compensation practices. If the penalty seems small, commentators suggest that employees could refuse to sign up for coverage and may prefer more salary rather than health insurance premium payments. However, employees may want health insurance coverage, for its own sake, as well as to avoid the individual mandate penalty. Thus, employees may place a higher value on coverage, and employers may have an incentive to provide health insurance coverage instead of higher salary. Commentators say that providing insurance may make more sense for the employer even if the employer mandate does not apply. Thus, employers cannot be indifferent to the individual mandate.

COMMENT

Some commentators calculate that if an employer's employees earn wages at or less than 250 percent of the FPL, it may pay for the employer to discontinue insurance coverage, increase the employee's pay, and have the employees purchase coverage through an exchange. Some employers have declared that they could obtain huge savings by ceasing insurance coverage and paying the employer mandate penalty.

Collection of penalty amounts. The penalty is included with the individual's income tax. The penalty is generally assessed and collected in the same manner as other tax penalties. Married couples are jointly and severally liable for the penalty for themselves and their dependents. However, enforcement is limited in two ways:

- The IRS cannot use liens or levies to collect any unpaid penalty; and
- Taxpayers are not subject to criminal prosecution or any additional penalty for failing to pay the penalty.

> **COMMENT**
>
> Some speculate that the IRS can only collect the penalty by offsetting income tax refunds. If the IRS intends to collect the penalty by offsetting refunds, employees might try to juggle (reduce) their withholding to avoid refunds that the IRS could offset.

THE PREMIUM TAX CREDIT

Beginning in 2014, taxpayers with household income between 100 percent and 400 percent of the federal poverty level (FPL) can qualify for a refundable health insurance premium assistance credit. The individual must enroll in a qualified health plan through an exchange. In addition to income, eligibility for the credit is based on family size and filing status. An individual cannot be claimed as a dependent and, if married, must file a joint return.

> **COMMENT**
>
> The Congressional Budget Office estimates that when the health care law is fully phased in, individuals will receive an average premium tax credit of more than $5,000 a year. The U.S. Department of Health and Human Services has indicated that savings could be as much as $9,900 for a family of four with an income of $33,525, and could still amount to $3,500 for a family with income of $78,225.

Effects of the Credit

The premium tax credit is of major importance to employers because it is the triggering mechanism for the employer mandate penalty. The premium tax credit also reduces the benefit to employees of obtaining health insurance coverage through their employer, thus encouraging them to obtain coverage through an exchange. Thus, the incentive will be strong for the employer to offer an affordable qualified group health plan.

Federal Poverty Level

The federal poverty level (FPL) is $22,050 for a family of four for 2010; $22,350 for 2011. Thus, a family can have substantial income—up to 400 percent of the FPL, or over $89,000—and still qualify for the credit. The FPL is adjusted annually so the figures will be higher in 2014 when the exchanges become operational. The FPL for computing the credit for a tax year is the FPL in effect on the first day of the initial or annual open enrollment period preceding that tax year.

EXAMPLE

A family of four has household income of $50,000 and purchases the benchmark plan. The income is 224 percent of the FPL. The premium for the benchmark plan is $9,000. The expected family contribution is $3,570. The premium tax credit equals $5,430 ($9,000 – $3,570). Thus, in fact, the actual family contribution is $3,570 (its out-of-pocket costs). If the family purchases a less expensive plan (e.g. premium of $7,500), the premium tax credit remains the same, but the family's out-of-pocket cost drops to $2,070.

Individuals having incomes below 100 percent of the FPL will generally be eligible for Medicaid and ineligible for the premium tax credit. Individuals on Medicare or who can enroll in "affordable" employer-provided coverage are also ineligible, regardless of whether the individual actually enrolls in employer-provided coverage. Coverage is not affordable if it costs more than 9.5 percent of household income or if the group health plan's share of the total cost of benefits is less than 60 percent. A taxpayer will not lose eligibility for the credit if the taxpayer's household income increases midyear. The cost of coverage could fluctuate if the taxpayer's family size changes during the year.

COMMENT

There is an exception for COBRA coverage provided by the employer. An individual must actually enroll in COBRA coverage to be considered eligible for minimum essential coverage.

Credit Amount

The credit equals the lower of:

- The amount paid by the taxpayer to the Exchange for coverage for the taxpayer, spouse, and dependents, or
- The difference between the premium for a benchmark plan (silver coverage, the second lowest cost plan) and the taxpayer's expected contribution.

The expected contribution is the "applicable percentage" for the taxpayer's level of household income, times that income.

COMMENT

By making the silver level the benchmark, taxpayers can get a larger credit than if the bronze level were the benchmark.

> **COMMENT**
>
> The applicable percentage ranges from 2 percent (for household incomes up to 133 percent of the FPL) to 9.5 percent (for incomes up to 400 percent of the FPL). For tax years after 2014, the initial and final applicable percentages will be adjusted to reflect the excess of premium growth over income growth for the preceding calendar year.

Advance Payment

Some employees will be entitled to an advance payment of the credit, calculated by the Department of Health and Human Services, though it will be paid by the Treasury Department. The advance credit will be calculated during an individual's open enrollment period and will be based on household income and tax status for the most recent tax year. Again, this could change, for example, if the individual gets married or divorced.

If the advance payment for the year exceeds the allowable credit, the excess is an increase in taxes owed for the year. The increase is limited to $400 for a married taxpayer and $250 for an unmarried taxpayer, if the taxpayer's household income is less than 400 percent of the FPL. Conversely, if the credit exceeds the advance payment, the taxpayer will be entitled to a refund.

> **COMMENT**
>
> Individuals who receive the credit must file an income tax return to reconcile the advance credit, even if the individual's income would normally be too low for a return to be filed.

OTHER CHANGES

The law makes other changes that will affect individuals, employers, and benefits. There will be a $2 per participant fee on health insurance (paid by the issuer) and self-insured plans (paid by the employer). There will be a cap on employee contributions to a health flexible spending account of $2,500. Commentators say this will eliminate the most "employee-friendly" health care alternative. There are new taxes on tanning services and medical devices. Employers must report the cost of coverage they provide. They also must provide plan summaries for self-insured group health plans and 60-days notice of any material modification in the plan. Employers also must give employees a notice describing coverage options through the exchanges.

STUDY QUESTIONS

---

9. One concern of employers is the premium tax credit because it is the triggering mechanism for the employer mandate penalty. *True or False?*

10. If the advance payment of the premium tax credit for the year exceeds the allowable credit, the excess is:

    a. An increase in taxes the taxpayer owes for that year

    b. Carried over as a tax credit for the following tax year

    c. Recovered by having the taxpayer file an amended income tax return for that year

---

CONCLUSION

The new health care law is far-reaching and complex. It creates tremendous uncertainty for many individuals, their families, employees, and employers. The federal government will continue to issue guidance and respond to problems identified by affected parties. The only certainty is that the law will continue to develop. Taxpayers, both employers and individuals, need to understand their new rights and responsibilities so that they can make appropriate decisions about health care coverage.

Expensing and Bonus Depreciation: Dealing with Sunsets

This chapter discusses the bonus depreciation deduction, focusing especially on the requirements for claiming bonus depreciation at a 100 percent rate. Bonus depreciation is compared to the expensing under Code Sec. 179. Special rules that allow taxpayer's to expense qualified real property under Section 179 are highlighted.

LEARNING OBJECTIVES

Upon completion of this chapter you will be able to:

- Identify the types of property that quality for bonus depreciation;
- Understand the acquisition and placed-in-service deadlines that apply to the 100 percent bonus rate;
- Understand how an asset's date of acquisition is determined;
- Understand special rules that apply to property having a longer production;
- Describe the election to claim the 100 percent rate on components of self-constructed property;
- Compute safe harbor luxury car depreciation on passenger cars eligible for a 100 percent rate;
- Describe how bonus depreciation interacts with other tax code provisions;
- Differentiate similarities and differences between bonus depreciation and the Section 179 allowance; and
- Describe the Section 179 election for qualified real property.

INTRODUCTION

The bonus depreciation deduction is one of the most important tax benefits available to businesses, large or small. The power of this incentive is at its maximum in 2011, because the bonus rate for qualifying assets acquired after September 8, 2010, and placed in service before 2012 is increased from 50 percent to 100 percent. For assets placed in service in 2012, the bonus rate drops to 50 percent. Unless Congress extends this tax incentive again, bonus depreciation will expire in 2013.

This chapter reviews the basic rules for claiming bonus depreciation, directing particular attention to the special requirements in order for the 100 percent rate to apply.

The statutory language implementing the 100 percent bonus deduction (Code Sec. 168(k)(5)) left many unanswered questions regarding qualification for the 100 percent rate. Most of these issues were tackled head-on by the IRS in Rev. Proc. 2011-26, which was issued on March 29, 2011. Rev. Proc. 2011-26 will be referenced throughout this chapter.

Taxpayers should not let the 100 percent bonus deduction overshadow the usefulness of the Section 179 expense deduction. In some cases it is preferable to claim a Section 179 expense deduction in place of bonus depreciation. There are also situations in which an asset will qualify for expensing under Section 179 but will not qualify for bonus depreciation at either the 50 percent or 100 percent rate. This chapter considers these and other issues surrounding Section 179 provisions that are relevant to the 2011 tax year, particularly the expiring election to treat qualified real property as Section 179 property.

BONUS BASICS

Before the chapter considers some of the more complex issues surrounding the bonus deduction, the types of property that qualify and do not qualify for bonus depreciation are discussed. In addition, the text reviews computation of the bonus deduction.

Types of Property Qualifying for Bonus Depreciation

Bonus depreciation may only be claimed on the following types of property (Code Sec. 168(k)(2)(A)):

- MACRS property with a recovery period of 20 years or fewer;
- MACRS water utility property;
- MACRS qualified leasehold improvement property; and
- Depreciable computer software, whether developed internally or purchased.

COMMENT

The modified accelerated cost recovery system (MACRS) is the primary system used to depreciate assets placed in service since 1987.

COMMENT

Computer software that is amortizable over 15 years under Section 197 does not qualify for bonus depreciation. Software is amortizable under Section 197 only if it is acquired in connection with the purchase of the assets of an entire trade or business. Off-the-shelf computer software is never considered a Section 197 intangible and, therefore, qualifies for bonus depreciation.

The regular MACRS recovery period (i.e., the general depreciation system (GDS) recovery period) is used to determine whether MACRS property has a recovery period of 20 or fewer years even if the straight-line MACRS alternative depreciation system (MACRS ADS) is elected and a longer recovery period applies.

COMMENT

The recovery period of an asset is the assigned number of years over which the cost of an asset is depreciated or recovered under MACRS. The MACRS ADS recovery period assigned to an asset is usually longer than the GDS recovery period.

Property That Does Not Qualify for Bonus Depreciation

The following property cannot qualify for bonus depreciation:

- Used property;
- Any property that must be depreciated using the MACRS ADS;
- Any property, except for computer software, that is not depreciated using MACRS (e.g., intangible property, property depreciated using the sum-of-the-years'-digits method, income-forecast method, or work hours method); and
- An asset placed in service and disposed of in the same tax year.

The following property must be depreciated under the MACRS ADS and, therefore, does not qualify for bonus depreciation:

- Property used predominantly outside of the United States, other than airplanes, vessels, containers, and vehicles used in transportation activities between the United States and foreign countries;
- Tangible property leased to a tax-exempt entity (tax-exempt use property);
- Property to the extent it is financed with tax-exempt bonds (tax-exempt, bond-financed property); and
- Listed property used *50 percent or less for business purposes* during the tax year.

Listed property includes:

- Passenger automobiles (e.g., cars, SUVs, trucks, and vans) subject to the Code Sec. 280F annual depreciation limitations because they have a gross vehicle weight rating (GVWR) less than 6,000 pounds;
- Any means of transportation, such as an airplane or vehicle not subject to the Code Sec. 280F limits;
- Property of a type that is generally used for recreation, amusement, or entertainment; and
- Computers or peripheral equipment.

A listed property must be depreciated using the MACRS ADS (and, therefore, does not qualify for bonus depreciation) if its business use is 50 percent or less in the tax year the listed property is placed in service. If business use drops to 50 percent or less in a later tax year during the ADS recovery period, depreciation—including the bonus deduction—is subject to recapture in an amount equal to the difference between the depreciation and bonus deductions previously claimed and the depreciation deductions that could have been claimed using ADS.

COMMENT

A property that must be depreciated using MACRS ADS in the tax year that it is placed in service does not qualify for bonus depreciation. However, if a taxpayer elects to use ADS to depreciate property for which ADS is not mandatory, bonus depreciation can be claimed.

EXAMPLE

Geoffrey Firth, a business owner taxpayer, places a car used 100 percent for business in service in 2011 and elects to depreciate the property using ADS. The car may qualify for bonus depreciation. If the car is used 50 percent or less in Geoffrey's business in 2011, the use of ADS is mandatory and the car cannot qualify for bonus depreciation.

COMMENT

Bonus depreciation is not subject to recapture if there is a decline in business use to 50 percent or less unless the asset on which bonus depreciation is claimed is a listed property.

Computation of Bonus Depreciation Allowance

The bonus deduction is equal to the applicable percentage (i.e., 50 percent or 100 percent) of the "unadjusted depreciable basis" of the qualified property (Reg. § 1.168(k)-1(d)(1)). *Unadjusted depreciable basis* is generally the cost reduced by any amount expensed under Section 179 and any other required basis adjustments (such as the basis adjustment for 50 percent of the investment credit) (Reg. § 1.168(k)-1(a)(2)(iii)).

EXAMPLE

MediCo places 7-year MACRS property costing $1 million in service on August 10, 2010. The 50 percent bonus rate applies because MediCo acquired the property before September 9, 2010. The company claims a $500,000 Section 179 expense deduction on the property. The bonus deduction is $250,000 (($1 million − $500,000 Section 179 expense) × 50% bonus rate). MACRS depreciation deductions are then claimed over the 7-year recovery period on the remaining $250,000 basis ($1,000,000 − $500,000 Section 179 expense − $250,000 bonus deduction = $250,000). If the 100 percent rate applied and MediCo claimed a $500,000 Section 179 deduction, the bonus deduction would have been $500,000 (($1,000,000 − $500,000 Section 179 expense) × 100%) and no regular depreciation would be claimed because the entire cost is claimed as a Section 179 expense and bonus deduction.

NOTE

The bonus deduction is claimed in the tax year that a qualifying depreciable asset is placed in service. The tax year that an asset is placed in service is not necessarily the same tax year that the asset is acquired.

Basis Adjustment for Tax Credits and "Section 1603 Payments" in Lieu of Energy Credit

Prior to a taxpayer computing the bonus deduction (or regular depreciation deductions), the basis of property is reduced by the amount of any credits claimed for the property that require an adjustment to basis such as the disabled access credit (Code Sec. 44), the energy credit (Code Sec. 48), or any payments received for specified energy property under Section 1603 of the *American Recovery and Reinvestment Tax Act of 2009,* Division B, Pub. L. 111-5, 123 Stat. 115 (Section 1603 payments) (Rev. Proc. 2011-26, Section 3.03(5)).

Energy credit. The basis of property for which an energy credit is claimed is reduced by 50 percent of the credit.

The energy credit applies to a variety of energy-production property, including energy produced from solar, wind, and geothermal sources. If a taxpayer takes a Section 1603 payment in lieu of an energy credit, the basis of the energy property is reduced by 50 percent of the grant before computing bonus depreciation and regular depreciation (Code Sec. 48(d)).

Rehabilitation credit. A taxpayer may claim bonus depreciation on rehabilitation expenditures (as defined in Code Sec. 47(c)(2)) that are not residential rental or nonresidential real property. The rehabilitation credit, however, may only be claimed on the cost (or other applicable basis) of the rehabilitation expenditures less the amount claimed as bonus depreciation. Accordingly, if the 100 percent bonus deduction is claimed, the credit cannot be claimed. If the 50 percent bonus rate applies, the credit may only be claimed on the cost remaining after reduction by the bonus allowance. A taxpayer claiming the rehabilitation credit must depreciate the remaining basis of the rehabilitation expenditures using an MACRS straight-line method (Reg. § 1.168(k)-1(f)(10)).

STUDY QUESTIONS

---

1. Which of the following assets does **not** qualify for bonus depreciation?

a. Computer software purchased at a brick-and-mortar store

b. A pick-up truck, regardless of weight, used less than 50 percent for business in the year it is placed in service

c. An electricity generation plant with an MACRS recovery period of 20 years

2. Before a taxpayer computes bonus depreciation, the cost of an asset is reduced by:

a. Any amount expensed under Section 179

b. 100 percent of any Section 1603 grant taken in lieu of the energy credit

c. The first-year depreciation deduction

ORIGINAL USE REQUIREMENT

The original use of the property must begin with the taxpayer after December 31, 2007, in order to claim bonus depreciation. However, the 100 percent bonus rate cannot apply unless the original use begins with the taxpayer after September 8, 2010 (Rev. Proc. 2011-26, Section 3.02(c)).

Original use refers to the *first use* to which the property is put (Reg. § 1.168(k)-1(b)(3)).

COMMENT

The original use requirement means that used property acquired by a taxpayer from another person does not qualify for bonus depreciation. An item of new inventory, such as a new car held by a dealer, is considered originally used by the purchaser. Similarly, a taxpayer who purchases an unfinished asset from an unrelated person that is under construction, such as a building, is considered the original user if the taxpayer completes construction and places the asset in service for the taxpayer's own use.

> **EXAMPLE**
>
> Machinal Corporation begins to construct a machine that is not long production property on September 1, 2009. Equip Corporation enters into a binding contract on October 1, 2010, to acquire the incomplete machine. Equip, an accrual-basis taxpayer, accrues $5 million paid for the incomplete machine when it takes possession on November 30, 2010. Equip spends an additional $10 million to complete construction and places the machine in service by December 31, 2011. Equip is considered the original user of the entire machine. The 100 percent bonus rate applies to the entire $15 million cost because the acquisition, placed-in-service, and original use requirements are satisfied.

Leased property purchased by a lessee from the lessor is considered originally used by the lessor.

> **EXAMPLE**
>
> Gareth Bronson, a sole proprietor, leases a new car in 2011 from LeaseCo. In 2013, Gareth purchases the car from LeaseCo. At first glance, it may seem that the original use of the car began with Gareth because the car was "new" when first leased to him. However, the original use of the car actually began with LeaseCo when it purchased the car and held it out for lease to customers. This was the first use to which the car was put. LeaseCo may claim bonus depreciation and regular depreciation deductions on the car while it is leased, and Gareth may claim deductions for the lease payments. When Gareth purchases the car in 2013, it is not eligible for a second round of bonus depreciation but may be eligible for expensing under Section 179 because "used" property qualifies for Section 179 expensing. Any amount not expensed by Gareth will be recovered as MACRS depreciation deductions over the vehicle's recovery period (subject to the Code Sec. 280F annual depreciation limitations, if applicable).

ACQUISITION AND PLACED-IN-SERVICE REQUIREMENTS

Bonus depreciation may only be claimed on qualifying property that satisfies "acquisition date" and "placed-in-service date" requirements (Code Sec. 168(k)(2)(A)).

General Rules

In general, a 50 percent bonus rate applies to property that is acquired after December 31, 2007, and before January 1, 2013, provided no written binding contract for the acquisition of the property (or for its construction, manufacture, or production by a third party) was in effect prior to January 1, 2008.

If the preceding requirements are satisfied and the qualifying property is acquired after September 8, 2010, and placed in service before January 1, 2012, a 100 percent rate applies.

EXAMPLE

ABC acquires and places assets in service on the dates shown. The applicable bonus rate based on these dates is provided.

- ABC acquires an asset on November 1, 2011, and places it in service on December 1, 2011. The 100 percent rate applies;
- ABC acquires an asset on November 1, 2011, and places it in service on January 1, 2012. The 50 percent rate applies;
- ABC acquires an asset on September 10, 2010, and places it in service on December 1, 2011. The 100 percent rate applies; and
- ABC acquires an asset on September 1, 2010, and places it in service on December 1, 2011. The 50 percent rate applies.

The placed-in-service deadlines for the 50 percent and 100 percent rates are extended one year for property with a "longer production period."

This means that long production property qualifies for the 50 percent rate if the asset is acquired after December 31, 2007, and before January 1, 2013 (or a written binding acquisition contract is entered into during this period), and placed in service before January 1, 2014.

The 100 percent rate applies if long production property is acquired after September 8, 2010, and before January 1, 2012 (or a written binding acquisition contract is entered into during this period), and is placed in service before January 1, 2013.

COMMENT

Longer production period property is property that:

- Has an MACRS recovery period of 10 years or greater;
- Costs more than $1 million; and
- Takes longer than one year to build.

The costs of production must be subject to the uniform capitalization rules under Code Sec. 263A. Certain transportation property, mainly commercial aircraft used to transport persons or property, is also considered longer production property (Code Sec. 168(k)(2)(B)). Longer production period property may qualify for bonus depreciation at the 100 percent rate if it is placed in service before January 1, 2013. The 50 percent rate applies if it is placed in service before January 1, 2014. These deadlines are one year longer than those that apply to other qualifying property. Special rules for longer production period property are discussed in more detail later.

Determining Bonus Depreciation Acquisition Date

The rules for determining the acquisition date of an asset are different for the 50 percent and the 100 percent rate. In addition, special rules apply in determining the acquisition date of property that a taxpayer constructs for its own use or contracts with another person to construct, produce, or manufacture for the taxpayer's use. These rules for *self-constructed property* are the same for 50 percent and 100 percent rates property. They are discussed later in this chapter.

Acquisition date rules for the 50 percent bonus rate. For purposes of the 50 percent rate, an asset is considered acquired on the date that the taxpayer takes physical possession or control of the property (Reg. § 1.48-2(b)(6); Reg. § 1.167(c)-1(a)(2))).

However, if a written binding contract for the acquisition was entered into after December 31, 2007, and before January 1, 2013, the requirement that a property must be acquired before January 1, 2013, is deemed satisfied (Code Sec. 168(k)(2)(A)(iii)).

COMMENT

The written binding contract rule for 50 percent rate property only appears relevant for long production property because all property other than long production property must be placed in service by the taxpayer before January 1, 2013, in order to qualify for the 50 percent rate. If a property is deemed acquired when reduced to physical possession or control, then it necessarily follows that it will have been acquired (i.e., reduced to physical possession or control) before January 1, 2013, if it is placed in service by the taxpayer before January 1, 2013. The placed-in-service deadline for long production property, however, is before January 1, 2014. In this situation, a taxpayer that places the long production property in service in 2013 will satisfy the before January 1, 2013, acquisition deadline without regard to the date of physical possession or any other factor if it has entered into a written binding contract before January 1, 2013.

EXAMPLE

Maximal Corporation enters into a written binding contract with Ephemeral Co. to purchase a machine that is long production property on March 1, 2012. The machine is delivered and placed in service by Maximal on November 1, 2013. The requirement that the machine be acquired before January 1, 2013, is deemed satisfied. Maximal may claim bonus depreciation at the 50 percent rate because it is deemed to have acquired the machine before January 1, 2013, and it placed the machine in service before January 1, 2014, the placed-in-service deadline for long production property.

EXAMPLE

ServiceCo Corporation enters into a written binding contract to purchase a machine that is not long production property on March 1, 2012. The machine is delivered and placed in service on January 10, 2013. Even though the machine is deemed acquired on March 1, 2012 (i.e., before the January 1, 2013, acquisition deadline), it does not qualify for bonus depreciation because it was not placed in service before January 1, 2013.

Acquisition date rules for the 100 percent rate. 100 percent rate property is considered acquired when its cost is paid for by a cash-basis taxpayer or incurred by an accrual-basis taxpayer. The paid or incurred test only applies when the return preparer is determining whether a property qualifies for the 100 percent rate (Section 3.02(1) of Rev. Proc. 2011-26).

COMMENT

An accrual-basis taxpayer generally incurs the cost of property when the property is "provided" to the taxpayer and the cost of services as the services are provided (Reg. § 1.461-4(d)(2)(i)). Taxpayers usually consider property as "provided" when it is delivered. A taxpayer, however, is also permitted to treat property as provided when title to the property passes. The method used by the taxpayer to determine when property is provided is a method of accounting that must be used consistently from year to year and cannot be changed without IRS consent (Reg. § 1.461-4(d)(6)(iii)).

EXAMPLE

Allen Hyde, a cash-basis taxpayer, takes delivery of and places a machine in service on December 15, 2011. He pays for the machine on January 15, 2012. The 100 percent bonus rate does not apply because the machine was not "acquired" before January 1, 2012. The machine was deemed acquired on the date of payment.

EXAMPLE

Amanda Regent acquires the same machine as Allen, but Amanda's company uses accrual-basis accounting. Her machine will qualify for the 100 percent rate because it is deemed acquired and placed in service before January 1, 2012. The machine was deemed acquired on December 15, 2011, when delivered to Amanda's company.

COMMENT

In a presentation at the American Bar Association's Tax Section meeting in Washington, D.C., on May 6, 2011, Brandon Carlton, Office of the Tax Legislative Counsel, U.S. Treasury Department—Office of Tax Policy, indicated that the principles of Code Sec. 461 and the related regulations are used to determine when a cost is paid or incurred. The payment test only applies to cash-basis taxpayers and the incurred test only applies to accrual-basis taxpayers. According to Mr. Carlton, the "3½ month rule" (Reg. § 1.461-4(d)(6)(ii)), applies for purposes of bonus depreciation. This rule allows a taxpayer to treat a prepaid amount as incurred if the property is expected to be provided to the taxpayer within 3½ months of the prepayment. If an accrual-basis taxpayer has used this rule consistently as a method of accounting, the rule applies to determine when an asset is acquired for purposes of bonus depreciation.

EXAMPLE

LoCo, an accrual-basis taxpayer, has used the 3½ month rule as an accounting method since it began business. LoCo pays for a new machine on September 1, 2010. The machine is delivered on November 1, 2010, and placed in service on February 7, 2011. For purposes of the 100 percent rate, the machine is considered acquired on September 1, 2010. The 100 percent bonus rate does not apply because the machine is considered acquired before September 9, 2010.

EXAMPLE

Deductco, also an accrual-basis taxpayer that uses the 3½ month rule, pays for a new machine on November 1, 2011. The machine is delivered on January 2, 2012, and placed in service on February 7, 2012. For purposes of the 100 percent rate, the machine is considered acquired on November 1, 2011. The 100 percent bonus rate does not apply, however, because the machine was placed in service in 2012.

Impact of pre-September 9 binding contract on 100 percent bonus. Bonus depreciation does not apply to any property that is subject to a written binding acquisition contract that was in effect prior to January 1, 2008 (Code Sec. 168(k)(2)(A)). This restriction is currently not a consideration in the vast majority of cases.

Among taxpayers and practitioners, there is some confusion regarding whether the 100 percent bonus rate can apply to property that is subject to a pre-September 9 written binding contract.

The legislative language for the 100 percent bonus rate does not address the issue. Similarly, Rev. Proc. 2011-26 provides no specific guidance. However, the Joint Committee Report states that property subject to a pre-September 9, 2010, binding contract may qualify for the 100 percent rate so long as the contract was not in effect prior to January 1, 2008 (Joint Committee on Taxation, Technical Explanation of the Revenue Provisions Contained in the *Tax Relief, Unemployment Insurance Reauthorization, and Job Creation Act of 2010* (JCX-55-10), December 10, 2010). Following the issuance of Rev. Proc. 2011-26, CCH contacted the Office of Associate Chief Counsel and was informally advised that the binding contract rule as interpreted by the Joint Committee applies.

STUDY QUESTIONS

---

3. Without regard to the extended placed-in-service date for property with a longer production period, the 100 percent bonus depreciation rate applies to property acquired:

   a. After September 8, 2010, and placed in service before January 1, 2012

   b. After December 31, 2010, and placed in service before January 1, 2012

   c. After December 31, 2007, and placed in service before January 1, 2012

4. For purposes of the 100 percent bonus rate, property is deemed acquired by:

   a. A cash- or accrual-basis taxpayer when it is placed in service

   b. A cash-basis taxpayer when possession is taken

   c. A cash-basis taxpayer when its cost is paid and by an accrual-basis taxpayer when its cost is incurred

---

PROPERTY WITH A LONGER PRODUCTION PERIOD

As previously discussed, the 50 percent rate and 100 percent rate placed-in-service deadlines for property with a longer production period are extended one year. Accordingly, the 100 percent rate applies to longer production property if the property is acquired after September 8, 2010, and before January 1, 2012, and placed in service before January 1, 2013. If the 100 percent rate does not apply, the 50 percent rate will apply to longer production property if it was acquired after December 31, 2007, and before January 1, 2013, and placed in service before January 1, 2014.

CAUTION

Section 3.02(1)(a) of Rev. Proc. 2011-26 provides that property with a longer production period meets the 100 percent rate acquisition requirement if it is acquired before *January 1, 2013* (rather than the "before January 1, 2012," deadline for other 100 percent rate property). This January 1, 2013, date, however, seems inconsistent with the statutory language of Code Sec. 168(k) (5). In a presentation at the American Bar Association's Tax Section meeting in Washington, D.C., on May 6, 2011, Brandon Carlton, Office of the Tax Legislative Counsel, U.S. Treasury Department—Office of Tax Policy, recognized the apparent inconsistency and indicated that the extended January 1, 2013, acquisition deadline stated in Rev. Proc. 2011-26 was only intended to apply to apply to long production property acquired pursuant to a written binding contract entered into after September 8, 2010, and before January 1, 2012, and to 2012 progress expenditures paid or incurred in connection with 100 percent rate property with a long production property.

Impact of Written Binding Contract to Acquire or Construct Longer Production Property

A written binding contract entered into after September 8, 2010, and before January 1, 2012, to acquire property with a longer production period or to have property with a longer production period manufactured, constructed, or produced for the taxpayer, will satisfy the requirement that the property must be acquired before January 1, 2012 in order to qualify for bonus depreciation at the 100 percent rate. The acquisition date requirement is satisfied regardless of when a taxpayer pays or incurs the cost of the property, construction begins, or physical possession is taken (Section 3.02(1) of Rev. Proc. 2011-26).

A written binding contract entered into after December 31, 2007, and before January 1, 2013, will satisfy the acquisition date requirement for the 50 bonus rate if the 100 percent rate does not apply.

EXAMPLE

Harry Rosen, a taxpayer, enters into a written binding contract to acquire a new stitching machine that is longer production property on October 19, 2011. The machine is constructed and delivered on December 15, 2012, and placed in service by the taxpayer on December 30, 2012. The machine is treated as acquired after September 8, 2010, and before January 1, 2012, because it is long production property that is subject to a written binding acquisition contract entered into after September 8, 2010, and before January 1, 2012. Because the machine was deemed acquired before January 1, 2012, and placed in service before the extended January 1, 2013, deadline for 100 percent rate longer production property it qualifies for the 100 percent rate. It does not matter whether Harry uses the cash basis or accrual basis or when construction of the stitching machine begins.

Progress Expenditures

Although longer production property placed in service during 2013 qualifies for a 50 percent bonus rate, no portion of the asset's basis relating to construction, production, or manufacture that occurs during 2013 (i.e., 2013 progress expenditures) will qualify for bonus depreciation.

In contrast, the entire basis of long production property placed in service during 2012 qualifies for the 100 percent rate (Section 3.02(1)(b) of Rev. Proc. 2011-26).

EXAMPLE

ComElect, a taxpayer, begins construction of an electric generation power plant (MACRS 20-year property) on November 1, 2010. The plant is long production property. Construction is completed in 2012 and ComElect places the plant in service before the end of 2012. The entire basis of the plant qualifies for the 100 percent rate. If the plant is placed in service in 2013, the 50 percent rate applies to the portion of the plant's cost attributable to construction that occurs on or after November 1, 2010, and before January 1, 2013. No bonus would be allowed for 2013 expenditures.

CAUTION

The allowance of the 100 percent rate on 2012 progress expenditures is clearly consistent with the statutory language and expressly allowed by Rev. Proc. 2011-26. However, the Joint Committee on Taxation's "Blue Book" (J.C.S.-2-11) (footnote 1597) indicates Congress did not intend to allow the 100 percent rate for 2012 progress expenditures and that a technical correction may be necessary. If the technical correction were enacted, a 50 percent rate would apply to 2012 progress expenditures and a 100 percent rate would apply to post-September 9, 2010, and pre-January 1, 2012, progress expenditures. For the time being at least, the IRS will also allow a taxpayer to claim the 100 percent rate on 2012 progress expenditures.

Extended Acquisition and Placed-in-Service Deadline for Noncommercial Aircraft

The acquisition dates, written binding contract rules, and extended placed-in-service deadlines, discussed earlier for 50 percent and 100 percent rate property with a longer production period, apply equally to certain noncommercial aircraft, such as a company aircraft used for transporting company officers (Code Sec. 168(k)(2)(C)).

To be treated like longer production property, the following conditions apply:

- The aircraft must be purchased by the taxpayer;
- The taxpayer must make a nonrefundable deposit of 10 percent of the cost or $100,000 (whichever is less) at the time of the contract to purchase;
- The aircraft must cost at least $200,000; and
- The aircraft must have a production period of at least four months.

COMMENT

The entire basis of a noncommercial airplane qualifies for bonus depreciation at the applicable 50 percent or 100 percent rate. The rule for longer production property that disallows 2013 progress expenditures from qualifying for the 50 percent bonus deduction does not apply to a noncommercial aircraft. Similarly, the potential technical correction that would disqualify 2012 progress expenditures from the 100 percent rate would not apply to noncommercial aircraft.

STUDY QUESTIONS

5. In order for property with a longer production period to qualify for 100 percent bonus depreciation, the property must be placed in service before:

   a. January 1, 2012
   b. January 1, 2013
   c. January 1, 2014

6. Progress expenditures paid or incurred during 2012 on longer production property that is placed in service before January 1, 2013, do not qualify for bonus depreciation at the 100 percent rate. *True or False?*

7. Longer production property constructed for a taxpayer by another person meets the acquisition date requirement for the 100 percent rate if the taxpayer entered into a written, binding contract for its acquisition:

   a. After December 31, 2007, and before January 1, 2013
   b. After September 8, 2010, and before January 1, 2013
   c. After September 8, 2010, and before January 1, 2012

SELF-CONSTRUCTED PROPERTY

Determining the Acquisition Date of Self-Constructed Property

Often a taxpayer will manufacture, produce, or construct an asset for its own use or enter into a written binding contract with a third party to construct the property for the taxpayer.

If a taxpayer enters into a written binding contract with another taxpayer to construct a property prior to the beginning of construction, then the property is considered self-constructed by the taxpayer and the special rules for determining the acquisition date of self-constructed property apply (Reg. §1.168(k)-1(b) (4)(iii)(A)).

In the case of self-constructed asset, the 100 percent bonus rate will only apply if the self-constructed asset is "acquired" by the taxpayer after September 8, 2010, and before January 1, 2012 (before January 1, 2013, in the case of property with a longer production period).

If an asset that is long production property or a noncommercial aircraft is specially constructed by another person for a taxpayer, the acquisition date requirement for the 100 percent rate is satisfied if the construction is pursuant to a written binding contract entered into after September 8, 2010, and before January 1, 2012. This special rule for binding contracts only applies to long production property and noncommercial aircraft.

Assuming that the acquisition date is not determined under the rule for binding written contracts, a self-constructed asset is deemed acquired when the manufacture, production, or construction begins (Code Sec. 168(k)(2)(E)(i)).

Manufacture, construction, or production of property begins when *physical work* of a significant nature begins. This involves a facts and circumstances test. Physical work does not include preliminary activities. Preliminary activities include expenses related to planning and designing, securing financing, exploring, and researching. If a building or structure with an MACRS recovery period of 20 years or fewer qualifies for bonus depreciation (e.g., a retail motor fuel outlet or electric power plant), preliminary work includes clearing a site, test drilling to determine soil conditions, or excavation to contour land (Reg. § 1.168(k)-1(b)(4)(iii)(B)).

In place of the facts and circumstances test, a taxpayer often elects a safe harbor that treats manufacture, construction, or production as beginning on the date that the taxpayer incurs (in the case of an accrual-basis taxpayer) or pays (in the case of a cash-basis taxpayer) more than 10 percent of the total cost of the property (excluding the cost of any land and preliminary activities such as planning or designing, securing financing, exploring, or researching).

When self-constructed property is manufactured, constructed, or produced for the taxpayer by another person, this safe harbor test must be satisfied by the taxpayer (Reg. § 1.168(k)-1(b)(4)(iii)(B)).

EXAMPLE

Sue Thompson, a cash-basis taxpayer, enters into a written binding contract with a third party on January 15, 2010, for the construction of a dough-blending machine that will be used in Sue's business. The machine is not long construction period property. Because the contract was entered into before construction began the machine is treated as self-constructed property. In order to qualify for the 100 percent rate, the construction of the machine must begin after September 8, 2010, and before January 1, 2012. Construction begins either when physical work of a significant nature begins or, applying the safe harbor, Sue pays for more than 10 percent of its cost. The machine must also be placed in service before January 1, 2012, in order for the 100 percent rate to apply. If it is placed in service during 2012, its cost qualifies for the 50 percent rate. If it is placed in service after 2012, no bonus deduction is allowed.

EXAMPLE

Joe Pfeiffer, an accrual-basis taxpayer, begins construction of an earth-grading machine that will be used in his own business on July 1, 2010. The machine is not property with a long production period. If physical work of a significant nature begins after September 8, 2010, or more than 10 percent of the total cost of the machine is incurred after September 8, 2010, the machine will qualify for bonus depreciation at the 100 percent rate provided that it is placed in service before January 1, 2012. If it is placed in service in 2012, a 50 percent rate applies. Joe may claim no bonus depreciation if he places the machine in service in 2013.

EXAMPLE

Assume that the earth-grading machine in the preceding example is constructed pursuant to a written binding contract entered into with EarthMove Inc. prior to the beginning of construction on July 10, 2010. Assume the contract is considered a contract to acquire property (i.e., the benefits and burdens of ownership are with EarthMove). As explained earlier, under the accrual method, Joe will incur no expenses until delivery of the property. Accordingly, the machine will qualify for the 100 percent rate if Joe elects the safe harbor method and the machine is delivered after September 8, 2010 and placed in service before January 1, 2012.

Components of Larger Self-Constructed Property—Special Election to Claim 100 Percent Bonus Depreciation

Even though a self-constructed property as a whole does not qualify for 100 percent bonus depreciation because construction, manufacture, or production of the property began before September 9, 2010, the taxpayer may make an election to claim 100 percent bonus depreciation on components it acquires or self-constructs that separately meet the requirements for the 100 percent rate. The election only applies if the larger self-constructed property does not qualify for the 100 percent rate because construction, manufacture, or production began before September 9, 2010 (Rev. Proc. 2011-26, Section 3.02(2)).

COMMENT

The special election for components only applies to components of a larger self-constructed property that would qualify for a 100 percent rate but for the fact that manufacture, production, or construction by the taxpayer began before September 9, 2010. Accordingly, the larger self-constructed property must be placed in service before January 1, 2012 (before January 1, 2013, for larger constructed property with a longer production period and noncommercial aircraft). The original use of the property must also begin with the taxpayer after September 8, 2010.

A *component* is any part used in the manufacture, construction, or production of the larger self-constructed property. A component for this purpose does not have to be the same as an asset for depreciation purposes or the same as the unit of property for purposes of other tax code sections (Rev. Proc. 2011-26, Section 3.02(2)). Thus, the 100 percent bonus allowance could be claimed on any part or piece of an asset that meets the 100 percent rate requirements even though that part is not a separately depreciable asset. Theoretically, for example, a taxpayer could choose a level of "granularity" in defining components as small as a nut or bolt. However, the level of granularity chosen should be consistently applied in determining whether a component qualifies for the 100 percent rate.

EXAMPLE

William Beaton, an accrual-basis taxpayer, began constructing a ship for his own use on March 10, 2010. The ship is long production property that qualifies for the extended January 1, 2013, placed-in-service deadline for the 100 percent rate. William placed the ship in service in August 2012.The ship does not qualify for the 100 percent rate only because construction began before September 9, 2010. William incurred $7 million for the cost of purchased components after September 8, 2010, and before January 1, 2013, and $5 million for the cost of self-constructed components the construction of which began after September 8, 2010, and before January 1, 2013. William incurred $10 million in costs for purchased components before September 9, 2010, and $5 million for self-constructed components, the construction of which began before September 9, 2010. The election to claim 100 percent bonus depreciation only applies to the $12 million attributable to components William purchased or self-constructed after September 8, 2010. The remaining $15 million of components qualify for bonus depreciation at a 50 percent rate because he incurred the cost of the purchased components before September 9, 2010, or began manufacture of the self-constructed components before September 9, 2010 (Rev. Proc. 2011-26, Section 3.04(3) Example 3).

The election to claim the 100 percent rate on a component must be made by the due date (including extensions) of the federal tax return for the taxpayer's tax year in which the larger self-constructed property is placed in service. The taxpayer attaches a statement to the return indicating that the taxpayer is making the election provided in Section 3.02(2)(b) of Rev. Proc. 2011-26 and whether the taxpayer is making the election for all or some eligible components. It is unnecessary for the statement to enumerate the components to which the election applies. Of course, a taxpayer should maintain adequate records to verify its position if there is an audit.

If the election is not made for a component that otherwise qualifies for the 100 percent rate, a 50 percent rate applies.

COMMENT

In a presentation at the American Bar Association's Tax Section meeting in Washington, D.C., on May 6, 2011, Brandon Carlton, Office of the Tax Legislative Counsel, U.S. Treasury Department—Office of Tax Policy, suggested that the costs of installing an asset that does not qualify for the 100 percent rate because construction began before September 9, 2010, may qualify separately as a "component" that is eligible for the 100 percent rate if the installation costs are paid or incurred before January 1, 2012 (before January 1, 2013 in the case of longer production property).

If the manufacture, construction, or production of a larger self-constructed property begins before January 1, 2008, the larger property and any acquired or self-constructed components of the larger property do not qualify for bonus depreciation at either the 50 percent or 100 percent rate (Section 2.04 of Rev. Proc. 2011-26).

STUDY QUESTIONS

8. An asset that is constructed by a taxpayer for its own use is considered acquired for purposes of bonus depreciation when:
   a. The asset is placed in service
   b. Construction of the asset begins
   c. Construction of the asset ends

9. Under an elective safe harbor, a taxpayer may treat a self-constructed asset as acquired for bonus depreciation when:
   a. More than 5 percent of the construction costs are paid or incurred
   b. More than 10 percent of the construction costs are paid or incurred
   c. Work of a significant physical nature begins

10. A taxpayer may be able elect to claim 100 percent bonus depreciation on a component of a larger self-constructed property if the self-constructed property does not qualify for 100 percent rate bonus depreciation solely because:
    a. The self-constructed property was not placed in service during 2011 (2012 if the property is longer production property)
    b. Construction began before September 9, 2010
    c. Construction began before January 1, 2008

INTERACTION OF BONUS DEPRECIATION WITH OTHER CODE PROVISIONS

An obvious effect of the 100 percent bonus deduction is a sharp reduction in taxable income. Accordingly, deductions (e.g. Section 199 manufacturing deduction), credits (e.g. general business credits), and other tax benefits that contain limits based on taxable income will be reduced if bonus depreciation is claimed. Additional interactions are discussed below.

Bonus Depreciation and the Alternative Minimum Tax

The bonus deprecation allowance is claimed in full for alternative minimum tax (AMT) purposes (Code Sec. 168(k)(2)(G)).

If the 50 percent rate applies, regular MACRS depreciation deductions are also allowed in full for AMT purposes. If the 100 percent rate applies, there will be no regular MACRS deductions because the entire cost of the bonus depreciation asset is deducted in the placed-in-service year.

CAUTION

Electing out of bonus depreciation on the 3-, 5-, 7-, and/or 10-year MACRS property classes can trigger an AMT liability. If an election out is made for any of these classes of property, an AMT adjustment is required. The adjustment is the difference between the regular tax depreciation deduction for the property using the 200 percent declining-balance method and the AMT deduction that is allowed using the 150 percent declining-balance method. A taxpayer that elects out of bonus depreciation for one of these property classes can avoid an AMT adjustment by electing to depreciate the property class using the MACRS 150 percent declining-balance, straight-line, or ADS method.

PLANNING POINTER

A taxpayer may prefer to elect out of bonus depreciation in order to reduce or eliminate a net operating loss (NOL). One reason for avoiding an NOL is that certain states have limited carryback and carryforward periods or have entirely eliminated NOL carrybacks and carryforwards.

Bonus Depreciation and Depreciation Recapture

Bonus depreciation, amounts expensed under Section 179, and regular depreciation deductions claimed on Section 1245 property are subject to recapture as ordinary income to the extent of any recognized gain from the disposition of the property. If the taxpayer claims bonus depreciation or the Section 179 allowance on Section 1250 property—for example, a qualified leasehold improvement—it is treated as an accelerated depreciation deduction. The difference between the depreciation (including the bonus and Section 179 deductions) claimed on the Section 1250 property through the recapture year and the amount of depreciation that would have been allowed using the straight-line method is recaptured as ordinary income to the extent of gain. In the case of individuals, estates, and trusts, any unrecaptured depreciation on Section 1250 property is treated as "unrecaptured Section 1250 gain" and taxed at a 25 percent rate.

Bonus Depreciation and the Mid-Quarter Convention

The MACRS mid-quarter convention applies if more than 40 percent of the basis of property other than MACRS 27.5-year residential rental and 39-year nonresidential real property is placed in service during the last four months of a taxpayer's tax year. In making this determination, basis does not include the portion of the cost of an asset that is expensed under Section 179. However, basis does include any portion of cost that is claimed as bonus depreciation (Rev. Proc. 2011-26, Section 3.03(4)).

EXAMPLE

Cal Roberts, a calendar year taxpayer, placed a used car costing $40,000 in service in June 2011 and furniture costing $50,000 in service in November 2011. The entire cost of the furniture qualifies for bonus depreciation at the 100 percent rate. The car does not qualify for bonus depreciation because it is used. Even though Cal claimed the full cost of the furniture as a bonus deduction, more than 40 percent of the total basis of the nonreal property placed in service in 2011 (computed without regard to bonus depreciation) was placed in service in the last quarter ($50,000 ÷ $90,000 = 55%). Therefore, the mid-quarter convention applies and the car must be depreciated using the mid-quarter convention even though the entire cost of the property placed in service in the last quarter was claimed as a bonus deduction.

Impact of 100 Percent Rate on Like-Kind Exchanges

Often taxpayers restructure the sale of a depreciated asset having a low basis as a like-kind exchange in order to defer the gain that would otherwise be recognized upon the sale. The federal tax benefit associated with a like-kind exchange, however, may be effectively eliminated if the exchange takes place in 2011, when the bonus rate is 100 percent.

EXAMPLE

Taxpayer Joan Simmons exchanges a sound-mixing machine with a fair market value of $10,000 and an adjusted basis of $4,000 for a new machine that has a $22,000 fair market value. She pays an additional $12,000 cash for the new mixer. The adjusted basis of the new machine is $16,000 ($4,000 + $12,000). The bonus depreciation rules allow bonus depreciation to be claimed on both the carryover basis ($4,000) and the boot ($12,000). Thus, Joan claims a $16,000 bonus deduction and the basis of the machine for purposes of determining future gain is $0.

If she simply sold the old machine and acquired a new mixer, Joan would have been taxed on $6,000 gain ($10,000 – $4,000) as ordinary income depreciation recapture and claimed a $22,000 bonus deduction against ordinary income. The basis of the new machine is $0 because Joan claimed its entire cost as a bonus deduction. Thus, $6,000 of the $22,000 bonus deduction offsets the $6,000 ordinary income recapture, leaving Joan a net $16,000 bonus deduction. The net tax benefit is the same with or without a like-kind exchange.

PLANNING POINTER

Many states have partially or completely decoupled from the federal system's bonus depreciation. Thus, a like-kind exchange may continue to save taxes at the state level even though federal bonus depreciation is claimed. Furthermore, because individual taxpayers are not allowed to claim state taxes in computing federal alternative minimum tax liability, an increased state tax liability (attributable to failure to structure a like-kind exchange) can trigger or increase the taxpayer's AMT liability.

Impact of 100 Percent Bonus Depreciation with Long-Term Contract Method of Accounting

A provision enacted by the *Small Business Jobs Act* (P.L. 111-240) has expired (Code Sec. 460(C)(6)(B)). That provision allowed taxpayers to compute depreciation as if 50 percent bonus depreciation had not been enacted when determining the percentage of completion under a long-term contract. The provision only applied to property with a recovery period of 7 years that was placed in service in 2010 (2011 in the case of longer production property that is 7-year transportation property).

Accordingly, the problem that this provision attempted to address—the acceleration of the percentage of the contract that was deemed completed in the year bonus depreciation was claimed—will become even more acute with respect to property placed in service in 2011 that qualifies for bonus depreciation at a 100 percent rate.

Leasehold Improvements, Restaurant Improvements, and Retail Improvements

Qualified restaurant property (Code Sec. 168(e)(7)) and qualified retail improvement property (Code Sec. 168(e)(8)) do not qualify for bonus depreciation. Bonus depreciation (100 percent in 2011 and 50 percent in 2012) may be claimed on qualified leasehold improvement property (Code Sec. 168(e)(6)). Some confusion has arisen as to whether bonus depreciation may be claimed on a restaurant improvement or retail improvement that also satisfies the definition of a leasehold improvement property. The IRS has definitively resolved the issue in favor of taxpayers. An improvement made by a lessor or a lessee that meets the definition of a *qualified leasehold improvement* and also meets the definition of either *qualified restaurant property* or *qualified retail improvement property* may qualify for bonus depreciation (Rev. Proc. 2011-26, Section 3.03(3)).

> **COMMENT**
>
> Qualified leasehold improvement property, qualified retail improvement property, and qualified restaurant property placed in service before January 1, 2012, are classified as MACRS 15-year property and any cost not claimed as a bonus deduction or Section 179 deduction is depreciated using the straight-line method. Unless Congress enacts extender legislation, these three types of property when placed in service after 2011 will be depreciated as MACRS 39-year nonresidential real property.

STUDY QUESTION

11. Which of the following does *not* apply to bonus depreciation?

    a. It is not allowed for AMT purposes

    b. It may be claimed on retail improvement property that is also leasehold improvement property

    c. For the mid-quarter convention calculation of whether more than 40 percent of the basis of property has been placed in service in the last quarter of a tax year, it does not reduce the basis of the property.

BONUS DEPRECIATION ELECTIONS

Election to Claim 50 Percent Bonus Depreciation in Place of 100 Percent

Section 4 of Rev. Proc. 2011-26 contained an election that allowed a taxpayer to claim a 50 percent bonus rate in place of the 100 percent rate for any class of MACRS property. However, this election only applied to a tax year that included September 9, 2010, and had to be elected by the due date (including extensions) of the federal tax return for the taxpayer's tax year that included September 9, 2010. Consequently, the deadline has expired for all calendar year taxpayers and most fiscal year taxpayers.

> **COMMENT**
>
> The Joint Committee on Taxation's Blue Book explanation (JCS-2-11, footnote 1597) indicates that Congress intended to allow a taxpayer to elect 50 percent bonus depreciation in place of the 100 percent rate for any class of property. A technical correction would be necessary. The IRS in Rev. Proc. 2011-26 allowed in a taxpayer to elect a 50 percent rate but only in a tax year that included September 9, 2010.

Election Not to Claim Bonus Depreciation

A taxpayer may elect out of bonus depreciation with respect to any class of property placed in service in a tax year. The election out applies to all assets in the property class that are placed in service in the tax year regardless of whether the 50 percent or 100 percent bonus depreciation rate applies.

EXAMPLE

DynoDrive, a 2011–2012 fiscal year corporation, places three machines (MACRS 5-year property) in service in 2011 that qualify for the 100 percent bonus rate and two machines in service in 2012 that qualify for the 50 percent rate. DynoDrive may elect not to claim bonus depreciation on all MACRS 5-year property placed in service during the 2011–2012 fiscal year. The election applies to all five machines (and to any other MACRS 5-year property that DynoDrive placed in service in the tax year). An election out cannot be made for a fewer number of machines.

PLANNING POINTER

An election out of 100 percent bonus depreciation in 2011 will spread the depreciation deductions for the cost of an asset into future years measured by the asset's depreciation period. This may be an appropriate strategy, for example, if a taxpayer has an expiring NOL carryforward and needs to "increase" its taxable income in 2011 by reducing deductions such as depreciation in order to take advantage of the NOL. Another reason for electing out is that a taxpayer expects to move into a higher tax bracket after 2011.

Elections for 2009–2010 Fiscal Year Taxpayers Who Did Not Claim 50 Percent Bonus Depreciation

The *Small Business Jobs Act* (P.L. 111-240) enacted on September 27, 2010, extended the 50 percent bonus depreciation allowance to apply to property placed in service in calendar year 2010 (2011 for long production property and noncommercial aircraft). Many 2009–2010 fiscal tax year taxpayers and taxpayers with a short 2010 tax year filed returns before enactment of the extension and understandably failed to claim the 50 percent bonus deduction on qualifying property placed in service before September 27, 2010.

Section 5 of Rev. Proc. 2011-26 provides procedures for claiming 50 percent bonus depreciation on this property, revoking an election out of bonus depreciation that was made on a fiscal year 2009–2010 return or a 2010 short tax year return, and electing not to claim bonus depreciation.

Filing Form 3115. Affected taxpayers will want to review Rev. Proc. 2011-26. In brief, taxpayers that failed to file an amended 2009–2010 fiscal year return or 2010 short tax year return still have time to file Form 3115, *Application for Change in Accounting Method*, to take the unclaimed bonus deduction into account as a Code Sec. 481(a) adjustment on a timely filed federal tax return for the *first or second* tax year after the 2009–2010 fiscal tax year or 2010 short tax year. The taxpayer, however, must continue to own the 50 percent rate property.

An election out of bonus depreciation that was made on a 2009–2010 fiscal year or short 2010 tax year return, however, had to be revoked on an amended return by June 11, 2011, or before the taxpayer filed its tax return for the first tax year succeeding the 2009–2010 fiscal tax year. An unrevoked election continues to apply to property placed in service in 2010 even though the return was filed before the property was placed in service.

Deemed election out. A deemed election out of bonus depreciation applies to a 2009–2010 fiscal-year taxpayer or 2010 short tax year taxpayer that timely filed its return and did not claim bonus depreciation on a class of property either on its original return or under the procedure provided in Rev. Proc. 2011-26. A deemed election out applies to all qualified property in the property class for which the deemed election applies placed in service in the 2009–2010 fiscal year or 2010 short tax year, including property that qualifies for the 100 percent rate.

EXAMPLE

EarlyFile, Inc., a fiscal year 2009–2010 taxpayer, timely filed its return without claiming bonus depreciation on an item of 5-year property placed in service in March 2010. No formal election out was made or revoked. It placed no other 5-year property in service in the 2009/2010 tax year. If EarlyFile does not timely elect to claim 50 percent bonus depreciation on the property by following the guidelines in Rev. Proc. 2011-26, the taxpayer is deemed to have made an election out.

STUDY QUESTION

12. A calendar year taxpayer may elect to claim 50 percent bonus depreciation in lieu of 100 percent bonus depreciation on qualified property placed in service in 2011. ***True or False?***

SAFE HARBOR BONUS FIX FOR VEHICLES SUBJECT TO DEPRECIATION CAPS

Safe Harbor Method of Accounting for "Luxury Cars"

Annual depreciation caps apply to "passenger automobiles" during the vehicle's depreciation period (Code Sec. 280F). A *passenger automobile* is any car, truck, or van with a gross vehicle weight rating (GVWR) of 6,000 pounds or less. A truck or van (including an SUV) with a GVWR in excess of 6,000 pounds is not considered a passenger automobile and, therefore, is not subject to these caps.

In general, the cap that applies to a passenger automobile for the tax year is compared to the depreciation deduction that would be allowed for the tax year computed as if the Code 280F provision had not been enacted (i.e., computed as if there were no caps in any tax year). In each tax year of the vehicle's recovery period, a taxpayer may deduct the lesser of the depreciation deduction computed without regard to the caps and the cap for the tax year.

An anomalous interaction between the 100 percent bonus depreciation deduction and the Code Sec. 280F "depreciation cap" provision would have prevented a taxpayer from deducting any depreciation on a vehicle after the tax year in which it was purchased.

First, however, the following example illustrates the problem in more detail.

EXAMPLE

Michael Ledford, a business taxpayer, buys a passenger automobile for $30,000 in January 2011. The first-year return deduction is $11,060 (the first year cap) because this is less than $30,000 (the 100% bonus deduction). In years two through six, the amount of depreciation Michael can claim on the return is $0, because depreciation computed without regard to the caps in each of these years ($0) is necessarily less than the cap for each of these years!

Tax Year	Cap	Deduction Without Regard to Cap	Return Deduction: Less of Col. 1 or 2
2011	$11,060	$30,000	$11,060
2012	$4,900	$0	$0
2013	$2,950	$0	$0
2014	$1,775	$0	$0
2015	$1,775	$0	$0
2016	$1,775	$0	$0
Total:			$11,060

COMMENT

Depreciation deductions disallowed during a vehicle's regular recovery period because of the caps are claimed annually beginning in the tax year after the end of the recovery period in an amount equal to the cap that applies in the fourth through sixth tax years. Thus, in the preceding example, the $18,940 difference between the cost of the vehicle ($30,000) and the amount actually claimed on the return during the six-year depreciation period ($11,060) is recovered at the rate of $1,775 per year. The $18,940 amount is referred to as the vehicle's "Section 280F unrecovered basis."

The example clearly illustrates that the interaction between 100 percent bonus depreciation and the caps produces an unfair result. The 100 percent rate was intended to encourage, not discourage, capital investments. The IRS, however, fixed this situation with a "safe harbor method" of accounting.

Safe-Harbor Depreciation

Under the IRS *safe-harbor method* of accounting for luxury automobiles, a taxpayer claims the first-year depreciation cap in the year of purchase on Form 4562, *Depreciation and Amortization,* because the first-year cap is less than the 100 percent bonus deduction. However, in the second through sixth tax years of the vehicle's depreciation period, a taxpayer claims on its return the amount of depreciation (taking the caps into account) that would be allowed if a 50 percent bonus depreciation rate had applied.

EXAMPLE

Under the safe harbor method, depreciation on the $30,000 vehicle placed in service in January 2011 is computed as follows:

Tax Year	Deduction Without Regard to Cap*	Return Deduction: Lesser of Col. 1 or 2
2011	$30,000	$11,060
2012	$4,800	$4,800
2013	$2,880	$2,880
2014	$1,728	$1,728
2015	$1,728	$1,728
2016	$864	$864
Total:		$23,060

> * The basis to which the MACRS table percentages are applied in 2012 through 2016 is $15,000 ($30,000 cost reduced by the $15,000 bonus deduction that could have been claimed in 2011 if a 50% bonus rate applied ($30,000 × 50% = $15,000)). Accordingly, without regard to the caps, 2012 depreciation is $4,800 ($15,000 × 32% second-year table percentage), 2013 depreciation is $2,880 ($30,000 × 19.2% third-year table percentage), 2014 and 2015 depreciation is $1,728 ($15,000 × 11.52% fourth- and fifth-year table percentages), and 2016 depreciation is $864 ($15,000 × 5.76% sixth-year table percentage).

To adopt the safe harbor method of accounting, a taxpayer only needs to complete Form 4562 by computing depreciation beginning in the *second* recovery year as if a 50 percent rate applied in the first recovery year. Taxpayers who filed a 2010 Form 4562 prior to issuance of the safe harbor method do not need to amend the 2010 return in order to adopt the safe harbor method on a vehicle placed in service in 2010. Such a taxpayer will have claimed a bonus deduction equal to the first-year cap on the 2010 return and this is the amount allowed under the safe harbor.

CAUTION

The table percentages may not be used under the safe harbor method after the first tax year if the amount of depreciation (including bonus depreciation) computed for the first tax year based on a 50 percent bonus depreciation rate is less than the first-year cap. In 2011, this rule can affect a new car that costs less than $18,433 or a new truck, van, or SUV that costs less than $18,767, assuming that the half-year convention and 200 percent declining balance method apply (the usual situation).

STUDY QUESTION

13. The safe harbor bonus depreciation "fix" for passenger automobiles placed in service in 2010 by a calendar year taxpayer is elected by:

   a. Amending the 2010 return
   b. Computing depreciation using the safe harbor method on the 2011 return
   c. Claiming no depreciation on the vehicle on the 2011 return

SECTION 179 EXPENSING ELECTION

In many cases, the Section 179 expensing deduction will take a back seat to bonus depreciation in 2011 because of the 100 percent bonus rate for qualified assets placed in service in 2011. However, many assets that do not qualify for bonus depreciation will qualify for expensing under Section 179. These include:

- Used assets and qualified retail improvements;
- Restaurant improvements; and
- Restaurant buildings.

When an asset qualifies for expensing under Section 179 or bonus depreciation, there may be a reason to choose one method over the other.

Section 179 Basics

The Section 179 dollar limitation is $500,000 for tax years beginning in 2010 and 2011.

The dollar limitation is reduced dollar for dollar by the cost of qualified Section 179 property placed in service during the tax year over an investment limitation. The investment limitation for 2010 and 2011 is $2 million. The dollar limit is completely phased out if $2.5 million or more of Section 179 property is placed in service in 2010 or 2011. The cost of Section 179 property that is claimed as a bonus deduction is taken into account in computing the phaseout. For example, if a calendar-year taxpayer placed $2.5 million of Section 179 property in service in 2011 and claimed $2 million of the cost of that property as a 100 percent bonus deduction, the $500,000 Section 179 dollar limit is still completely phased out.

The total cost of Section 179 property that may be expensed for any tax year cannot exceed the total amount of taxable income derived from the active conduct of any trade or business during the tax year, including employee salaries and wages. An amount disallowed as the result of the taxable income limitation is carried forward.

Generally, Section 179 property consists only of new or used Section 1245 property that is acquired by purchase. Off-the-shelf computer software placed in service in 2010 or 2011, however, may be expensed.

Section 179 property does not include:

- Air conditioning or heating units;
- Property used predominantly outside of the United States;
- Property used predominantly to furnish lodging or used predominantly in connection with furnishing lodging;
- Property used by certain tax-exempt organizations unless used in connection with the production of income subject to the tax on unrelated trade or business income; and
- Property used by governments and foreign persons.

$250,000 Section 179 Deduction for Leasehold Improvements, Restaurant Improvements, and Retail Improvements

For a tax year beginning in 2010 or 2011, a taxpayer may elect to treat the entire cost of "qualified real property" as Section 179 property and expense up to $250,000 of the cost under Section 179 (Code Sec. 179(f), as added by the *Small Business Jobs Act of 2010* (P.L. 111-240)). The cost of qualified real property that is expensed reduces the overall $500,000 "dollar" limitation.

Qualified real property is qualified leasehold improvement property (Code Sec. 168(e)(6)), qualified restaurant property (Code Sec. 168(e)(7)), and qualified retail improvement property (Code Sec. 168(e)(8)). These types of property also qualify for a 15-year MACRS depreciation period if placed in service before 2012.

Qualified leasehold improvements, retail improvements, and restaurant property defined. *Qualified leasehold improvements* are Section 1250 improvements to the interior portion of nonresidential real property that is at least three years old and which is placed in service by a lessor or lessee (unrelated to each other), pursuant to or under the terms of a lease.

Qualified leasehold improvements do not include:

- Elevators and escalators;
- The enlargement of a building;
- Internal structural framework; or
- Structural components that benefit a common area used by different lessees of the same building, such as stairways, hallways, lobbies, common seating areas, interior and exterior pedestrian walkways and pedestrian bridges, loading docks and areas, and rest rooms.

Qualified retail improvements are defined similarly except that the improvement must be made to the interior portion of the building that is open to the general public and used in the retail trade or business of selling tangible personal property to the general public (e.g., the stock room in back of retail space does not qualify because it is not open to the general public). The property does not need to be leased. The improvement may be made by the owner, owner-lessor, or lessee.

Qualified restaurant property is any Section 1250 property that is an improvement to a building if more than 50 percent of the building's square footage is devoted to preparation of and seating for on-premises consumption of prepared meals. A restaurant building is also qualified restaurant property.

EXAMPLE

Vanessa Halbert, a taxpayer with a 2011 calendar tax year, places $500,000 of qualified real property and $50,000 of other Section 179 property in service in 2011. She may elect to treat the qualified real property as Section 179 property and expense a maximum of $300,000 ($250,000 qualified real property and $50,000 of other Section 179 property).

COMMENT

Generally, only Section 1245 property (new or used) and off-the-shelf computer software is eligible for expensing under Section 179. The temporary expensing election for qualified real property is a significant exception to this rule.

CAUTION

An election to treat qualified real property as Section 179 property applies to all qualified real property placed in service during the tax year. If a taxpayer has placed a significant amount of qualified real property in service and elects to treat it as Section 179 property, the election can trigger the investment limitation and cause a reduction or elimination of the $500,000 dollar limit.

EXAMPLE

Ron Jackson places $50,000 of used Section 179 machinery and a $3 million restaurant building in service in 2011. If Ron makes the election, he may not expense any amount because the $500,000 annual limitation would be reduced to $0 by reason of the investment limitation. In this situation, Ron should not make the election to treat qualified real property as Section 179 property so that he can claim a $50,000 Section 179 deduction on the remaining used property.

No carryforward to tax year beginning in 2012. The amount of a carryforward of a Section 179 deduction that it attributable to qualified real property may not be carried forward to a tax year that begins after 2011. This means that a taxpayer that elects to treat qualified real property placed in service in a tax year beginning in 2011 as Section 179 property may not elect to expense an amount that would generate a carryforward attributable to the qualified real property.

> **EXAMPLE**
>
> BuyTech Corp., a calendar year taxpayer, places $1 million of qualified real property in service in 2011 and no other Section 179 property is placed in service. BuyTech's taxable income for 2011 is $400,000. If the corporation elects to treat its qualified real property as Section 179 property, it may only elect to expense $400,000. BuyTech may not elect to expense $500,000 and generate a $100,000 Section 179 carryforward.

A taxpayer may have a Section 179 carryforward in 2011 that is attributable to qualified real property that was placed in service in a tax year that began in 2010. If this carryforward cannot be used in 2011, it also cannot be carried forward to 2012. Instead, the amount of the carryforward is treated as property that is placed in service on the first day of the 2011 tax year.

> **EXAMPLE**
>
> TeleTouch Corp. has a $100,000 Section 179 carryforward from 2010 that is attributable to qualified real property. The corporation has no taxable income in 2011. The Section 179 carryforward may not be carried forward to 2012. Instead, TeleTouch is treated as if it had placed $100,000 of qualified real property in service on January 1, 2011, and may claim MACRS depreciation deductions.

A pro-rata allocation rule is made to determine the amount of a carryforward that is attributable to qualified real property if a carryforward was generated in a tax year in which both qualified real property and other types of Section 179 property were expensed.

Summary of Features: Section 179 and Bonus Depreciation Compared

A taxpayer may have a choice between expensing the entire cost of an asset under Section 179 and claiming the entire cost as a 100 percent bonus deduction if the asset is placed in service in 2011. Many times there are no advantages between one choice and the other. For example, both deductions are allowed in full for AMT purposes. However, certain important distinctions do exist.

Bonus depreciation only applies to new property with a recovery period of 20 years or fewer. The Section 179 deduction can be claimed on new or used Section 1245 property without regard to the length of the recovery period. Also, qualified real property placed in service in a tax year beginning in 2010 or 2011 may be expensed under Section 179. Only qualified leasehold improvements (a type of Section 179 qualified real property) are eligible for bonus depreciation and the Section 179 deduction.

TAX POINTER

Generally, a taxpayer should first expense property that does not qualify for bonus depreciation.

EXAMPLE

Lindsay McGee, a business taxpayer, places $500,000 of used property and $500,000 of new property in service in 2011 that qualify for expensing under Section 179. If she expenses the used property and claims bonus depreciation on the new property, her total deduction is $1 million. If Lindsay expenses the new property, she may not claim bonus depreciation on the used property. Her total deduction is limited to $500,000 plus the first-year depreciation deduction on the used property.

The amount of the bonus deduction is unlimited. In 2011, a $500,000 Section 179 dollar cap applies. Moreover, the $500,000 amount is subject to the investment limitation reduction discussed above.

TAX POINTER

Some states have decoupled from federal bonus depreciation but not Section 179. In this situation it may be advantageous to claim a Section 179 deduction in lieu of bonus depreciation.

Unless an election out is made, bonus depreciation applies to all qualifying property within an MACRS asset class (e.g., all 5-year property). Section 179 is elective and far more "targeted" since a taxpayer may elect to expense particular qualifying assets and is not even required to expense the entire cost of a qualifying asset.

Net operating losses. The Section 179 deduction is also limited to the amount of taxable income derived from all of a taxpayer's active trades and businesses (including wages from employment). There is no taxable income limitation on the bonus deduction. Therefore, unlike the Section 179 deduction, a bonus deduction can create or increase a net operating loss. However, any Section 179 allowance that is disallowed on account of the taxable income limitation may be carried forward indefinitely (with the exception of a Section 179 carryforward attributable to qualified real property) until the taxpayer has sufficient taxable income to offset the carryforward.

Recapture. The Section 179 expense deduction and bonus deduction are both treated as "depreciation" deductions and therefore are recaptured as ordinary income to the extent of gain when a Section 1245 asset is sold or otherwise disposed.

One potential advantage of the bonus deduction, however, is that if business use falls to 50 percent or less, a portion of the Section 179 deduction is subject to recapture but the bonus deduction is not. An exception to this rule, however, is that recapture will also apply to a portion of bonus depreciation upon a decline of business use to 50 percent or less if the asset is a listed property described in Code Sec. 280F, such as a car, truck, airplane, or other means of transportation.

Mid-quarter convention. A final distinction between the bonus deduction and the Section 179 allowance, previously mentioned, is that the Section 179 deduction reduces the basis of property for purposes of determining whether the mid-quarter convention applies. The bonus deduction does not. Thus, a taxpayer may be able to avoid the mid-quarter convention by expensing property placed in service in the final quarter instead of claiming the bonus allowance or, alternatively, trigger the mid-quarter convention by expensing property placed in service in the first three quarters.

TAX POINTER

If the mid-quarter convention applies, an asset placed in service within the first two quarters of a tax year receives a greater first-year depreciation deduction than would otherwise be allowed if the half-year convention applies. Smaller deductions are claimed on assets placed in service in the last two quarters. Depending upon a taxpayer's situation, triggering the mid-quarter convention can accelerate first-year depreciation deductions. The utility of this planning tool is limited if the 100 percent bonus deduction is available.

STUDY QUESTIONS

14. All of the following statements describe the election to expense qualified real property *except:*

    a. The election only applies to the tax years beginning in 2011 and 2012

    b. No amount of a Section 179 carryforward attributable to qualified real property may be carried forward to a tax year beginning in 2012

    c. No more than $250,000 of qualified real property may be expensed

---

15. Bonus depreciation and the Section 179 allowance are:

   a. Not allowed for AMT purposes

   b. Subject to ordinary income depreciation recapture

   c. Allowed to be claimed on used property

CONCLUSION

The 100 percent bonus depreciation deduction for qualifying assets acquired placed in service before January 1, 2012, is an unprecedented tax break for taxpayers in the position to purchase depreciable property during 2011. Bonus depreciation reverts to a 50 percent rate in 2012—a generous deduction but not nearly as compelling as the 100 percent rate. Determining whether an asset qualifies for the 100 percent rate can be somewhat complex, particularly when property is self-constructed or is property with a longer production period that qualifies for an extended placed-in-service deadline. However, Rev. Proc. 2011-26 has removed much of the uncertainty in a way generally favorable to taxpayers.

CPE NOTE: When you have completed your study and review of chapters 1–3, which comprise Module 1, you may wish to take the Quizzer for this Module.

For your convenience, you can also take this Quizzer online at **www.CCHGroup.com/TestingCenter**.

Information Reporting: Increasing Demands

This chapter explores several new information reporting requirements, an area that continues to expand with respect to both domestic and foreign transactions. Many of these new requirements place relatively onerous demands across a wide swath of taxpayer groups. Large employers, banks and other financial institutions, investment brokers, and U.S taxpayers with investments abroad—large and small alike—for example, are all affected. The penalties for noncompliance can be quite onerous, as well, making a thorough knowledge of the new requirements all the more important. This chapter will hopefully impart that knowledge.

LEARNING OBJECTIVES

Upon completion of this chapter you will be able to:

- Understand the rationale behind Congress and the IRS' ongoing efforts to expand information reporting, both at home and abroad;
- Identify key provisions of the health care information reporting requirements
- Articulate the obligations placed upon many banks and other financial institutions by the payment card processing rules;
- Differentiate between a payment card transaction and a third-party network transaction
- Identify key provisions of the broker reporting rules;
- Identify who must file a Form TD F 90-22.1, what types of accounts must be reported, and the consequences of failing to do so; and
- Identify the withholding and reporting requirements imposed on foreign financial institutions.

INTRODUCTION

As part of what seems a never-ending effort to close the "tax gap," Congress and the Internal Revenue Service continue to expand the information reporting requirements, both domestically and abroad. With an estimated $350 billion in uncollected taxes falling into the gap every year, it is easy to understand the reasons for the collection initiatives. By being able to locate and collect excess monies already owed, Congress can, in effect, increase revenues without having to deal with the messy politics of tax hikes.

Information reporting is useful to the IRS, meanwhile, because it provides the agency the ability to match what is reported by one taxpayer with the amount provided by another, and pounce upon discrepancies. As a result, these reporting efforts are likely to expand even further. The year 2011 proved a banner tax year, with several new requirements taking effect—and more in the offing. This chapter examines the most important among the new provisions.

INFORMATION REPORTING AT HOME

Cost of Employees' Group Health Insurance Coverage

The Patient Protection and Affordable Care Act, signed into law on March 30, 2010, requires employers to inform their employees of the cost of their applicable employer-sponsored health care coverage. This information, which is to be reported on Form W-2, is required for the employees' informational benefit only, supposedly to enable a greater appreciation of the amount of benefits bestowed upon them—at least in part by the tax system, either as tax-free benefits paid for by the employer or employee-paid benefits paid from pretax salary. That reporting must begin with 2012 Forms W-2, for tax year 2012, that is, the forms that employers are generally required to provide their employees in January 2013 and then filed with the Social Security Administration (SSA). Employers are accordingly not mandated to report the cost of coverage on any forms required to be furnished to employees prior to January 2013 (the due date for providing 2012 W-2s). Nevertheless, should an employer so choose, it may voluntarily furnish the information on 2011 Forms W-2.

Employers filing fewer than 250 W-2 Forms with the IRS need not report the applicable information for 2011 or 2012, with a possibility of the extension of relief beyond that time. *Applicable employer-sponsored coverage* for an employee means coverage under any group health plan made available to the employee by an employer that is excludible from the employee's gross income under Code Sec. 106.

Certain types of coverage described in Code Sec 9832(c)(1) are not subject to the reporting requirements under this general W-2 information requirement for health care benefits:

- Coverage only for accident insurance, disability income insurance, or any combination of the two;
- Coverage issued as a supplement to liability insurance;
- Liability insurance, both general and automobile;
- Workers' compensation or similar insurance;
- Automobile medical payments insurance;
- Credit-only insurance; and
- Other types of regulation specified insurance coverage under which benefits for medical care are secondary or incidental to other insurance benefits.

Also excluded are:

- Any coverage under a separate policy, certificate, or contract of insurance that provides benefits, substantially all of which are for the treatment of the mouth or eye;
- Any coverage the payment for which is not excludible from gross income and for which a deduction under Code Sec. 162(l) is not allowable, including:
  - Coverage only for a specified disease or illness; and
  - Hospital indemnity or other fixed indemnity insurance.

STUDY QUESTION

> **1.** Beginning with Form W-2 for the 2012 tax year, employers preparing at least 250 W-2s must include:
>
> **a.** Cost of the employees' employer-sponsored health care coverage
> **b.** The benefits paid for workers' compensation or disability income
> **c.** Coverage for a specified disease or illness

Income Received Through Payment Card Processing

New Code Sec. 6050W, added by the *Housing and Economic Recovery Act of 2008* and the regulations promulgated under it, provide that banks and other payment settlement services must report gross annual receipts for each merchant. The requirements, which took effect on January 1, 2011, dramatically alter the landscape for large banks, financial institutions, and third-party payment processors, all of which must now report transactions related to all payment cards. It also indirectly means that merchants are more likely to be called upon by the IRS to explain payment amounts that they either did not report, or reduced through expense deductions and other offsets.

The new section obligates merchant acquiring entities and third-party settlement organizations to file information returns for each calendar year reporting all payment card and third-party network transactions with participating payees taking place in that year. Statements must also be provided to each participating payee on or before January 31 of the year following the year for which the return was filed. The 2008 act also amended Code Sec. 3406 to provide that amounts reportable under Code Sec. 6050W are subject to backup withholding. Certain payors must, therefore, deduct and withhold income tax from a "reportable transaction" if the payee fails to provide its taxpayer identification number (TIN) to the payor on a required return or if notified by the IRS that the TIN furnished by the payee is incorrect. The backup withholding requirements apply to all amounts paid after December 31, 2011.

Definitions/Nuts and Bolts

By the terms of the new law, any "payment settlement entity" making payment to a "participating payee" in settlement of "reportable payment transactions" must make an annual return. Included on this return must be the gross amount of the reportable transactions, and the name, address and taxpayer identification number (TIN) of the payee. The term "Payment settlement" entity means, in the case of a "payment card transaction," a "merchant acquiring entity;" and, with respect to a "third-party network transaction," a "third-party settlement organization." *These special terms are defined, below.*

Merchant acquiring entity. The Code defines *merchant acquiring entity* as the bank or other organization with the contractual obligation to make payment to participating payees in settlement of reportable payment card transactions, whereas *third-party settlement organization* means the central organization bearing the contractual obligation to make payment to participating payees of third-party network transactions.

Payment card transaction. A *reportable payment card transaction,* meanwhile, is any transaction in which a payment card is accepted as payment and any transaction that is settled through a third-party payment network. The IRS has provided guidance to help interpret the meaning of this term in the context of both payment card transactions and third-party network transactions, as well as to assist in the determination of the gross amount of the transaction to be reported. For each participating payee, the gross amount is the total dollar amount of the reportable payment transactions in the aggregate for each participating payee, without regard to any adjustments for credits, cash equivalents, refunded amounts, discounts, or anything else.

> **COMMENT**
>
> In situations in which two or more persons qualify as payment settlement entities for any reportable payment transaction, only the payment settlement entity that in fact makes the payment in settlement is obligated to report the payment, that is, only the entity that actually submits the instruction to transfer the settlement funds. This party may designate a different person to satisfy the reporting obligation, but doing so will not absolve the obligated party of liability.

> **COMMENT**
>
> Each participating payee must report the gross amount of the reportable payment transactions in the *aggregate* for each month of the calendar year, as well as the calendar year as a whole.

A *de minimis* exception exists for payments made by third-party settlement organizations to certain participating payees. Accordingly, a third-party settlement organization must report payments made to a participating payee only if its aggregate payments to that payee from third-party network transactions exceed $20,000 and the number of such transactions is greater than 200.

> **NOTE**
>
> Although it weighed the possibility, the IRS has decided against extending this exception to payment card transactions.

A *payment card transaction* is any transaction in which a payment card is accepted as payment, whereas a *payment card* means a card issued pursuant to an agreement or arrangement that provides for:

- One or more issuers of such cards;
- A network of persons unrelated to each other, and to the issuer, who agree to accept the cards as payment; and
- Standards and mechanisms for settling the transactions between the merchant acquiring entities and the persons who agree to accept the cards as payment.

> **COMMENT**
>
> When two or more persons qualify as payment settlement entities for any reportable payment transaction, only the payment settlement entity that makes the payment in settlement is obligated to report the payment, that is, only the entity that actually submits the instruction to transfer the settlement funds. This party may designate a different person to satisfy the reporting obligation, but doing so will not absolve the obligated party of liability.

> **EXAMPLE**
>
> In payment card transactions, funds generally do not pass directly from the cardholder to the provider of goods and services. A credit card organization, such as Visa, may direct the transfer of funds from the card issuing bank through the debit of funds that the issuing bank has on account with, say, a Federal Reserve Bank, and a credit of those same funds to the merchant or service provider's bank—the *merchant acquiring bank*—which then makes payment to the goods or services provider to settle the transaction. The information reporting requirements of Code Sec. 6050W reflect the fact that it is the merchant acquiring bank that is in the best position to file the information return to the provider of the goods or services.

NOTE

The definition of *payment card* in the Code Sec. 6050W regulations is broader than elsewhere in the regulations, specifically Reg. § 31.3406(g)-1(f)(2)(i), which simply defines it as a card issued by a credit card organization.

STUDY QUESTIONS

2. A third-party settlement organization must report payments made to a participating payee only if its aggregate payments to that payee from third-party network transactions exceed _____ and the number of such transactions is greater than _____.

   a. $5,000; 100
   b. $10,000; 150
   c. $20,000; 200

3. Which participant in a payment card transaction is in the best position to file the information return to the party that provided the good or services?

   a. Credit card organization
   b. Merchant acquiring bank
   c. Card issuing bank

Participating payee. A *participating payee* means:
- For a payment card transaction, any person who accepts a payment card as payment; and,
- For a third-party network transaction, any person who accepts payment from a third-party settlement organization in settlement.

COMMENT

The definition of *participating payee* includes any governmental unit, as well as any agency or instrumentality of any governmental unit. As a result, payments that are made to a governmental unit through the use of, for example, transit cards or electronic toll collection systems are included within the scope of Code Sec. 6050W if the payments meet the other requirements.

Third-party Network Transactions

Under Code Sec. 6050W(c)(3), a *third-party network transaction* as any transaction settled through a third-party payment network. Code Sec. 6050W(d)(3), in turn, states that a third-party network is any arrangement or agreement that:

- Involves the establishment of accounts with a central organization by a substantial number of persons who
  — Unrelated to the organization,
  — Provide goods or services, and
  — Have agreed to settle transactions for the provision of these goods or services pursuant to the arrangement or agreement;
- Provide standards and mechanisms for settling the transactions; and
- Guarantee those providing goods and services pursuant to the arrangement or agreement that they will be paid for the provision of the goods or services.

The tax code specifically provides that a third-party payment network does not include any agreement or arrangement that provides for the issuance of payment cards.

Central organization. A *central organization* is one that provides a network enabling buyers to transfer funds to sellers that have established accounts with the organization and a contractual obligation to accept payments through the network.

> **EXAMPLE**
>
> Typically, healthcare networks include covered members, participating providers, and a health care facility of some type, each of which may be a primary party to the organization's agreements with other network parties. Nevertheless, because the purpose of a health care network is not to enable buyers to transfer funds to sellers, they are not third-party payment networks.

Shared service organizations. Although an in-house accounts payable department is not a third-party payment network, so called shared service organizations (SSOs) that act as independent contractors in connection with the accounts payable to purchasers, may be, if:

- A substantial number of unrelated providers of goods and services maintain established accounts with the SSO; and
- This arrangement allows purchasers to transfer funds to providers contractually obligated to accept them.

EXAMPLE

Because they process electronic payments between buyers and sellers, automated clearing house networks are not third-party payment networks. Electronic payment facilitators, on the other hand, may contract with third parties to settle transactions on behalf of a payment settlement network. In cases in which an electronic payment facilitator, or other third party, makes payment with respect to reportable transactions, and on behalf of the payment settlement entity, the required return must be made by the electronic payment facilitator in the payment settlement entity's place.

Third-party settlement organization. A *third-party settlement organization* is the central organization that has the contractual obligation to make payment to participating payees of third-party network transactions.

Foreign Address Exclusion from Participating Payee Classification

Importantly, the Code specifically excludes any person with a foreign address from being classified as a participating payee and, therefore, it would appear, at first glance, that U.S. payment settlement entities are absolved of responsibility for reporting payments made to those with foreign addresses.

Recently promulgated regulations, however, clarify and narrow this exclusion The new regs state that a payment settlement entity that is a U.S. payor or middleman is not required to report payments to participating payees with a foreign address, but only as long as, prior to payment, the payee has provided the payment settlement entity with documentation upon which the entity may rely to treat the payment as made to a foreign person.

COMMENT

The relevant standard against which the foreign person is to be evaluated is that provided in Reg. § 1.1441-1(e)(1)(ii).

In contrast, a payment settlement entity that is not a U.S. payor or middleman is not required to report payments to participating payees that do not have a U.S. address as long as that entity neither knows, nor has reason to know, that the participating payee in question is a U.S. person.

Given the importance of this distinction, then, a U.S. payor or U.S. middleman is:

- A citizen or resident of the United States, a domestic partnership, corporation, estate, or trust, including any foreign offices of any of these;

- The government of the United States or the government of any state or political subdivision, or any agency or instrumentality of any of these;
- A controlled foreign corporation;
- A foreign partnership, if at any time during its tax year, one or more of its partners are U.S. persons (as defined in Reg. § 1.1441-1(c)(2)) who, in the aggregate hold more than 50 percent of the income or capital interest in the partnership or if, at any time during its tax year, it is engaged in the conduct of a trade or business in the United States;
- A foreign person 50 percent or more of the gross income of which, from all sources for the three-year period ending with the close of its taxable year preceding the collection or payment (or such part of such period as the person has been in existence), was effectively connected with the conduct of trade or business within the United States; or
- A U.S. branch of a foreign bank or a foreign insurance company.

> **COMMENT**
>
> The IRS has provided transitional relief to help alleviate the burden that will be involved for some taxpayers in redocumenting existing participating payees. For payments made pursuant to contractual obligations entered into before January 1, 2011, a payment settlement entity that is a U.S. payor or middleman may rely on a foreign address as long as the U.S. payor or middleman neither knows, nor has reason to know, that the payee is a U.S. person. For this limited purpose, a contract renewal will not result in a new contractual obligation unless there is a material modification.

> **COMMENT**
>
> A presumption also exists under which a U.S. payor or middleman making payment outside the United States to an offshore account need not report the payments to a participating payee with a foreign address only if the name of that payee indicates that it is a foreign per se corporation and the payment settlement entity neither knows, nor has reason to know, that the payee is a U.S. person in disguise.

Payment settlement entities other than U.S payors or middlemen need not make an information return if the participating payee does not have a U.S. address and if the entity does not, and has no reason to, know that that payee is a U.S person.

COMMENT

In situations in which the participating payee has both a foreign and a U.S. address, the latter trumps. That is to say, if the participating payee has any U.S. address, the non-U.S. payment settlement entity may treat the participating payee as a foreign person only if the non-U.S. payment settlement entity has in its possession documentation upon which it may rely to treat the payee as a foreign person.

Time, Manner, and Form for Reporting

The IRS has created a new form specifically to be used for reporting under Code Sec. 6050W. Accordingly, Form 1099-K, *Merchant Card and Third-party Payments,* requires annual reporting for each participating payee of the gross amount of their aggregate reportable payment transactions, both for the calendar year and by each month of the calendar year.

Backup Withholding

Section 3091(c) of the *Housing and Economic Recovery Act of 2008* amended Code Sec. 3406 to provide that all amounts reportable under Code Sec. 6050W, and paid to participating payees after December 31, 2011, are subject to backup withholding.

COMMENT

A *participating payee* specifically includes any governmental unit.

The regulations under Code Sec. 3046 have also been amended to state that, with respect transactions that would otherwise be reportable under both Code Secs. 6041 and 6050W, Code Sec. 6050W trumps, so long as a certain *de minimis* thresholds are met.

COMMENT

Payment settlement entities reporting under Code Sec. 6050W are better situated to perform backup withholding for third-party network transactions than are payors under Code Sec. 6041, for several reasons. First, backup withholding is often difficult for payors in third-party network transactions because an invoice may or may not be issued. Second, payors do not generally make payment directly to the provider of goods and services, but rather to the third party, who in turn pays the provider making it impossible to determine with certainty the amount required to be reported under Section 6041.

STUDY QUESTIONS

4. If the participating payee does not have a U.S. address and the payment settlement entity (other than a U.S payor or middleman) does not know and has no reason to know, the payee is a U.S. person, the payment settlement agency is not required to file an information return. *True or False?*

5. Starting on January 1, 2012, under Code Sec. 3406 all reportable amounts (per Code Sec. 6050W) paid to participating payees are subject to backup withholding. *True or False?*

BROKER REPORTING RULES

As a result of recent changes in the law, many brokerage customers will see something new when they gaze upon their 1099-B forms early next year. In the past, of course, brokers were required to report to their clients, and the IRS, amounts reflecting the gross proceeds of any securities sales taking place during the preceding calendar year. In keeping with a broader move toward greater information reporting requirements, in general, however, new legislation now makes it incumbent upon brokers to provide their clients, and the IRS, not only with sales information but also the adjusted basis in the lots of securities purchased by their clients after certain dates, as well as the date on which the securities were acquired.

Although certainly an onerous new requirement for the brokerage houses, this information should simplify the lives of many ordinary taxpayers by relieving them of the often difficult matter of calculating their stock bases. Of course, it also eliminates the opportunity for taxpayers to fraudulently inflate the basis of a security and therefore to lower the amount of gain reported on the sales transaction.

When calculating gain or loss on the sale of stock, all taxpayers must employ a relatively simple formula. By the terms of this calculus, gain equals amount realized (how much was received in the sale) less adjusted basis (generally, how much was paid to acquire the securities plus commissions). By requiring brokers to provide their clients with both variables in the formula, Congress has lifted a heavy load from the shoulders of many investors.

Broker Returns

Section 403 of the *Energy Improvement and Extension Act of 2008* amended the Internal Revenue Code, and added to it new Code Secs. 6045A and 6045B. Accordingly, Code Sec. 6045(g) now provides that every broker required to file a return under Code Sec 6045(a) reporting the gross proceeds from the sale of any covered security must now also include in the return the customer's adjusted basis in the security and whether any gain or loss is long or short term. Regulations define a *broker* as any U.S. or foreign person that, in the ordinary course of a trade or business, stands at the ready to effect sales on behalf of others.

> **COMMENT**
>
> With respect to sales effected at an office outside the United States, however, the term includes only those persons that qualify as "U.S. Payors" or "middlemen," as delineated in the regulations under Code Sec 6049 (discussed earlier). In addition, certain "exempt foreign persons" are also relieved of the reporting requirements.

STUDY QUESTION

6. The *Energy Improvement and Extension Act of 2008* added new sections to the tax code to require brokers who must file a return reporting gross proceeds from selling covered securities to add:

   a. The customer's adjusted basis in the security and whether any gain is long or short term

   b. The same information for "exempt" foreign persons as for U.S. persons

   c. Additional clarification about the covered securities, such as their high and low prices for the date of trade and their 52-week price range

Covered and Specified Securities

Code Sec. 6045(g) further provides that a *covered security* is any specified security acquired on or after the applicable date, if the security was:

- Acquired via a transaction in the account in which it is held; or
- Transferred to the account from another and in which the security was a covered security, but only if the receiving broker also receives a statement satisfying the mandates of Code Sec. 6045A (discussed below).

> **COMMENT**
>
> A covered security is a specified security acquired for cash. Thus, stock acquired through the exercise of rights distributed by an issuer is a covered security. Restricted stock granted by an employer, on the other hand, is not.

A *specified security*, meanwhile, includes virtually every conceivable financial instrument subject to a basis calculation, including:

- Share of stock in a corporation;
- Note, bond, debenture, or other evidence of indebtedness;
- A commodity or commodity derivative if so deemed by the IRS; and
- Any other financial instrument for which the Treasury Secretary determines basis reporting is appropriate.

Applicable Dates

The new requirements take effect in three stages:

- For stock in a corporation, with the twin exceptions of a regulated investment company (RIC) stock or stock acquired through a dividend reinvestment plan (DRP), the applicable date is January 1, 2011;
- For stock in a RIC or acquired in connection with a DRP, the operative date is January 1, 2012; and
- For all other specified securities, the applicable date is January 1, 2013.

Gifted and Inherited Securities

Under Code Sec. 6045(g)(3)(A)(iii), a covered security includes all transferred securities that are covered securities in the account from which they are transferred, so long as the receiving broker also is in receipt of a transfer statement. Accordingly, gifted and inherited securities that were covered securities in the account(s) of a donor or decedent will remain covered securities when transferred to the account(s) of the recipient, provided they are accompanied by a transfer statement.

Transfer statements for gifted securities. Transfer statements for gifts must indicate:

- That the transfer consists of gifted securities;
- The adjusted basis of those securities in the hands of the donor (i.e., carryover basis);
- The donor's original acquisition date;
- The date of the gift and the fair market value of the gift on that date, if readily ascertainable.

On a subsequent disposition of the securities, the selling broker must apply the relevant basis rule for gifts, such as, for example, the rules disallowing loss on the sale of gifted securities to the extent of any built-in loss at the time of the gift.

Transfer statements for inherited securities. For inherited securities, on the other hand, the transferring broker must report adjusted basis equal to the fair market value of the securities on the date of death, unless the broker receives different instructions from the estate representative. If the transferring broker neither knows nor can readily ascertain the fair market value of a security on the decedent's date of death, that broker may treat the security as if it were uncovered. Likewise, if the transferring broker is unable to identify which securities in a joint account have been transferred from the decedent, the broker may treat each security in the account as uncovered.

Reporting Method

Brokers must report a customer's adjusted basis for any security other than RIC or DRP stock using the first-in, first-out (FIFO) method, unless the customer notifies the broker requesting lot relief and adequately identifies the securities to be sold or transferred at the time of the sale or transfer. Other acceptable methods for purposes of the basis calculation include specific identification and the average basis method. The difference in tax consequences can be significant.

> **COMMENT**
>
> A customer's standing orders for sales and transfers of stock will serve as adequate identification for both disposition types.

In contrast, a broker must report the adjusted basis of RIC or DRP stock in accord with its default method under Code Sec 1012, unless the customer directs otherwise and elects another acceptable method.

STUDY QUESTION

> **7.** The transfer statement required of brokers differs for gifted and inherited securities in that:
>
> **a.** The statement for gifted securities must include the adjusted basis in the hands of the donor and the donor's acquisition date, whereas the statement for inherited securities uses the securities' fair market value on the date of the donor's death
>
> **b.** Gifted securities use the donor's original basis upon the securities' acquisition, whereas inherited securities use the fair market value of securities on the date the recipient receives the securities
>
> **c.** Gifted securities are taxed using the average basis method, whereas inherited securities are taxed using the LIFO method

Dividend Reinvestment Plans

As their name would suggest, dividend reinvestment plans allow investors the opportunity to reinvest all, or a portion, of any dividends received back into additional shares, or fractions of shares, of identical stock. Plans will qualify as DRPs, if their written plan documents specify that at least 10 percent of every dividend paid is reinvested in identical stock (10 percent rule).

> **COMMENT**
>
> Stock will be deemed identical if it has the same CUSIP number, except that stock in a DRP can never be identical to stock outside the DRP.

While offering investors many advantages, one historical drawback to DRPs has been their tendency to obligate participants to keep track of their cost bases for many small purchases of stock, and maintain records of these purchases, sometimes over the course of many years. Going forward, however, taxpayers will be able to average the basis of stock held in a DRP acquired on or after January 1, 2011.

> **COMMENT**
>
> The average basis method will only apply while the stock is held as part of the DRP. Accordingly, if the stock is transferred to another account, each share of stock will have a basis in the receiving account equal to its basis in the DRP immediately before the transfer.

> **COMMENT**
>
> The regulations do not define *dividend,* providing only that dividends subject to Code Sec. 316 are subject to the 10 percent reinvestment requirement. Nevertheless, DRPs may average the basis of stock acquired through the reinvestment of other distributions that are not dividends under Code Sec. 316.

RIC Stock

Under Code Sec. 1012(c)(2), RIC stock acquired before January 1, 2012, is treated as held in a separate account from RIC stock acquired after that date. Nevertheless, a RIC may elect to treat all stock in the RIC held by the stockholder as one account, on a stockholder-by-stockholder basis (a *single-account election*). When this election applies, the average basis of the customer's stock is computed by averaging the basis of all stock acquired, regardless of its acquisition date, and all shares are considered covered securities.

Wash Sales

Code Sec. 6045(g)(2)(B)(ii) provides that a broker must apply the wash sale rules of Code Sec. 1091 when reporting the adjusted basis of a covered security if the purchase and sale that resulted in the wash sale occurred in the same account and in *identical*, as opposed to substantially similar, securities. By the terms of Code Sec. 1091, *wash sales* are sales of stock or securities in which losses are realized, but not recognized, because the seller also acquires substantially identical stock or securities 30 days before or after sale. Disallowed losses are reflected in the basis of acquired stock or securities. Nonrecognition applies only to losses; gains are recognized in full.

EXAMPLE

On January 5, 2011, Susan Jenson buys 100 shares of Apple common stock for $350 per share. She holds this stock until August 5, when, in the midst of a general market swoon, the price of Apple stock drops to $320 per share. Fearing further losses, Susan sells her 100 shares at that price, realizing a $3,000 loss (350 × 100 – 320 × 100), in the process. On August 11, the market begins to rebound and, with it, the price of Apple stock. Not wanting to miss out on any future gains, and with the price at $340, Susan buys another 100 shares of Apple common. Because she made a sale and purchase of, in this case, identical securities within 30 days of the sale that generated the loss, a wash sale occurred, and Susan will be unable to recognize her $3,000 loss.

COMMENT

The question of what constitutes a material difference between securities for purposes of the wash sale rules is similar to the question of when properties are materially different so that the parties exchanging the properties must realize gain or loss on the exchange. The Supreme Court has held that properties are materially different for gain or loss realization purposes when they embody legally distinct entitlements. With respect to the wash sale rules, factors to be considered in determining whether securities are substantially identical include their:

- Earning power or interest rate;
- Value of assets—tangible or intangible—or security; and
- Conditions of retirement, or, in the case of bonds, maturity dates and earlier call provisions.

Short Sales

In the past, brokers reported the gross proceeds of short sales in the year in which the short position was opened. The new rules, however, require that brokers report short sales for the year in which the short sale is closed.

> **EXAMPLE**
>
> Concerned with the pace of the economic recovery, Jessica Hallberg decides, on August 31, 2011, to sell short 1000 shares of Microsoft common stock. She is able to borrow the shares from her broker and, on that date, when the price per share is $30, the trade is executed. She takes a $30 basis in her short position (less brokerage commissions) and reaps $30,000 from the sale. Jessica's insight proves correct and, by May 8, 2012, the price of Microsoft has plunged to $20 per share. On that date, she decides to close her position and buys to cover 1,000 shares for a total cost of $20,000 (plus brokerage commissions). Under prior rules, this transaction would be reported in 2011 (the year in which the position was opened). Now, however, brokers will be obligated to report the short sale in 2012.

S Corporations

Under preexisting law, broker reporting on Form 1099-B was not required for brokers' corporate customers, including S corporations. Section 6045(g) (4), however, now requires brokers to report all sales of covered securities, acquired on or after January 1, 2012, by S corporations (other than financial institutions).

> **COMMENT**
>
> Whether an entity qualifies as an S corporation is determined by referencing the definition set forth in Code Sec. 1361(a).

> **NOTE**
>
> The 1099-B reporting requirements continue to be inapplicable to sales by C corporations.

In addition, the new regulations have eliminated the "eyeball test" that allowed a broker to rely solely on a customer's name to determine whether that customer was a corporation exempt from reporting. However, the regulations do retain the "actual knowledge test," which absolves brokers from having to obtain an exemption certificate from customers the broker knows is exempt. Finally, it bears mention that the regulations do retain a limited eyeball test for insurance companies and foreign corporations, because neither is eligible to be an S corporation.

Options

By the terms of Code Sec 6045(h)(1), if a covered security is acquired or disposed in connection with the exercise of an option that was bought or sold in the same account, the amount received or paid in the option's acquisition must be treated as an adjustment to gross proceeds or adjusted basis. Reporting of gross proceeds and basis is required when there is an expiration of or closing transaction in an option on a specified security or an exercise of a cash-settled option on a specified security. As noted, the new reporting requirements do not apply to any option granted or acquired before January 1, 2013.

Transfer Statements

Under new Code Sec. 6045A, a broker or other applicable person that transfers to another broker a covered security must also transfer to the receiving broker a written statement that allows the receiving broker to satisfy the new broker reporting requirements. This statement must be furnished to the broker accepting custody no later than 15 days after the transfer of the covered security.

Issuer Reporting

An issuer of specified securities must file a return, according to forms or regulations prescribed by the Treasury Secretary, describing any organizational action, including, but not limited to, stock splits and reorganizations, that affects the basis of the specified security, under newly added Code Sec 6045B. The issuer also must note the quantitative effect of the action and any other information the IRS may prescribe. This return is to be filed within 45 days after the date of the organizational action. If the action takes place in December, however, the return must be filed by January 15 of the following year.

Finally, Code Sec. 6045B(c) states that the issuer must, by January 15 of the year following the action, also furnish to each nominee (or certificate holder, if none), as of the record date of the action, a written statement including the:

- Name, address, and telephone number of the person responsible for filing the return;
- The information required to be reported; and
- Any other information the IRS may require.

Foreign Intermediaries and Securities

Qualified intermediaries that are not U.S payors or middlemen, as described in Regulation 1.6049-5(c)(5), and above, will not be deemed brokers with respect to transactions effected at an office outside the United States.

> **COMMENT**
>
> Recent changes to the tax code will impose certain information reporting requirements on foreign financial institutions that enter into an agreement with the IRS under Code Sec. 1471(b). Persons who enter into such agreements will have the ability to elect to report certain information required under Code Secs. 6041, 6042, 6045, and 6049. It is likely that, in such cases, the agreement would specify the extent of the foreign person's reporting requirements.

INFORMATION REPORTING ABROAD

The *Foreign Account Tax Compliance Act* (FACTA), enacted in 2010 as part of the *Hiring Incentives to Restore Employment Act* (HIRE Act), adds a new Chapter 4 to the tax code and imposes far-reaching withholding and reporting requirements on "foreign financial institutions," as well as certain nonfinancial foreign entities. The overarching goal of these new requirements is to ensure compliance with the new reporting requirements imposed upon U.S. persons with respect to their ownership interests in most foreign accounts.

Foreign Financial Accounts

In a development sure to ensnare many an unwary taxpayer, the U.S. Department of the Treasury, acting on behalf of the Financial Crimes Enforcement Network (FinCEN), has issued final regulations relating to the reporting of foreign financial accounts by certain U.S. persons (RIN 1506-AB08, see *CCH Federal Tax Weekly,* Issue No. 9 (March 3, 2010)). To reflect changes required by the regulations, both Form TD F 90-22.1, *Report of Foreign Bank and Financial Accounts* (FBAR), and its corresponding instructions, have also been revised. The regulations took effect on March 28, 2011, and applied to FBARs required to be filed by June 30, 2011, with respect to foreign financial accounts maintained in calendar year 2010, as well as to FBARs filed in all future years. Their promulgation helps illustrate the Internal Revenue Service's aggressive commitment to ensuring disclosure of foreign financial information by American citizens and residents.

COMMENT

Because the FBAR requirements are Treasury, and not IRS, imposed, Form TD F 90-22.1 must be received, and not merely postmarked, by the annual June 30 deadline.

Who Must File an FBAR?

The Bank Secrecy Act (BSA) provides that the Secretary of the Treasury "shall require a resident or citizen of the United States, or a person in, and doing business in, the United States, to…keep records and file reports, when the… person makes a transaction or maintains a relation for any person with a foreign financial agency." Generally, the regulations clarify the matter by requiring every person subject to the jurisdiction of the United States, and possessed of signatory or other authority, over a securities, bank, or other financial account in a foreign financial institution, to report each year in which the relationship exists. The Treasury Secretary is further directed to prescribe the specific information to be reported and the form upon which such information will be supplied.

A Form TD F 90-22.1, accordingly, must be filed anytime the value of a person's foreign accounts exceeds $10,000 no later than June 30 of each calendar year for any qualifying accounts maintained during the previous calendar year.

The new instructions to the FBAR delineate those persons required to file:

- United States citizens;
- United States residents; and
- Corporations, partnerships, limited liability companies, and trusts created, organized, or formed in the United States, or under the laws of the United States.

COMMENT

To determine the status of an alien, the residency tests of Code Sec. 7701(b) are used. An expanded definition of *United States* applies for FBAR, however: not only the States, and District of Columbia, but all U.S. territories and possessions, as well. Indian lands are also included.

COMMENT

Code Sec. 7701(b) allows individuals to make certain elections with respect to their tax status. Certain legal permanent residents, for example, may opt, under a tax treaty, to be treated as nonresidents for tax purposes. These elections will not relieve these individuals of their FBAR responsibilities. The elective provisions of Code Secs. 6013(g) and 6013(h) are also of no consequence in determining an individual's status.

STUDY QUESTIONS

8. Under FinCEN final regulations for reporting foreign financial accounts, which of the following is *not* required to file Form TD F 90-11.1?
   a. United States residents (noncitizens) holding any amount in foreign accounts
   b. U.S. citizens, corporations, and limited liability companies
   c. Trusts holding values of less than $10,000 and created under foreign laws

What Types of Accounts Must Be Reported?

Prior to the promulgation of the new regulations, some confusion existed over when a particular account would be deemed "foreign" under the FBAR requirements. Although stopping short of drawing a brightline rule, FinCEN did provide some additional clarity by stating that, as a general rule, an account will not be considered foreign if it is maintained with a financial institution located in the United States. Thus, for example, individuals purchasing portfolio securities in a foreign corporation, through a U.S.-based brokerage account, will not have foreign accounts under the FBAR requirements. Similarly, individuals with assets at U.S.-based financial institutions, usually banks, that act as global custodians and hold most, or all, of the depositor's funds abroad will not be obligated to file.

COMMENT

Such accounts, often referred to as "omnibus accounts," typically pool the assets of several investors in cash and securities in non-U.S. markets. Generally held in the name of the global custodian, they afford the depositors no legal right to access the investors' holdings without going through the global custodian bank. Were a specific custodial agreement developed to grant a US person direct access to their foreign-held assets, however, that person would be deemed to have a foreign financial account.

The new regulations also specifically provide that the following all qualify as foreign financial accounts:
- Bank accounts
  — Savings deposits,
  — Demand deposits,
  — Checking, or
  — Any other accounts maintained with a person in the business of banking;
- Securities accounts: Accounts maintained with a person in the business of buying, selling, holding, or trading stock or other securities;

- Other financial accounts, including
  - Accounts maintained with a person in the business of accepting deposits as a financial agency, and
  - Insurance policies with a cash value and annuity policies;
- Accounts maintained with a person acting as a broker or dealer for futures or options   transactions in any commodity listed on, or subject to the rules of, a commodity exchange or association; and
- Mutual, or similarly pooled, funds that issue shares to the general public and feature regular net asset value determinations and redemptions.

COMMENT

Bank accounts include time deposits, such as certificates of deposit accounts, that allow individuals to deposit funds with a banking institution and redeem the initial amount, plus a specified rate of interest, after some prescribed period of time.

COMMENT

The FBAR reporting requirements apply only to policies that have a cash value, but, like other account types, are not limited to those that pay an income stream.

COMMENT

Because hedge and private equity funds are generally neither available to the general public nor possessed of regular net value determinations, they are beyond the reach of the FBAR requirements. FinCEN has, nevertheless, reserved the right to address investment companies other than mutual, or similarly pooled, funds at a later date.

Excepted Accounts

The new regulations except from the FBAR reporting requirements certain other accounts, including:

- Accounts of departments or agencies of the United States, Indian Tribes, or any political subdivision of a state;
- Accounts of an international financial institution of which the United States is a member;
- Accounts held or maintained by a U.S. military banking facility; and
- Correspondent accounts maintained by banks solely for the purpose of bank-to-bank settlements.

COMMENT

Exempt entities, including pension and welfare benefit plans, are notably not excluded from the FBAR requirements.

What Qualifies as a Financial Interest?

Under the restated FBAR regulations, U.S. persons will be deemed to have a financial interest in each bank, securities, or other financial account in a foreign country for which the persons are the owner of record, or holder of legal title, regardless whether the account is maintained for them or another person's, benefit. If foreign financial accounts are maintained in the name of more than one U.S. person, each named U.S. person will be considered to have a financial interest in the account.

A U.S. person will also have a financial interest in a foreign account when the account is titled in any of the following persons:

- An individual acting on behalf of a U.S. person in his or her capacity as attorney, agent, or nominee with respect to the account;
- A corporation in which the U.S. person owns more than 50 percent of the corporation's stock by vote or value, either directly or indirectly;
- A partnership in which the U.S. person directly or indirectly owns a greater than 50 percent share of the interest in profits or capital;
- Any other entity in which the U.S. person owns more than 50 percent of the voting power, equity or asset value, or interest in profits;
- Trusts in which the U.S. person is the grantor and has an ownership interest for purposes of U.S. tax; and
- Trusts in which the U.S. person has either a greater than 50 percent present beneficial interest in the asset value, or receives more than 50 percent of trust income;

"Signature Authority"

Few areas have generated as much confusion as FBAR's reporting requirement for those possessing signature, or other, authority over foreign financial accounts. In essence, an individual possesses the requisite authority whenever a foreign financial institution will act upon the receipt of a direct communication from that individual with respect to the disposition of assets.

> **COMMENT**
>
> In a particularly contentious area, FinCEN declined to provide an exemption for employees with signature authority over, but no underlying financial interest in, the foreign financial accounts of their employers. The agency did, however, truncate the recordkeeping requirements for such individuals. FinCEN has no expectation that these individuals personally maintain records for their employers' foreign accounts.

The regulations do provide a series of exceptions, however, for:

- Officers or employees of banks examined by the federal banking agencies;
- Financial institutions examined by the Securities and Exchange Commission (SEC) or the Commodity Futures Trading Commission; and
- Officers and employees of Authorized Service Providers, to the extent that such individuals have authority over accounts owned or maintained by an SEC registered and examined investment company and has no financial interest in the account.

Also excluded from the requirement are officers and employees of entities with any class of equity securities listed on a national exchange, as long as those individuals have no financial interest in the account. Finally, excluded are officers and employees of U.S. corporations having a class of equity securities registered under Section 12(g) of the Securities Exchange Act.

Special Rules

In an effort to simplify FBAR filings in certain cases, FinCEN has adopted a series of special rules. Thus, for example, U.S. persons having a financial interest in 25 or more foreign financial accounts must report only basic information. Similarly, the filing of consolidated reports will be permitted in some cases. Participants and beneficiaries in certain retirement plans are also not required to file a FBAR with respect to foreign financial accounts held by the plan. Nor are certain trust beneficiaries obligated to file.

> **COMMENT**
>
> The exemption does not apply to retirement plans, or participants and beneficiaries that exceed the 50 percent ownership threshold. An FBAR must be filed.

Penalties

Although the civil penalties for a willful failure to comply with the FBAR requirements are understandably severe—namely, up to the greater of $100,000 or the amount in the account at the time of the violation—even be exempt from the Chapter 4 withholding requirements and the type of information and identification to be collected and reported by those affected by the new requirements. The IRS intends to issue proposed regulations based on Notice 2010-60 and to publish draft information reporting and certification forms.

STUDY QUESTIONS

> 9. Employees who hold signature authority over foreign financial accounts of their employers but have no underlying financial interest in the accounts are exempt from FBAR's signature authority reporting requirements. ***True or False?***
>
> 10. The *Foreign Account Tax Compliance Act* (FATCA) rules for nonfinancial foreign entities will apply to payments made after:
>   a. December 31, 2011
>   b. December 31, 2012
>   c. January 1, 2014

CONCLUSION

On April 14, 2011, President Obama signed into law the *Comprehensive 1099 Taxpayer Protection and Repayment of Exchange Subsidy Overpayments Act of 2011*; and, in the process, repealed the expanded 1099 information reporting requirements that were contained in the *Patient Protection and Affordable Care Act*. These requirements would, among other things, have required reporting to the IRS of any payments of $600 or more made by any nonexempt corporation in return for any type of property and, required reporting by landlords of all payments made with respect to rental property that was not part of a trade or business.

Such actions, however, should be considered anomalous, as the clear trend overwhelmingly favors more, rather than less, information reporting. In the same month as the repeal bill was signed, for example (April 2011), IRS Chairman Douglas Shulman delivered a speech in Washington, D.C., in which he set forth his ideas for the future of tax collection. In his vision, the IRS would receive all information returns from third parties (W2s, 1099s, etc) before any individual taxpayers filed their returns. Taxpayers or their professional return preparers could then access that information, via the Web, and download it into their returns, using commercial tax software. Taxpayers would then add any self-reported and supplemental information to their returns before filing them. The IRS would then embed this core third-party information into pre-screening filters and would immediately reject any return that did not match up with its records.

Although such dramatic changes likely remain years away, the number of information reporting documents the IRS receives annually can be expected to continue its rise. Forty years ago, the number stood at 360 million. Today it is over 2 billion. And, in the wake of the changes this chapter has examined, it is sure to even larger in 2012, and beyond.

New IRS Requirements for Return Preparers

The chapter explores the new IRS requirements for individuals who prepare federal tax returns for compensation. The IRS has mandated that all paid return preparers use an IRS-assigned Preparer Tax Identification Number (PTIN). Certain paid preparers will be required to successfully complete a competency examination (expected to begin in late 2011) and continuing education (expected to begin in 2012). Additionally, final Circular 230 rules bring all paid return preparers under Circular 230 and a 2009 federal law mandates that specified tax return preparers file clients' returns electronically unless otherwise exempt.

LEARNING OBJECTIVES

Upon completion of this chapter you will be able to:

- Describe the IRS's new return preparer oversight initiative;
- Understand the mandatory Preparer Tax Identification Number (PTIN) rules;
- Understand the final Circular 230 Regulations;
- Describe the new designation "registered tax return preparer";
- Identify which paid return preparers are exempt from competency testing and continuing education; and
- Understand the IRS's requirements for mandatory electronic filing by specified tax return preparers.

INTRODUCTION

According to the IRS, a majority of individuals rely on paid tax return preparers to assist them in filing their federal income tax returns. The IRS reported that between 1993 and 2005 the number of taxpayers who prepared their own returns without outside assistance fell by more than two-thirds. For 2008, more than 87 million federal income tax returns were prepared by paid tax return preparers. Effective for 2011, all paid preparers (a definition that may exclude certain support staff) must use a Preparer Tax Identification Number (PTIN). The IRS also is scheduled to begin competency testing in late 2011 and require continuing education in 2012 for preparers who seek the new designation of registered tax return preparers. Specified tax return preparers under a 2009 law must file returns electronically, unless exempt.

PREVIOUS OVERSIGHT OF PREPARERS

In 2009, the IRS estimated that between 900,000 and 1.2 million individuals prepared federal tax returns for compensation. The level of oversight of the preparer traditionally depended on whether the preparer held a professional license, such as certified public accountant (CPA) and attorney, or the preparer was enrolled to practice before the IRS (enrolled agent or EA). Unenrolled preparers—individuals who are not CPAs, EAs, or attorneys—were traditionally subject to minimal oversight by the IRS.

Unenrolled Return Preparers

According to the IRS, the majority of paid federal income tax return preparers are unenrolled preparers. An *unenrolled return preparer* is an individual other than an attorney, CPA, enrolled agent, or enrolled actuary who prepares and signs a taxpayer's return as the preparer, or who prepares a return but is not required (by the instructions to the return or regulations) to sign the return. An unenrolled return preparer is permitted to appear as a taxpayer's representative only before customer service representatives, revenue agents, and examination officers, with respect to an examination regarding the return he or she prepared. An unenrolled return preparer cannot:

- Represent a taxpayer before other offices of the IRS, such as Collection or Appeals. This includes the IRS Automated Collection System (ACS) unit;
- Execute closing agreements;
- Extend the statutory period for tax assessments or collection of tax;
- Execute waivers;
- Execute claims for refund; or
- Receive refund checks.

COMMENT

All paid return preparers are subject to various penalties under the Internal Revenue Code and criminal sanctions. For example, Code Sec. 6694(a) imposes a civil penalty on a preparer who prepares a return that understates the taxpayer's liability when the understatement was due to a position that the preparer knew or reasonably should have known was unreasonable. The penalty is increased under Code Sec. 6694(b) if the understatement is due to the preparer's willful attempt to understate liability or reckless or intentional disregard for the rules.

Calls for Regulation

In recent years, various organizations, lawmakers, and others have called for greater regulation of return preparers. In 2006, the Taxpayer Advocacy Panel recommended licensing of all paid return preparers. The IRS Electronic Tax Administration Advisory Committee (ETAAC) recommended that the IRS establish threshold standards for return preparers in 2008. Several bills were also introduced in Congress to require the registration of all paid return preparers (the 2007 Taxpayer Protection and Assistance Bill (Sen. 1219); the 2008 Taxpayer Bill of Rights (H.R. 5716)).

In 2009, the IRS began a process of exploring proposals to regulate all paid return preparers. The IRS invited representatives from the tax preparation industry, the tax professional community, government agencies, and consumer advocates to attend three public meetings. The IRS also issued Notice 2009-60, requesting public comments on, among other topics, minimum levels of education and training necessary to provide tax return preparation services, whether return preparers should be subject to a code of ethics and special provisions for CPAs, EAs, and attorneys.

COMMENT

The IRS received more than 500 responses to Notice 2009-60. According to the IRS:

- 89 percent of respondents favored registration of paid return preparers;
- 90 percent of respondents favored minimum testing requirements for paid return preparers; and
- 98 percent of respondents favored establishment of ethics standards for paid return preparers.

STUDY QUESTIONS

1. Throughout the mid-1990s to mid-2000s, the number of taxpayers who used paid tax preparers for assistance in preparing their tax returns:

   a. Declined sharply

   b. Was steady year to year

   c. Increased substantially

2. Comments to Notice 2009-60 by the IRS recommended all of the following *except:*

   a. Establishing ethics standards for paid return preparers

   b. Expanding peer reviews from CPAs only to all paid return preparers

   c. Minimum testing requirements for paid return preparers

THREE PRONGS RESULTING FROM RETURN PREPARER OVERSIGHT INITIATIVE

The IRS Return Preparer Oversight Initiative

The IRS announced the results of its return preparer review in 2010. The IRS's return preparer oversight initiative has three prongs:

- Mandatory use of Preparer Tax Identification Numbers (PTINs) by all return preparers who prepare for compensation certain federal tax returns (beginning January 1, 2011);
- Competency testing for return preparers who prepare returns for compensation and are not certified public accountants (CPAs), enrolled agents (EAs), attorneys, or otherwise exempt from testing (expected to begin in October 2011); and
- Continuing education for return preparers who prepare returns for compensation and are not certified public accountants (CPAs), enrolled agents (EAs), attorneys, or otherwise exempt from continuing education (expected to begin in 2012).

Preparer Tax Identification Numbers (PTINs)

Effective January 1, 2011, all return preparers who prepare federal tax returns for compensation must obtain or renew a PTIN. The PTIN requirement applies to all federal tax returns except for:

- Form SS-4, *Application for Employer Identification Number;*
- Form SS-8, *Determination of Worker Status for Purposes of Federal Employment Taxes and Income Tax Withholding;*
- Form SS-16, *Certificate of Election of Coverage under FICA;*
- Form W-2 series of returns;
- Form W-7, *Application for IRS Individual Taxpayer Identification Number;*
- Form W-8BEN, *Certificate of Foreign Status of Beneficial Owner for United States Tax Withholding;*
- Form 870, *Waiver of Restrictions on Assessment and Collection of Deficiency in Tax and Acceptance of Overassessment;*
- Form 872, *Consent to Extend the Time to Assess Tax;*
- Form 906, *Closing Agreement On Final Determination Covering Specific Matters;*
- Form 1098 series;
- Form 1099 series;
- Form 2848, *Power of Attorney and Declaration of Representative;*
- Form 3115, *Application for Change in Accounting Method;*
- Form 4029, *Application for Exemption From Social Security and Medicare Taxes and Waiver of Benefits;*

- Form 4361, *Application for Exemption From Self-Employment Tax for Use by Ministers, Members of Religious Orders and Christian Science Practitioners;*
- Form 4419, *Application for Filing Information Returns Electronically;*
- Form 5300, *Application for Determination for Employee Benefit Plan;*
- Form 5307, *Application for Determination for Adopters of Master or Prototype or Volume Submitter Plans;*
- Form 5310, *Application for Determination for Terminating Plan;*
- Form 5500 series;
- Form 8027, *Employer's Annual Information Return of Tip Income and Allocated Tips;*
- Form 8288-A, *Statement of Withholding on Dispositions by Foreign Persons of U.S. Real Property Interests;*
- Form 8288-B, *Application for Withholding Certificate for Dispositions by Foreign Persons of U.S. Real Property Interests;*
- Form 8508, *Request for Waiver From Filing Information Returns Electronically;*
- Form 8717, *User Fee for Employee Plan Determination, Opinion, and Advisory Letter Request;*
- Form 8809, *Application for Extension of Time to File Information Return;*
- Form 8821, *Tax Information Authorization;* and
- Form 8942, *Application for Certification of Qualified Investments Eligible for Credits and Grants Under the Qualifying Therapeutic Discovery Project Program.*

PTIN application process. The IRS has created an online PTIN application process. Alternatively, preparers can submit a paper application (Form W-12, *IRS Paid Preparer Tax Identification Number (PTIN) Application*). The minimum age to obtain a PTIN is 18. The online system generally assigns a PTIN as soon as the applicant has completed the application process. The IRS has advised that it takes four to six weeks to process paper applications.

Each preparer must have his or her own PTIN and each may only obtain one PTIN. Preparers applying for a PTIN must provide their Social Security number (SSN). The IRS has made an exception for U.S. citizens who have a conscientious objection to obtaining an SSN for religious reasons. The IRS also carved out an exception for permanent non-U.S. citizens who are ineligible to obtain an SSN. In both cases, the IRS requires these preparers to give supplemental documentation to verify their identity and substantiate their eligibility for a PTIN.

Religious objection. U.S. citizens who have a conscientious objection to obtaining a social security number for religious reasons must complete Form W-12, *IRS Paid Preparer Tax Identification Number (PTIN) Application,* either online or on paper, and a paper Form 8945, *PTIN Supplemental Application For U.S. Citizens Without a Social Security Number Due to Conscientious Religious Objection.* Applicants must submit documentation to substantiate identity, U.S. citizenship, and status as a member of a recognized religious group.

> **COMMENT**
>
> Individuals who have an Individual Taxpayer Identification Number (ITIN) are ineligible for a PTIN unless they are foreign persons with a permanent non-U.S. address.

Penalties. Preparers who prepare returns for compensation and who do not obtain and use a PTIN may be subject to penalties. For example, the IRS may impose penalties under Code Sec. 6695, seek an injunction to prevent the individual from preparing returns, or take other disciplinary action.

> **CAUTION**
>
> A PTIN is not the same as an Electronic Filing Identification Number (EFIN). An EFIN is a number issued by the IRS to individuals or firms that have been approved as authorized IRS e-file providers. It is included with all electronic return data transmitted to the IRS.

Fees. The IRS charges $64.25 to obtain or renew a PTIN. A third-party vendor is paid a portion of the fee for the costs of administering the online PTIN application system.

> **COMMENT**
>
> The IRS has reduced the EA registration and renewal fee from $125 to $30 to account for the reallocation of portions of the EA renewal processes to the PTIN application and renewal process.

PTIN renewal. PTINs that were obtained for the 2011 filing season will expire on December 31, 2011. The IRS expects that renewal will be available in mid-October 2011. Preparers who applied for their PTINs on paper will be able to renew either online or on paper. Preparers must renew their PTIN before January 1, 2012.

COMMENT

In July 2011 the IRS reported that approximately 100,000 individuals prepared returns for compensation during the 2011 filing season but failed to follow new PTIN requirement. The IRS plans to contact these individuals and remind them of the PTIN requirement. The letters explain the new PTIN rules. inform preparers of how to register for a new PTIN, renew an old PTIN, and get assistance.

EXAMPLE

Zachary Jacobson works as an office manager for a small tax preparation firm. Zachary prepares invoices for services provided by the firm to its clients. Zachary does not prepare returns for clients or compute their tax liabilities. Zachary is not a tax return preparer for purposes of the PTIN requirement and does not need to obtain a PTIN.

EXAMPLE

Bashir Jamal and Danielle Toulouse, both studying accounting at a local college, work as part-time paid interns for a small CPA firm. Bashir and Danielle perform data entry from the tax organizer that clients fill out and assemble the documentation that the clients have submitted. When more information is needed, Bashir and Danielle may telephone clients to gather information missing from the tax organizer. Bashir and Danielle do not assist in the preparation of clients' returns. Bashir and Danielle are not return preparers for purposes of the PTIN requirement and they do not need PTINs.

EXAMPLE

Priscilla Anderson is a retired attorney. During filing season, Priscilla volunteers at a local community center to assist senior citizens in the preparation of their federal income tax returns. Priscilla is not a return preparer for purposes of the PTIN requirement because she does not prepare returns for compensation and, thus, does not need to obtain a PTIN.

The PTIN regulations also carve out from the definition of tax return preparer for individuals who provide only typing, reproduction, or other mechanical assistance in the preparation of a return.

Foreign preparers. A foreign preparer who does not have and is not eligible to obtain a Social Security number and is neither a citizen of the U.S. nor a resident alien of the United States must submit Form W-12, *IRS Paid Preparer Tax Identification Number (PTIN) Application,* either online or on paper, and a paper Form 8946, *PTIN Supplemental Application For Foreign Persons Without a Social Security Number.* Only preparers that have a foreign (non-U.S.) address may file this form.

Interns. If an intern does not receive compensation, the intern is not required to obtain a PTIN. If an intern engages in tax return preparation activities that make the intern a tax return preparer and the intern is compensated for these activities, the intern must obtain a PTIN.

STUDY QUESTIONS

3. Which rule of the IRS return preparer oversight initiative became effective January 1, 2011?

    a. Mandatory testing of all paid return preparers

    b. Mandatory use of PTINs by preparers (with certain exceptions) of certain federal returns

    c. Mandatory continuing education for return preparers not exempted from continuing education.

4. If multiple paid preparers are involved in preparing or reviewing a tax return, whose PTIN is used to submit the return?

    a. The preparer with the greatest seniority in the firm

    b. The signing preparer responsible for the return's accuracy

    c. Each preparer involved with the return must list his or her PTIN on the return

CIRCULAR 230

In June 2011, the IRS released final Circular 230 regulations. Circular 230 contains the rules of practice before the IRS. The final regulations, among other provisions:

- Extend the rules of practice in Circular 230 to cover all paid tax return preparers;
- Clarify professional standards;
- Establish the new Registered Tax Return Preparer designation; and,
- Set the eligibility requirements to become a Registered Tax Return Preparer (among other provisions).

Eligibility to Practice Before the IRS

Attorneys. An *attorney* is any person who is a member in good standing of the bar of the highest court of any state, territory, or possession of the United States, including a Commonwealth, or the District of Columbia. An attorney, not currently under suspension or disbarment from practice before the IRS is eligible to practice before the IRS. *Good standing* means current eligibility to practice before the court. A license to practice law issued in, or by, a foreign jurisdiction does not confer eligibility to practice before the IRS. If an attorney is eligible to practice before the IRS, he or she may represent taxpayers located in any United States jurisdiction with respect to all matters administered by the IRS.

CPAs. A *certified public accountant* is any person who is duly licensed to practice as a certified public accountant in any state, territory, or possession of the United States, including a Commonwealth, or the District of Columbia. A license to practice accountancy as a public or registered accountant, or some other title not conferring "certified public accountant" status, issued under the laws of any United States jurisdiction, does not necessarily confer eligibility to practice before the IRS. A certified public accountant in other than active status as a certified public accountant has the burden of establishing that he or she is nevertheless duly qualified. A license to practice accountancy issued in, or by, a foreign jurisdiction does not confer eligibility to practice before the IRS. If a certified public accountant is eligible to practice before the IRS, he or she may represent taxpayers located in any United States jurisdiction with respect to all matters administered by the IRS.

Enrolled agents. An *enrolled agent* (EA) is an individual who has earned the privilege of practicing before the IRS. Enrolled agents, like attorneys and CPAs are unrestricted as to which taxpayers they can represent, what types of tax matters they can handle, and which IRS offices they can practice before.

Enrolled retirement plan agents. *Enrolled retirement plan agents* (ERPAs) are authorized to represent taxpayers under the IRS Employee Plans Determination Letter program, the Employee Plans Compliance Resolution System, and the Employee Plans Master and Prototype and Volume Submitter programs. ERPAs also may represent taxpayers on matters related to Form 5500 filings, but not on actuarial issues. If an enrolled retirement plan agent is eligible to practice before the IRS, he or she may represent taxpayers located in any United States jurisdiction but only with respect to those matters specifically involving retirement plans.

STUDY QUESTIONS

5. Circular 230 final regulations establish the new designation:

   a. Enrolled retirement plan agent

   b. Registered tax return preparer

   c. Enrolled agent

6. If an association in a foreign jurisdiction issues a license to practice accountancy to an individual, he or she is granted the CPA designation upon establishing a practice in the United States. *True or False?*

Expansion of Circular 230 to All Preparers

Before the IRS issued final Circular 230 regulations in 2011, a return preparer generally was not subject to the provisions in Circular 230 unless the preparer was a CPA, EA, attorney, or other type of practitioner identified in Circular 230. The final Circular 230 regulations provide that *all* preparers who prepare federal returns for compensation are subject to Circular 230.

EXAMPLE

During the past six filing seasons, Mario Hernandez has prepared Forms 1040 and accompanying schedules for individuals for compensation. Mario is not an attorney, CPA, or EA. Previously, Mario would not have been subject to Circular 230 because he was not an attorney, CPA, EA, or other type of practitioner identified in Circular 230. The final Circular 230 regulations provide that all preparers who prepare federal returns for compensation, such as Mario, are subject to Circular 230.

Enforcement of Circular 230 Rules

Traditionally, the IRS Office of Professional Responsibility (OPR) enforced the preparer rules in Circular 230. In the final Circular 230 regulations, the IRS removed references to OPR. The IRS explained that the final regulations are intended to give it the flexibility to adjust return preparer oversight between OPR and the new IRS Return Preparer Office.

OPR is composed of four units:

- *Case Development and Licensure Branch, Washington, D.C.*—This unit reviews disciplinary cases for jurisdiction, recommends the disposition of questionable applications for enrollment, and oversees OPR's Office of Practitioner Enrollment.
- *Enforcement & Oversight Branch I, Washington, D.C.*—This unit investigates practitioner misconduct with respect to possible violations of the Circular 230 regulations, recommends disciplinary sanctions, negotiates

settlements, and assists the IRS Associate Chief Counsel (General Legal Services) in presenting contested cases before administrative law judges and with appeals to the Appellate Authority.

- *Enforcement & Oversight Branch II, Washington, D.C.*—This unit provides administrative support to the Joint Board for the Enrollment of Actuaries, an independent federal board established pursuant to the *Employee Retirement Income Security Act of 1974* by the Secretary of Labor and the Secretary of the Treasury. The Joint Board, pursuant to its authority under ERISA, acts on applications for enrolled actuary status and, as appropriate, suspends or terminates the enrollment of actuaries who violate the Joint Board's regulations.

- *Office of Practitioner Enrollment, Detroit*—This unit processes applications for initial enrollment as an enrolled agent or as an enrolled retirement plan agent and, on three-year cycles, processes applications for renewal of enrollment.

Competency examination. The IRS clarified in the final Circular 230 regulations that competency testing to attain the designation registered tax return preparer will initially be limited to those individuals preparing individual tax returns (Form 1040 series tax returns and accompanying schedules) for compensation. Preparers who do not prepare individual returns for compensation will not be required to complete the initial competency test or become a registered tax return preparer at this time, the IRS has indicated. However, the IRS left open the door to requiring testing outside the Form 1040 series in the future.

Limited practice. Circular 230 traditionally has provided for limited practice before the IRS by certain individuals. Taxpayers can choose to represent themselves. An individual may also represent another taxpayer if the two are in a special relationship, such as immediate family members. An unenrolled tax preparer who prepares and signs a taxpayer's tax return as the preparer, or who prepares a tax return but is not required to sign the tax return, may represent the taxpayer before:

- Revenue agents;
- Customer service representatives; or
- Similar officers and employees of the IRS during an examination of the tax year or period covered by that return.

The unenrolled preparer, however, cannot represent taxpayers before:

- IRS Appeals;
- Revenue officers;
- Chief Counsel; or
- Similar officers or employees of the IRS or the Department of Treasury.

The final Circular 230 regulations delete the limited practice authorization as it relates to unenrolled preparers. The IRS removed the limited practice authorization for unenrolled preparers as that category of preparer will no longer be recognized. Unenrolled preparers will have to become registered tax return preparers or seek another recognized designation.

Privilege. For tax advice, the same common-law protections of confidentiality that apply to a communication between a taxpayer and an attorney apply to a communication made between a taxpayer and a federally authorized tax practitioner to the extent that the communication would be considered a privileged communication if it were between a taxpayer and an attorney. In the final Circular 230 regulations, the IRS explained that the Code Sec. 7525 practitioner privilege does not apply to communications between a taxpayer and a registered tax return preparer because the advice a registered tax return preparer provides ordinarily is intended to be reflected on a tax return and is not intended to be confidential or privileged.

Table 1. Requirements for Return Preparers

Category	PTIN	Competency Exam*	Continuing Education**
CPAs	X		
Attorneys	X		
Enrolled Agents	X		
Registered Tax Return Preparers	X	X	X
Supervised Preparers	X		
Non-1040 Form Series Preparers	X		

*Scheduled to begin in October 2011.
**Scheduled to begin in 2012.
Source: IRS.

STUDY QUESTIONS

7. Competency testing to attain the registered tax return preparer designation will initially be limited to:

   a. Preparers who prepare corporate, partnership, and LLC returns
   b. Preparers who prepare individual tax returns in the Form 1040 series
   c. Preparers who are currently an unenrolled preparer

8. Final Circular 230 regulations _____ the limited practice exception as it relates to unenrolled preparers:

   a. Delete
   b. Retain
   c. Retain for one year

REGISTERED TAX RETURN PREPARERS

One of the most significant changes in the enhanced oversight of return preparers under the final Circular 230 regulations is the new designation the IRS created: "registered tax return preparers." *Registered tax return preparers* are individuals who obtain or renew a PTIN, pass an IRS competency test and compliance/suitability checks, and satisfy continuing education requirements.

Practice Rights of Registered Tax Return Preparers

Preparers who earn the designation registered tax return preparer will enjoy certain practice rights before the IRS. Generally, registered tax return preparers may represent taxpayers before:

- Revenue agents;
- Customer service representatives; or
- Similar officers and employees of the IRS (including the Taxpayer Advocate Service) during an examination if the registered tax return preparer signed the tax return or claim for refund for the tax year or period under examination.

Registered tax return preparers may *not* represent taxpayers before:

- IRS Appeals;
- Chief Counsel; or
- Similar officers or employees of the IRS or the Department of Treasury.

> **COMMENT**
>
> The conduct of a registered tax return preparer in connection with the preparation of the return, claim for refund, or other document, as well as any representation of the client during an examination, will be subject to the standards of conduct in Circular 230. Inquiries into possible misconduct and disciplinary proceedings relating to registered tax return preparer misconduct will be conducted under the provisions in Circular 230.

Compliance and Suitability Check

Individuals seeking the designation registered tax return preparer will be subject to suitability and compliance checks. The IRS explained in the final Circular 230 regulations that:

- The compliance check will be limited to an inquiry regarding whether the individual seeking the designation registered tax return preparer has filed all required returns and whether the individual has failed to pay, or make proper arrangements with the IRS for payment of, any federal tax debts; and

- The suitability check will be limited to an inquiry regarding whether the individual seeking the designation registered tax return preparer has engaged in any conduct that would justify suspension or disbarment of any practitioner under Circular 230.

If the individual does not pass the tax compliance or suitability check, he or she will not be designated as a registered tax return preparer. An individual who fails the compliance and suitability check will be able to file a written protest within 30 days of the IRS's determination. An individual who is initially denied status as a registered tax return preparer for failure pass a compliance and suitability check may reapply after the initial denial if the individual becomes current in his or her tax liabilities.

Certificates

The IRS intends to issue certificates or cards to individuals who earn the designation registered tax return preparer. Registered tax return preparers must have both a valid registration card or certificate and a current and valid PTIN number to practice before the IRS. In describing their designation, registered tax return preparers may not use the term "certified" or imply an employer/employee relationship with the IRS.

> **COMMENT**
>
> The term *registered tax return preparer* is not without its critics. Some practitioners have cautioned that the term registered tax return preparer signifies an endorsement from the IRS. In response, the IRS made a small change in wording in the final Circular 230 regs. The proposed Circular 230 regulations would have allowed preparers to use the phrasing "designated as a registered tax return preparer with the Internal Revenue Service" when describing their designation. The final Circular 230 regulations remove the word *with* and replace it with the word *by*. A preparer may use the wording "designated as a registered tax return preparer by the Internal Revenue Service."

> **COMMENT**
>
> In May 2011 the IRS estimated that 600,000 to 700,000 individuals will apply to become registered tax return preparers.

Mechanics of Competency Testing

The IRS has explained on its website that the competency exam:
- Initially will be available only in English;

- Will be resource-assisted; certain resources will be permitted at the test site. The IRS has not yet described what type of resources will be allowed at the test site;
- Will provide those tested with basic information about the forms and schedules that will be covered by the return preparer examination (but the IRS will not offer any preparation courses).

Applicants will need to physically go to a testing site, authenticate their identity, and take the test in person at the testing site.

Continuing Education

Preparers who are required to complete the IRS competency examination are also required to complete continuing education coursework. The IRS has set the continuing education requirement for registered tax return preparers at 15 hours annually. The 15 hours of continuing education for registered tax return preparers breaks down as follows:

- 10 hours of federal tax law;
- 3 hours of federal tax law updates; and
- 2 hours of ethics

The IRS has not imposed a continuing education requirement for registered tax return preparers for 2011. Continuing education for registered tax return preparers will begin in 2012.

STUDY QUESTIONS

9. The compliance check for an individual seeking the designation registered tax return preparer under Circular 230 rules will be limited to all of the following *except:*

    a. Whether the preparer has filed all required returns
    b. Whether the individual has arranged or completed payment of federal tax debts
    c. The individual's conduct

10. Which of the following is *not* a requirement for the registered tax return preparer?

    a. A valid registration certificate or card
    b. Supervision by a CPA, EA, attorney, or other authorized tax preparer
    c. A current, valid PTIN

SUPERVISED PREPARERS, NON-FORM 1040 SERIES PREPARERS, STATE-CERTIFIED PREPARERS

Certain preparers, such as CPAs, enrolled agents, and attorneys in good standing, are not required to complete the IRS competency testing and continuing education requirements for registered tax return preparers. Also exempt from competency testing and continuing education requirements for registered tax return preparers are supervised preparers and non-Form 1040 series return preparers. However, supervised preparers and non-Form 1040 series preparers must obtain a PTIN.

Supervised Preparers

In Notice 2011-6 and on its website, the IRS described who is exempt from competency testing and continuing education because they are *supervised preparers* or if they do not prepare Form 1040 series returns. Supervised preparers for purposes of the exemption from IRS competency testing and continuing education are:

- Individuals who do not sign, and are not required to sign, tax returns as a paid return preparer but are:
- Employed by attorney or CPA firms; *or*
- Employed by other recognized firms that are at least 80 percent owned by attorneys, CPAs, or enrolled agents; and
- Who are supervised by
  - — An attorney,
  - — A certified public accountant,
  - — An enrolled agent,
  - — An enrolled retirement plan agent, or
  - — An enrolled actuary.

> **EXAMPLE**
>
> Joshua Stewart is a CPA and wholly owns a small tax return preparation business. Joshua only prepares Form 1040 series returns. Joshua hires Misha, who is not a CPA, EA, or attorney, to assist in the preparation of clients' returns. Misha works under Joshua's supervision. Misha is a return preparer for purposes of the PTIN requirement and must obtain a PTIN. However, Misha is treated as a supervised preparer for purposes of competency testing and continuing education requirements because Misha is supervised by a CPA works for a firm that is at least 80 percent owned by CPAs

The IRS also described some limitations on supervised preparers. Supervised preparers may not:

- Sign any tax return they prepare or assist in preparing;
- Represent taxpayers before the IRS in any capacity; or
- Identify themselves as registered tax return preparers.

REMINDER

Supervised preparers must obtain or renew a PTIN. The IRS advised the supervised preparer to provide the PTIN of his or her supervisor when obtaining or renewing a PTIN. The supervisor's PTIN must be a valid and active PTIN.

COMMENT

For purposes of Notice 2011-6:

- A *CPA firm* is a partnership, professional corporation, sole proprietorship, or any other association that is registered, permitted, or licensed to practice as a certified public accounting firm in any state, territory or possession of the United States, including Puerto Rico and the District of Columbia;
- A *law firm* is a partnership, professional corporation, sole proprietorship, or any other association that is registered, permitted or licensed to practice law in any state, territory or possession of the United States, including Puerto Rico and the District of Columbia; and
- A *recognized firm* is a partnership, professional corporation, sole proprietorship, or any other association—other than a law firm or CPA firm—that has one or more employees engaged in practice before the IRS and that is 80 percent or a greater percent owned by one or more attorneys, CPAs, EAs, enrolled actuaries, or enrolled retirement plan agents authorized to practice before the IRS.

Non-Form 1040 Series Preparers

Because the IRS initially indicated that competency testing would be limited to individual income tax returns (Form 1040 series returns), the IRS, at this time, is exempting non-Form 1040 series preparers from competency testing. However, non-Form 1040-series preparers must obtain a PTIN. *Non-Form 1040 series preparers,* the IRS explained, are individuals who do not prepare, or assist in the preparation of, any Form 1040 series tax return or claim for refund, except a Form 1040-PR or Form 1040-SS, for compensation. Non-Form 1040 series preparers may:

- Sign any tax return they prepare or assist in preparing; and
- Represent taxpayers before revenue agents, customer service representatives, or similar officers and employees of the IRS (including the Taxpayer Advocate Service) during an examination if the individual signed the tax return or claim for refund for the taxable year under examination

Non-Form 1040 series preparers may not:

- Prepare or assist in preparing any Form 1040 series tax return or claim for refund, except a Form 1040-PR or Form 1040-SS, for compensation; or
- Identify themselves as registered tax return preparers.

COMMENT

Non-Form 1040 series preparers must certify that they do not prepare, or assist in the preparation of, any Form 1040 series tax return or claim for refund, except a Form 1040-PR or Form 1040-SS, for compensation when they obtain or renew a PTIN.

EXAMPLE

Elijah Stern works for a small payroll processing firm that provides Form W-2 filing. He prepares Form W-2 series of returns for clients of the firm. He prepares no other returns for clients. Elijah is a non-Form 1040 series return preparer for purposes of competency testing and continuing education. However, Elijah must obtain or renew a PTIN.

State-Certified Preparers

California, Maryland, Oregon, and New York register return preparers under state law. Individuals who are *certified return preparers* under state law must successfully pass the IRS's competency testing and complete continuing education requirements to prepare any federal tax return for compensation unless they are CPAs, EAs, attorneys, supervised preparers, or non-1040 series return preparers. The IRS is not "grandfathering" preparers who are state-certified from competency testing and continuing education based on their state certification.

COMMENT

California requires any individual who prepare tax returns for a fee and who is not a CPA, EA, or attorney to register with the California Tax Education Council (CTEC). CTEC-registered preparers are the largest group of professional tax preparers in California, numbering approximately 40,000 individuals.

Registered and Licensed Public Accountants

In some states, a *registered or licensed public accountant* (LPA) has the same rights and privileges as a certified public accountant. An LPA in those states generally:

- Is eligible to practice before the IRS by virtue of the public accountant's license; and

- Will not be required to complete the IRS competency testing and continuing education requirements to become a registered tax return preparer to prepare returns for compensation.

> **COMMENT**
>
> The IRS has posted a nonexhaustive list of states where an LPA has the same rights and privileges as a CPA on its website: Alabama, Alaska, Arkansas, California, Colorado (Registered Public Accountants only), Connecticut, Hawaii, Idaho, Maine, Montana, New Hampshire, New Jersey, New York, North Dakota, Ohio, Oklahoma, Pennsylvania, Rhode Island, South Carolina (Public Accountants only), South Dakota, Tennessee, Vermont, and West Virginia.
>
> LPAs in the following states do not have the same rights and privileges as a certified public accountant and, therefore, will be required to pass the return preparer examination and satisfy the CPE requirements for tax return preparers to prepare any federal tax return for compensation: Delaware, Illinois, Iowa, Kansas, Michigan, Oregon (unless the person qualified for, and applied to take, the Uniform CPA examination before January 1, 2002), and South Carolina (Accounting Practitioners).
>
> The IRS has advised LPAs in other states to review the laws of the state in which they are licensed to determine whether they have the same rights and privileges as a certified public accountant.

Enrolled Retirement Plan Agents and Enrolled Actuaries

Enrolled retirement plan agents and *enrolled actuaries* must obtain a PTIN if they are compensated for preparing, or assisting in the preparation of, all or substantially all of a federal tax return or claim for refund. However, they are not required to become a registered tax return preparer if they do not prepare Form 1040 series returns.

STUDY QUESTIONS

> **11.** Individuals who are certified return preparers under state law and who prepare certain federal returns for compensation:
>
> **a.** Must complete IRS competency testing and continuing education requirements
>
> **b.** Are exempt from competency testing and continuing education
>
> **c.** Are treated as "grandfathered preparers" for purposes of competency testing and continuing education
>
> **12.** Licensed public accountants (LPAs) have the same rights and privileges as a CPA in some, but not all, states. *True or False?*

MANDATORY ELECTRONIC FILING

Individual taxpayers have the option to file their individual federal income tax returns on paper or electronically. The IRS prefers that taxpayers file their returns electronically because the IRS can process electronically filed returns much more quickly and at significantly less cost than paper returns. The IRS has mandated that certain taxpayers, such as large corporations, electronically file their returns. However, the IRS cannot by law require individual taxpayers to electronically file their returns. The IRS can use other methods to persuade individual taxpayers to move from paper filing to electronic filing. In 2011, the IRS discontinued mailing paper return packages to individual taxpayers to encourage individuals to electronically file their 2010 federal income tax returns.

In 2009, Congress passed the *Worker, Homeownership and Business Assistance Act* (P.L. 111-92) (2009 Worker Act). The 2009 Worker Act requires that specified tax return preparers electronically file covered returns if they prepare and file the returns for taxpayers for compensation. A *covered return* for this purpose includes any individual income tax return, whether for an individual, estate, or trust. An individual who provides tax assistance under a Volunteer Income Tax Assistance (VITA) program, a person who merely prepares a return of the employer (or of an officer or employee of the employer) by whom the person is regularly and continuously employed, or a person who prepares a return as a fiduciary for any person is not a "specified tax return preparer." The IRS issued final regulations, transition relief, and related guidance on mandatory electronic filing by specified tax return preparers in 2011 (TD 9518, Notice 2011-26, Notice-27, Rev. Proc. 2011-25).

Phase-in

The IRS decided to phase-in the mandatory electronic filing requirement over two years to accommodate "small" preparers:

- For calendar year 2011, a *specified tax return preparer* is a tax return preparer who reasonably expects to file (or if the tax return preparer is a member of a firm, the firm's members in the aggregate reasonably expect to file) 100 or more covered returns during calendar year 2011; and
- Beginning January 1, 2012, a *specified tax return preparer* is a tax return preparer who reasonably expects to file (or if the tax return preparer is a member of a firm, the firm's members in the aggregate reasonably expect to file) 11 or more individual income tax returns in calendar year 2012 and future calendar years.

Number of Covered Returns Preparers Reasonably Expect to File

A specified tax return preparer should estimate the number of covered returns he or she reasonably expects to prepare and file (or if the specified tax return preparer is a member of a firm, the firm reasonably expects to prepare and file) in the calendar year. Excluded from this estimate should be the number of returns that the specified tax return preparer reasonably expects his or her clients (or the firm reasonably expects its clients) will choose to have completed in paper format and will submit by mail or otherwise deliver to the IRS themselves. Additionally, a specified tax return preparer should exclude from this estimate the number of returns he or she expects not to be able to electronically file because the form is not accepted in IRS e-file.

EXAMPLE

Isabelle Valdez is an accountant who recently graduated from college with an accounting degree and has opened her own business. Isabelle has not prepared individual income tax returns for compensation in the past and does not plan to focus her business on individual income tax return preparation. Isabelle has no plans to, and does not, employ or engage any other tax return preparers. Isabelle estimates that she may be asked by some clients to prepare and file their individual income tax returns for compensation, but Isabelle expects that the number of people who do ask her to prepare and file their returns to be very small (no more than 7 in 2012). In fact, Isabelle prepares and files 6 individual returns for clients in 2012. Due to a growing client base, and based upon her experience in 2012, Isabelle expects that the individual tax returns she will prepare and file in 2013 will at least double, estimating she will prepare and file 12 Form 1040 returns in 2012. Isabelle is not a specified return preparer for purposes of the electronic filing mandate because she reasonably expects to file 10 or fewer returns in 2012 and Isabelle is not required to electronically file the individual returns she prepares and files in 2012. In 2013, however, Isabelle is a specified tax return preparer for purposes of mandatory electronic filing because she reasonably expects to file more than 10 individual returns.

EXAMPLE

Tyler Wadsworth is a solo general practice attorney in a small county. His practice includes the preparation of wills and assisting executors in administering estates. As part of his practice, Tyler infrequently prepares and files Forms 1041, *U.S. Income Tax Return for Estates and Trusts,* for executors. In the past three years, he prepared and filed an average of 5 Forms 1041 each year and never exceeded more than 7 Forms 1041 in any year. Based on Tyler's prior experience and his estimate for 2012, made prior to the time he first files an individual income tax return in 2012, Tyler reasonably expects to prepare and file no more than 5 Forms 1041 in 2012.

Due to the unforeseen deaths of several of his clients in late 2011, Tyler actually prepares and files 12 Forms 1041 in 2012. Tyler does not find out about these deaths until after he has already filed the first Form 1041 in 2012 for another client. Tyler is not required to electronically file these returns in 2012. He is not a specified tax return preparer for calendar year 2012 because prior to the time he filed the first Form 1041 in 2012, Tyler reasonably expected to file 10 or fewer individual income tax returns in 2012.

Firms

The IRS requires members of firms to compute the number of returns in the aggregate that they reasonably expect to file as a firm. If that number is 100 or more in calendar year 2011 (11 or more in 2012 and thereafter), then all members of the firm must e-file the returns they prepare and file. This is true even if a member prepares and files fewer than the threshold on an individual basis.

COMMENT

Fiduciaries, the IRS has explained on its website, that file returns are not considered tax return preparers and are therefore not covered by the electronic filing mandate.

Client Choice

A client of a specified tax return preparer may request to independently file a return on paper. Starting in 2012, the client who insists on filing a return on paper—and not the specified tax return preparer—must physically mail or otherwise deliver the paper return to the IRS after the specified tax return preparer has prepared the return. Further, a client's request to independently file a return on paper must be made in writing. The IRS has instructed specified tax return preparers to attach Form 8948, *Preparer Explanation for Not Filing Electronically,* to the client's return. The IRS has posted sample language on its website:

My tax return preparer [INSERT PREPARER'S NAME] has informed me that [INSERT PREPARER'S NAME] may be required to electronically file my [INSERT TAX YEAR] individual income tax return [INSERT TYPE OF RETURN: Form 1040, Form 1040A, Form 1040EZ, Form 1041, Form 990-T] if [INSERT PREPARER's NAME] files it with the IRS on my behalf (for example, submits it by mail to the IRS). I understand that electronic filing may provide a number of benefits to taxpayers, including an acknowledgment that the IRS received the returns, a reduced chance of errors in processing the returns, and faster refunds. I do not want to have my return electronically filed, and I choose to file my return on paper forms. I will mail or otherwise submit my paper return to the IRS myself. My preparer will not file or otherwise mail or submit my paper return to the IRS.

COMMENT

An e-mail message from the taxpayer, the IRS explained, is insufficient to demonstrate a taxpayer's choice to independently file a return on paper. However, a copy of a hand-signed and dated statement attached as a scanned document to an e-mail will satisfy the requirement that the request be in writing.

COMMENT

In Notice 2011-27, the IRS created an exception for calendar year 2011— and only for 2011—that allows either taxpayer mailing or preparer mailing of paper returns. The exception does not apply to 2012 and beyond. During 2011, a specified tax return preparer may mail the return in paper format at the request of the taxpayer, pursuant to a statement signed and dated by the taxpayer, and retained by the preparer. The IRS said that it will consider the following language sufficient:

I do not want to have my income tax return electronically filed, and I choose to have my return filed on paper forms. I have asked my tax return preparer to mail my paper return to the IRS on my behalf.

STUDY QUESTIONS

13. The *Worker, Homeownership and Business Assistance Act* requires that specified paid tax return preparers electronically file _____.

   a. Covered returns
   b. The Form 5500 and 8288 series of returns
   c. Form 8508

---

14. The threshold number of aggregated returns of a preparer firm that requires members to file electronically is _____ in calendar year 2011 and _____ in 2012 and thereafter.
   a. 100; 11
   b. 250; 20
   c. 250; 100

Hardship Waivers as Exemption from Mandatory e-filing

A specified tax return preparer may seek a hardship waiver from mandatory electronic filing. The decision to grant or deny a waiver is solely at the discretion of the IRS.

Specified tax return preparers should not expect the IRS to liberally grant hardship waivers, the IRS has cautioned. The fact that a specified tax return preparer does not have a computer or appropriate software or does not desire to obtain or use a computer or software is not, standing alone, an undue hardship. The IRS stated that an undue hardship waiver request based solely on this fact or personal desire, without any further explanation or justification, will be denied.

Approved waivers will be valid for one calendar year. If the IRS grants a waiver, the specified tax return preparer should attach Form 8948, *Preparer Explanation for Not Filing Electronically*, to the client's returns. If an undue hardship waiver request is denied, the specified tax return preparer may ask the IRS to reconsider the denial.

Administrative Exemptions from Mandatory e-filing

The IRS has provided certain administrative exemptions to mandatory electronic filing by specified return preparers:

- *Exempt preparers*—these specified tax return preparers are exempt from mandatory electronic filing:
  - Members of certain religious groups. A specified tax return preparer who is a member of a recognized religious group that is conscientiously opposed to its members using electronic technology, including for the filing of income tax returns electronically, and that has existed continuously since December 31, 1950;
  - Foreign preparers without Social Security numbers—a specified tax return preparer who is a foreign person without a Social Security number and is therefore ineligible to file electronically because the IRS e-file program currently does not accept foreign tax return preparers without Social Security numbers who live and work abroad; and
- *Preparers ineligible for IRS e-file*—a tax return preparer who is currently ineligible for the IRS e-file program due to an IRS sanction. To qualify for this exemption, the tax return preparer must have received a letter

from the IRS enforcing the sanction and the sanction must be in effect for some or all of the calendar year in which the individual income tax return or returns are being filed. This exemption ends on the date the sanction period ends or the date the IRS accepts the tax return preparer into the IRS e-file program, whichever date occurs first.

Exempt Returns Due to Preparer's Technological Difficulties

The following individual income tax returns are exempt from the electronic filing requirement under and the corresponding regulations, due to technological difficulties experienced by a specified tax return preparer:

- *Rejected returns*—a return that a specified tax return preparer attempted to e-file but was unable to e-file because the return was rejected and the specified tax return preparer attempted but could not resolve the reject condition or code;
- *Forms or schedules not supported by software*—a return prepared by a specified tax return preparer whose e-file software package does not support one or more forms or schedules that are part of the return; and
- *Other technological difficulties*—a return or returns prepared by a specified tax return preparer who experiences a short-term inability to electronically file the return or returns due to some other verifiable and documented technological problem.

Exempt Returns due to IRS Limitations

For all specified tax return preparers, the following individual income tax returns and attachments to returns are exempt from the electronic filing requirement, due to IRS barriers or other systemic limitations that currently prevent the returns and attachments from being filed electronically:

- *Returns currently not accepted electronically*—this category includes any individual income tax return that is not currently accepted electronically by IRS e-file or that the IRS has instructed taxpayers not to file electronically, including
  - Form 1040-NR, U.S. Nonresident Alien Income Tax Return,
  - Form 1041-QFT, U.S. Income Tax Return for Qualified Funeral Trusts,
  - Form 990-T, Exempt Organization Business Income Tax Return,
  - All amended individual income tax returns, such as Form 1040X, Amended U.S. Individual Income Tax Return,
  - A fiscal year return for Form 1040, U.S. Individual Income Tax Return,
  - A fiscal year return for Form 1041, U.S. Income Tax Return for Estates & Trusts, for certain periods (fiscal year Form 1041 returns ending during any month after June 30 of the current processing year),

— Form 1041 claiming a refund amount equal to or greater than $10 million,

— Form 1041 with a dollar amount over $99 billion, and

— Other Forms 1041 not accepted by IRS e-file for any other limitation listed in IRS Publication 1437, *Procedures for the Form 1041 e-file Program U.S. Income Tax Returns for Estates and Trusts*;

■ *Required documentation or attachments not accepted electronically*—any required documentation or attachments that the IRS does not yet provide the capability to file electronically.

> **COMMENT**
>
> The IRS has referred preparers to Publication 1346, *Electronic Return File Specifications and Record Layouts for Individual Income Tax Returns*, for forms in the Form 1040-series that the IRS currently accepts electronically.

IRS LETTERS AND VISITS TO PREPARERS

In 2010 and 2011, the IRS sent letters to more than 10,000 return preparers to remind them of their obligation to prepare accurate tax returns on behalf of their clients. The letters were sent preparers who complete large volumes of tax returns. The IRS identified preparers who in its view "may need assistance in meeting their required responsibilities." The IRS followed-up with in-person visits to approximately 2,500 recipients of the letters to further discuss their responsibilities as a return preparer. The visits took place at the preparers' offices.

Purpose of the IRS Contact

The IRS explained that the purpose of the letters and visits was to improve the accuracy and quality of filed tax returns and to heighten awareness of preparer responsibilities. The letters also reminded tax return preparers of the consequences of filing incorrect returns, such as:

■ Monetary penalties;

■ Suspension or expulsion from participation in IRS e-file;

■ Civil injunctions barring the return preparer from preparing tax returns; and

■ Referral for criminal investigation.

> **COMMENT**
>
> A preparer's professional designation or lack of one was not a factor in determining who received a letter or who was selected for a visit.

COMMENT

The IRS intends to continue its outreach letter and in-person visit initiative in future years. The IRS has not indicated as of the time this course was published how many preparers the IRS will contact by letter and visit in future years.

Visits

During the in-person office visits, the IRS confirmed that preparers were complying with requirements regarding the maintenance of records, signing, and furnishing identifying number on returns that they prepare. The IRS also asked preparers to make available all tax forms prepared in 2011, including all relevant documents. Relevant documents include, but are not limited to, worksheets, interview notes, correspondence, and a copy of the returns prepared for clients. No additional advance preparation is required, but the IRS will provide a link to educational material where practitioners can review their obligations as return preparers.

Penalties

IRS revenue agents making the visits are authorized to assess return preparer penalties during the visits. If violations are found, the revenue agent may determine it is appropriate to impose penalties. The IRS has explained on its website that revenue agents look to whether the preparer:

- Provided the client with a copy of the tax return;
- Signed the tax return as required by regulations;
- Furnished their identifying number as required by regulations;
- Retained a copy or list of returns and claims for refund as required by regulations;
- Filed correct information returns; and
- Properly refused to endorse or negotiate a refund check that was issued to a taxpayer.

Clients

The IRS has indicated it will generally not contact clients of the preparer. During the visits, the focus is on the return preparer's activity, not on the taxpayers' reporting compliance. The IRS is inspecting the taxpayers' returns to ensure the return preparer's compliance with the requirements subject to penalty under Code Sec. 6695 for failure to:

- Furnish a copy of the return to the taxpayer;
- Sign the return;
- Furnish identifying number; and
- Retain a copy or list of all returns prepared.

Taxpayers generally will not be contacted as a result of a FY2011 return preparer visit. Taxpayer contacts resulting from these visits will be to confirm potential violations of the return preparer that may result in penalties against the tax return preparer.

Figure 1. Sample Preparer Letter from IRS

Dear Return Preparer:

The Internal Revenue Service is taking steps to ensure tax return preparers are meeting their obligations with respect to the preparation of tax returns and claims for refund. We are sending this letter to a segment of the return preparer community to heighten awareness of preparer responsibilities and increased IRS oversight of tax return preparers.

We will be visiting a smaller segment of the return preparer community beginning in December to confirm these tax return preparers are complying with current return preparer requirements. If we select you for a visit, an IRS representative will contact you to schedule an appointment and to provide you with additional information about what you can expect during the visit.

It is important you are aware of your responsibilities as a tax return preparer, including new preparer tax identification number (PTIN) requirements that are effective for tax returns and claims for refund prepared after December 31, 2010. We, therefore, encourage you to review the enclosure, "Responsibilities of a Tax Return Preparer." If you need additional information, visit our website at **www.irs.gov/taxpros**.

Sincerely,

IRS

STUDY QUESTION

15. Starting in 2012, an individual taxpayer cannot request to file a return on paper independently of any return preparer. *True or False?*

CONCLUSION

The three prongs of the IRS oversight initiative are a significant change in the governance of return preparers. All preparers who prepare certain federal tax returns for compensation must use a PTIN. Paid return preparers who are not CPAs, EAs, attorneys, or otherwise exempt must successfully pass an IRS competency examination, subject to transition rules until 2014 for provisional PTIN holders. Paid return preparers who are not CPAs, EAs, attorneys, or otherwise exempt must complete mandatory continuing education, which the IRS anticipates requiring beginning in 2012. The IRS is expected to flesh-out more details about competency testing and continuing education.

Additionally, the IRS has revised its rules of practice effective August 2, 2011, to bring all return preparers under Circular 230 and the 2009 Worker Act requirements effective starting in calendar year 2011 that specified tax return preparers electronically file covered returns if they prepare and file the returns for taxpayers for compensation.

MODULE 2: COMPLIANCE-DIRECTED CHANGES — CHAPTER 6

Electronic Filing: Current Rules and Future Challenges

This chapter explores the development and growth of electronic tax return filing (e-filing). The chapter covers the mandatory e-filing requirements and discusses the IRS e-file program and the IRS's challenges in advancing e-filing in the future.

LEARNING OBJECTIVES

Upon completion of this chapter you will be able to:

- Explain the IRS's e-file mandate;
- Discuss key features of the IRS e-file program;
- Describe the mandatory e-file requirements for businesses and the consequences of not complying;
- Describe the mandatory e-file requirements for tax return preparers and the consequences of not complying; and
- Explain future challenges for the IRS in advancing e-filing.

INTRODUCTION

The electronic filing of tax returns began over two decades ago. Today electronic filing is more the norm, for both individuals and businesses, but it is not required for everyone. The IRS e-filing program is in place to actively promote e-filing. Taxpayers should be aware of the features and rules of the IRS e-file program. Taxpayers should also be aware of when e-filing is required and the consequences of noncompliance.

IRS E-FILE HISTORY

The year 1986 was a historic one in the world of federal tax. Congress passed the Tax Reform Act of 1986 (P.L. 99-514), which overhauled the Internal Revenue Code, and the IRS began a pilot project to process tax returns electronically.

The initial pilot program involved simple individual income tax returns for which refunds were due and resulted in 25,000 returns e-filed. In 1988, the pilot was expanded to include Form 1065, *U.S. Return of Partnership Income*, and Form 1041, *U.S. Income Tax Return for Estates and Trusts*. By 1990, the IRS e-file program expanded nationwide and the number of returns filed reached 4.2 million.

E-file was subsequently expanded to include other types of returns including Form 941, *Employer's Quarterly Tax Return* and Form 944, *Employer's Annual Tax Return*, for small businesses in 2003; and business and information returns such as Form 1120, *U.S. Corporation Income Tax Return*, Form 1120S, *U.S. Income Tax Return for an S Corporation* and the Form 990 series in 2004 (FS-2011-10, June 10, 2011).

In 2011, more than 100 million individual tax returns were filed electronically. This was approximately three out of every four individual tax returns (IR-2011-64, June 9, 2011). The IRS also reported that, as of April 17, 2011, almost 1 billion tax returns had been e-filed since the e-file program went national in 1990.

The 80 Percent Goal

The *IRS Restructuring and Reform Act of 1998* (P.L. 105-206) (RRA 98) provided a huge boost to the IRS's efforts to promote electronic filing. Congress mandated that the IRS develop a strategic plan to promote electronic filing and set a goal for the IRS to have at least 80 percent of the federal tax and information returns filed electronically by the year 2007 (Act Sec. 2001 of P.L. 105-206; Code Sec. 6011(f)). Congress backed up its mandate with the necessary funding for the IRS to move forward quickly on its electronic initiatives, cognizant that those advances would both raise compliance levels and lower eventual overall administrative costs.

The Electronic Tax Administration is the group of IRS officials responsible for the mandate's implementation. The Electronic Tax Administration Advisory Committee (ETAAC) provides input to the IRS on its strategic plan and assists in devising strategies to advance electronic filing and the broader Electronic Tax Administration vision. The ETAAC members are chosen for their expertise in the electronic exchange of tax administration information. The RRA 98 also established the IRS Oversight Board, which is charged with overseeing the IRS (Code Sec. 7802(c)(1)(A)). Both the ETAAC and the IRS Oversight Board must annually report to Congress on the IRS's progress in meeting its goal.

Because the IRS did not meet its e-filing goal by 2007, the IRS Oversight Board set a new goal that called for a combined e-file rate of 80 percent for all major tax returns filed by individuals, businesses, and tax-exempt organizations by 2012. *Major returns* are returns for which the filers account for income, expenses, and/or tax liabilities, including:

- Individual income tax returns;
- Employment tax returns;
- Partnership returns;
- Trust, estate and gift tax returns;

- Real estate mortgage investment conduit returns;
- Exempt organization returns; and
- Excise tax returns (IRS Oversight Board, *Electronic Filing 2010 Annual Report to Congress*).

Excluded are amended returns, payment vouchers, and requests for extensions.

E-filing Benefits

The e-file mandate came about because Congress realized that e-filing had enormous benefits. A major benefit is that e-filing reduces the cost of processing a return. In 2009, the IRS's estimated cost of processing a paper return was $3.29 compared to 19 cents for an electronic return ("Electronic Tax Return Filing: Improvements Can Be Made Before Mandate Becomes Fully Implemented" (GAO-11-344), March 2011).

Additional benefits of e-filing include higher accuracy rates, improved convenience, and faster processing and refunds for taxpayers.

E-filing also provides increased information that can improve the IRS's compliance programs and increase enforcement revenue.

E-FILE BASICS

In many cases, an individual or business entity may still choose to file either an electronic or paper return. The IRS is authorized to provide standards in its regulations for determining which returns must be filed electronically (Code Sec. 6011(e)). By statute, however, the IRS can mandate electronic filing only in limited circumstances, involving large businesses, exempt organizations, and individual returns filed by certain preparers. Through highlighting the convenience and efficiencies of electronic filing to the taxpayer—including faster refunds—however, the IRS hopes to accomplish by persuasion what it might not be able to accomplish otherwise.

The requirements and procedures for e-filing a tax return will vary depending upon the type of return filed. The IRS e-file program covers the electronic filing of most major returns. The IRS's Filing Information Returns Electronically (FIRE) Program covers e-filing of information returns.

IRS E-file Program

In a typical e-file situation, a taxpayer or the taxpayer's return preparer will use tax preparation software to file the federal income tax return, which is then submitted electronically to a transmitter. The transmitter then sends the return to the IRS. In most cases, the process of e-filing involves a third-party participant referred to as an "Authorized IRS e-file Provider."

Authorized IRS e-file Providers. An *Authorized IRS e-file Provider* is a participant in the IRS e-file program. Table 1 lists the five categories of Authorized IRS e-file Providers.

Table 1. e-file Provider Categories

Category	Description
Electronic Return Originator (ERO)	Originates the electronic submission of returns it either prepares or collects from taxpayers who want to e-file their returns
Intermediate Service Provider	Receives the return information from the ERO or taxpayer or tax-exempt organization that files electronically using commercial tax preparation software, processes the information and either sends the information to the Transmitter or sends the information back to the ERO, taxpayer or tax-exempt organization
Software Developer	Develops software to format electronic return information according to IRS specifications, and/or to transmit electronic tax return information directly to the IRS
Transmitter	Transmits electronic information directly to the IRS
Reporting Agent	Accounting service, franchiser, bank service bureau, or other entity that acts as an agent for the electronic filing of employment tax returns, makes federal tax deposits and federal tax payments, and submits information on the deposits and payments electronically

These categories are not mutually exclusive. For example, an ERO could, at the same time, perform the functions of a Transmitter, Software Developer, or Intermediate Service Provider, depending on the function performed.

Each category of provider has specific responsibilities that relate to its e-file activity. For example, an ERO must timely originate the electronic submission of the return and submit required paper documentation to the IRS. The ERO must also provide copies to the taxpayer, retain records, and make records available to the IRS.

Participation in IRS e-file provider program. Sole proprietors, businesses, and organizations that wish to become Authorized IRS e-file Providers must apply for acceptance in the e-file program. The application is made on Form 8633, *Application to Participate in IRS e-file Program*. The form can be completed online through the IRS e-Services website, after registering for IRS e-Services.

IRS e-Services is a suite of products for tax professionals and taxpayers that do business with the IRS electronically, including:

■ Registration;

■ E-file application;

■ Preparer Taxpayer Identification Number (PTIN);

- Taxpayer Identification Number (TIN) Matching Application; and
- E-filing incentive products.

Once a suitability check is passed, the IRS will assign an electronic filing identification number (EFIN).

An applicant may be denied participation in the program (e.g., for indictment or conviction of a crime or failure to file timely and accurate tax returns or pay tax) and is entitled to an administrative review of the denial. Several courts have held that denying an individual participation in the e-file program does not constitute a violation of the individual's due process rights (*S.B. Ekanem*, DC Md., 98-1 USTC ¶50,247; *N. Sabat*, DC Pa., 2000-1 USTC ¶50,328).

Applicable IRS rules. Rev. Proc. 2007-40 is the official set of rules that govern IRS e-file and the electronic filing for major returns such as the Form 1040 series, the Form 1120, and the Form 990 series. The rules also apply to the electronic filing of extensions of time to file individual, business, and exempt organization returns, as well as certain state returns.

The IRS may post additional e-file rules to its website, **http://www.irs. gov,** or include the rules in e-file publications or other guidance. Publication 3112, *IRS e-file Application and Participation*, provides detailed information about entering the IRS e-file program.

Authorized IRS e-file Providers must follow all of the rules governing the IRS e-file program provided in the publications and notices. All Authorized e-file Providers must:

- Follow advertising standards;
- Display "doing business as" information at all locations and sites where information is obtained from the taxpayer for purposes of electronic filing;
- Cooperate with the IRS's efforts to monitor Authorized IRS e-file Providers and investigate electronic fraud and abuse;
- Ensure against the unauthorized use of an EFIN and/or ETIN;
- Ensure the security of taxpayer information; and
- Make any required changes to the e-file application in a timely manner.

Safeguarding taxpayer information is a top priority for the IRS. Authorized IRS e-file Providers are currently required by the Federal Trade Commission (FTC) Safeguards Rule to have a comprehensive information security program. The Safeguards Rule, which was implemented as a result of the *Gramm-Leach-Bliley Act* (P.L. 106-102), requires companies that collect personal information from their customers to develop a written information security program. The program must be appropriate to its size and complexity, the nature and scope of its activities, and the sensitivity of customer information.

Penalties. An Authorized IRS e-file Provider's failure to follow the rules of the e-file program can result in penalties and sanctions.

The civil tax return preparer penalties can be applied in the appropriate situation, just as when a paper return is filed. For example, civil penalties may be imposed if the understatement of tax liability on a return prepared by a tax return preparer is due to an unreasonable position or if certain recordkeeping and signature requirements are not complied with (Code Secs. 6694 and 6695).

A *tax return preparer* for purposes of imposing these penalties is someone who prepares for compensation (or employs persons to prepare for compensation) all or a substantial portion of a return or refund claim. The phrase includes preparers of income, estate and gift tax, employment tax, excise tax, and exempt organization returns (Code Sec. 7701(a)(36)(A); Reg. § 301.7701-15).

CAUTION

An Authorized IRS e-file Provider will not be a tax return preparer if the services are limited to typing, reproduction or other mechanical assistance (mechanical assistance exception) in preparing the return or refund claim. If the provider alters the return, other than to make a nonsubstantive change, the exception will not apply. A nonsubstantive change is a change or correction limited to a:

- Transposition error;
- Misplaced entry;
- Spelling error; or
- Arithmetic correction (Reg. § 301.7701-15(f)(1)(viii); Rev. Proc. 2007-40).

All Authorized IRS e-file Providers are considered tax return preparers for purposes of the civil and criminal penalties for knowingly or recklessly disclosing tax return information (Code Secs. 6713 and 7216; Reg. § 301.7216-1).

A *tax return preparer* for purposes of these disclosure penalties is broader than the general definition of a tax return preparer. The definition includes persons providing auxiliary services in connection with the preparation of tax returns, and specifically includes a person who develops software used to prepare and file a tax return and any Authorized IRS e-file Providers.

Tax return information for purposes of the disclosure penalties includes information furnished in connection with the preparation of a taxpayer's return, either directly from the taxpayer or a third party. Tax return information also includes information received from the IRS, such as an acknowledgment of acceptance or notice of rejection of an electronically filed return (Reg. § 301.7216-1(b)(3)).

> **EXAMPLE**
>
> Jan Templeton purchases computer software to help her prepare her return. When Jan loads the software on her computer, she is prompted to provide registration information. The software provider is the tax return preparer and the registration information is tax return information.

Disclosure of tax return information among Authorized IRS e-file Providers is allowed in limited situations, such as when an ERO passes on information to an Intermediate Service Provider or Transmitter for the purpose of having the electronic return formatted and transmitted (Code Sec. 7216(b); Reg. § 301.7216-2). Additionally, a tax return preparer that provides tax preparation software may use the taxpayer's tax return information (e.g., information obtained through registration) to update for changes in the tax law or test and ensure the software's technical capabilities without the taxpayer's consent.

Sanctions. Sanctions for violating the rules and requirements of the IRS e-file program may include a written reprimand, suspension, or expulsion from the program, or any other sanction depending upon the severity of the infraction. The provider has a right to administrative review of the sanction.

STUDY QUESTIONS

> 1. All Authorized e-file Providers must have a comprehensive information security program in place, as required by:
>
>   **a.** The IRS
>   **b.** The Federal Trade Commission's Safeguards Rule
>   **c.** Reporting agents
>
> 2. The civil and criminal penalties for knowingly and recklessly disclosing tax return information apply to e-file Software Developers and Transmitters as well as Intermediate Service Providers, Reporting Agents and EROs. *True or False?*

Modernized e-File (MeF)

In 2004, the IRS introduced the Modernized e-File (MeF) electronic filing system. The system allows the filing of most business, tax-exempt organization, and individual returns through the Internet. MeF is scheduled to completely replace the IRS's Legacy e-file system in October 2012. MeF is a more flexible system that uses the widely accepted Extensible Markup

Language (XML) format. MeF has following advantages over the Legacy e-file system:

- Faster acknowledgments (within minutes or hours rather than 24-48 hours under the legacy system);
- Improved error code explanations;
- Year-round electronic filing;
- E-filing of prior year and amended returns;
- Use of XML that enables data accuracy and enhanced protection of taxpayer information;
- Facilitation of attaching forms and schedules to the return, along with other documents in portable document format (PDF);
- An integrated payment option; and
- A single point of submission and retrieval of state return information.

The IRS began using the MeF system in 2004 for business information returns. The first phase of Form 1040 MeF began in filing season 2010. Form 1040 and 22 other forms and schedules were included in this first phase.

Table 2. 2010 Individual Forms in MeF System

1040	Schedule EIC	2210	8829
Schedule A	Schedule M	2441	8863
Schedule B	Schedule R	4562	8880
Schedule C	Schedule SE	4868	8888
Schedule D	1099-R	8283	W-2
Schedule E	2106	8812	

Individual E-File Signatures

The IRS e-signature process for individual returns requires the individual to obtain a Personal Identification Number (PIN). The PIN is used to sign the return and the Declaration of Taxpayer. There are two ways to create an IRS e-signature PIN:

- The Self-Select PIN method; and
- The Practitioner PIN method.

If a joint return is filed, each taxpayer must have his or her own PIN (FS-2011-7, January 14, 2011).

Practitioner PIN method. The *Practitioner PIN method* is used by individuals who use an ERO (i.e., a volunteer or paid tax preparer) to file their return. The taxpayer authorizes the preparer to enter or generate a five-digit PIN on the individual's behalf. The taxpayer must sign Form 8879, *IRS e-file Signature Authorization*. The ERO may enter the taxpayer's PIN in the electronic record before the taxpayer signs Form 8879, but the form must be signed and dated before the ERO originates the electronic submission of the return. Taxpayers may also enter their own PIN in the electronic record, but they must still sign Form 8879. The preparer will retain the form and it is not mailed to the IRS (FS-2011-7, January 14, 2011; Publication 1345, *Handbook for Authorized IRS e-file Providers of Individual Income Tax Returns*).

COMMENT

A preparer may use an electronic signature pad for Form 8879.

Self-Select PIN method. The *Self-Select PIN* method is used by taxpayers who prepare their own returns. Taxpayers select five digits to enter as their PIN. To verify their identity, individuals must provide their prior year's adjusted gross income or PIN, and date of birth.

The IRS may issue a temporary Electric Filing PIN (EFP) for taxpayers who do not have their prior year AGI or PIN. The EFP can be used in place of the prior year's PIN.

Business E-File Signatures

The electronic return must be signed by an authorized tax return signer of the entity type (corporation, partnership, or exempt organization).

The MeF system provides two ways to create an IRS e-signature PIN: the Practitioner PIN method and the Scanned Form 8453 Signature method (Publication 4163, *Modernized e-File (MeF) Information for Authorized IRS e-file Providers for Business Returns*).

Practitioner PIN method for businesses. Only taxpayers using an ERO can use the Practitioner PIN method. The taxpayer will choose a five-digit self-selected PIN, which the taxpayer can authorize the ERO to input into the software or the taxpayer can enter the PIN directly. A Form 8879, unique to the parent entity must be signed. For example, Form 8879-C, *IRS e-file Signature Authorization for Form 1120*, is used by corporations.

Form 8453 signature method. If the return is filed through an ISP and/or Transmitter, and an ERO is not used, the authorized signer of the entity must sign the appropriate Form 8453. The form is then scanned and attached as a PDF file.

Form 8453 is unique for each parent entity. For example, Form 8453-C, *U.S. Corporation Income Tax Declaration for an IRS e-file Return*, is used by a corporation. The form has the same legal effect as if the taxpayer had actually and physically signed the return.

If an ERO is used, the ERO can use either the appropriate Form 8879 or Form 8453 to obtain authorization to file the return.

STUDY QUESTIONS

---

3. Individuals who use an ERO (free or paid tax return preparer) may agree to have the preparer generate a five digit PIN on their behalf using the:

  a. Self-Select PIN method

  b. Practitioner PIN method

  c. Form 8453 signature method

4. If an entity files its return through an ISP or Transmitter without using an ERO, the return's signer can sign the _____, which is scanned and attached to the return as a PDF file.

  a. Form 8453 for its entity type

  b. Form 8879-C for its business

  c. Form MeF

E-FILING BY INDIVIDUALS

At the end of the primary 2011 filing season, about 80 percent of all individual income tax returns (Forms 1040, 1040-A, 1040-EZ and 1040-SS) were filed electronically (Publication 3415, *Electronic Tax Administration Advisory Committee,* June 2011). Congress has provided, however, that the IRS may not require individuals to e-file their income tax returns. An individual income tax return includes the income tax return of an estate or trust. In 2010, the IRS did cease sending paper forms to taxpayers in an effort to move taxpayers toward electronic filing. Additionally, individual returns must be electronically filed by a return preparer who reasonably expects to file 100 or more individual income tax returns in calendar year 2011, and more than 10 returns in calendar years 2012 and following (Code Sec. 6011(e)(1), (3), as described later in the chapter).

Taxpayers who prepare their own returns using a personal computer and commercial tax preparation software usually choose to have their tax information processed by an Intermediate Service Provider that either forwards the information to a Transmitter or sends the information back to the taxpayer for online filing. However, they may choose to print out their completed returns and mail them to the IRS.

> **COMMENT**
>
> The following IRS publications govern IRS e-file for individuals:
>
> - Publication 1345, *Handbook for Authorized IRS e-file Providers of Individual Income Tax Returns;*
> - Publication 1346, *Electronic Return File Specifications and Record Layouts for Individual Income Tax Returns;* and
> - Publication 1436, *Test Package for Electronic Filers of Individual Income Tax Return.*

IRS Free File Program

Individual taxpayers may take advantage of Free File, which is offered through a partnership between the IRS and Free File Alliance, LLC, a group of private sector tax software companies (IR-2010-5; Publication 910, *IRS Guide to Free Tax Services*).

Taxpayers having adjusted gross incomes of a certain amount or less (e.g., 2010 adjusted gross income of $58,000) can use brand-name tax preparation software to complete and file their tax returns for free (**http://www.irs.gov/freefile**). Many companies also offer state tax preparation for a fee or for free.

Free File Fillable Forms are available to all taxpayers who are comfortable completing the electronic version of IRS paper forms without software support. The forms are also filed for free, but state tax form filing is not available.

> **COMMENT**
>
> Note that the forms are not filed directly with the IRS. In either case, a member of the Free File Alliance, LLC, is transmitting the data to the IRS. The "Choose Fillable Forms" button indicates that the taxpayer will be linking to a private company and that the IRS is not endorsing its products, services or security policies. In fact, 100 percent of federal e-files for individuals are handled by the commercial tax preparation industry.

Federal/State Electronic Filing Program

The Federal/State e-file is a cooperative tax filing between the IRS and most states. Federal and state individual income taxes are filed electronically at one time. The tax preparation software places the return information in separate federal and state packets, which are transmitted to the states. The IRS then forwards the state return to the appropriate state.

According to the IRS website, as of February 2011, 37 states and the District of Columbia participate in the federal/state e-filing program (**http://www.irs.gov/efile**).

VITA and TCE

The Volunteer Income Tax Assistance (VITA) program offers free help in preparing returns to moderate and low-income individuals. The Tax Counseling for the Elderly Program (TCP) provides free tax help to people age 60 and older.

Most VITA and TCE sites provide free electronic filing for returns and accompanying forms and schedules that are included in the VITA or TCE training course. The IRS, industry and non-profits acting together have delivered impressive benefits to lower and middle-income taxpayers. Both the IRS Free File program and the IRS VITA and TCE programs produced roughly 6 million electronically filed returns in the 2011 filing season.

E-Filing Not Permitted

There are a number of individual returns that are currently not accepted by IRS e-file or that the IRS has instructed taxpayers not to file electronically. These forms include:

- Form 1040-NR, *U.S. Nonresident Alien Income Tax Return;*
- Form 1040X, *Amended U.S. Individual Income Tax Return;* and
- Form 1040, *U.S. Individual Income Tax Return,* for a fiscal year.

In addition, when one files individual returns electronically, certain schedules and attachments must be filed on paper. Form. 8453, *U.S. Individual Income Tax Transmittal for an IRS e-file Return,* must be filed with the forms or documents.

STUDY QUESTIONS

5. Individual taxpayers who prepare their own tax returns using commercial tax preparation software and a computer submit returns for processing by:

   a. An ISP
   b. The Software Developer that sold the tax package to the taxpayer
   c. Reporting Agent

6. Which type of taxpayer can use e-filing?

   a. Nonresident aliens filing Form 1040-NR
   b. Free File program users
   c. Individuals with a fiscal year

E-FILING BY BUSINESSES

Businesses, including individuals with a Schedule C business, usually have the choice of filing paper or electronic returns. However, the IRS is authorized to issue regulations mandating e-filing if an entity (other than an estate or trust) files at least 250 returns during the calendar year. In the case of a partnership, the IRS is authorized to issue regulations mandating e-filing for partnerships having more than 100 partners. In determining which returns must be e-filed, the IRS must consider the ability of the taxpayer to comply with the requirement at reasonable cost. The IRS can waive the e-filing requirements if they would subject the taxpayer to undue hardship (Code Sec. 6011(e)(2)).

COMMENT

Another mandatory e-file requirement is just around the corner. *The Hiring Incentives to Restore Employment Act of 2010* (P.L. 111-147) mandated the IRS to require the e-filing of certain returns by financial institutions, regardless of the 250-return threshold (Code Sec. 6011(e)(4)). It is expected that the regulations will require all or most financial institutions to e-file with respect to certain withholding obligations involving foreign financial institutions and persons, for returns filed for tax years ending after December 31, 2012 (Notice 2010-60).

COMMENT

The following publications govern e-file for businesses: Publication 4163, *Modernized e-File Information for Authorized e-file Providers for Business Returns* and IRS Publication 4164, *Modernized e-file (MeF) Guide for Software Developers and Transmitters.*

Corporations

The majority of corporations currently are not required to e-file their income tax returns. E-filing of Form 1120, *U.S. Corporation Income Tax Return*, is required for corporations that:

- Have assets of at least $10 million at the end of the tax year, listed on Schedule L, *Balance Sheets per Books;* and
- File at least 250 returns during the calendar year ending with or within the tax year.

All members of a controlled group of corporations must file their returns electronically if the aggregate number of returns required to be filed by the group is at least 250 (Reg. § 301.6011-5(a)).

The e-filing requirement applies to all the Form 1120 series (e.g., Form 1120-F, *U.S. Income Tax Return of a Foreign Corporation* and Form 1120S, *U.S. Income Tax Return of an S Corporation*). The e-filing requirement applies to all related forms, schedules and statements required to be attached and amended and superseding forms (Reg. § 301.6011-5(d)(4)).

All types of returns filed by the corporation, including information returns (such as Form W-2, *Wage and Tax Statement*, Form 1099 series, etc.), employment tax returns and excise tax returns, are taken into account in determining the threshold (Reg. § 301.6011-5(d)).

Corrected returns, amended returns, and returns filed with the Form 1120 series form are not counted.

EXAMPLE

Jar, Inc., a fiscal year corporation has assets of $10 million. Jar's fiscal year ends July 30. During the calendar year ending December 31, 2011, Jar is required to file one Form 1120, 130 Forms W-2, 130 Forms 1099-DIV, Dividends and Distributions, one Form 940, Employer's Annual Federal Unemployment (FUTA) Tax Return, and four Forms 941, Employer's Quarterly Federal Tax Return. All of these returns are counted toward the 250-return threshold. Because Jar is required to file 266 returns during the calendar year that ended within its tax year ending July 30, 2012, it meets the 250-return threshold and must file its Form 1120 electronically for its tax year ending July 30, 2012.

Exempt Organizations

Exempt organizations are subject to rules similar to those that apply to corporations. An exempt organization with assets of at least $10 million at the end of the tax year must e-file Form 990, *Return of Organization Exempt From Income Tax*, if it meets the 250-return threshold during the calendar year that ends with or within the tax year (Reg. § 301.6033-4).

COMMENT

Form 990-EZ is not required to be e-filed because it can only be filed by an exempt organization with total assets of less than $500,000 at the end of the year.

Private foundations and charitable trusts are required to e-file Form 990-PF, *Return of Private Foundation or Section 4947(a)(1) Nonexempt Charitable Trust Treated as a Private Foundation*, regardless of asset size, if the 250-return threshold is met.

For annual periods beginning after 2010, certain exempt organizations with annual gross receipts of less than $50,000 may submit a Form 990-N, *Electronic Notification (e-postcard) for Tax Exempt Organizations Not Required to File Form 990 or Form 990-EZ* (Code Sec. 6033(i); Rev. Proc. 2011-15). The e-postcard contains only a brief statement of identifying information.

Large Partnerships

Partnerships with more than 100 partners are required to e- file their Form 1065 (or Form 1065 B, *U.S. Return of Income for Electing Large Partnerships*), along with Schedules K-1 and any other related forms and schedules that must be attached to the form (Reg. § 301.6011-3).

A partnership has more than 100 partners if over the course of the partnership's tax year, the partnership has over 100 partners, regardless of whether a partner was a partner for the entire tax year or whether the partnership had more than 100 partners on any one day during the tax year. The partner must have a direct interest in the partnership, but there is no distinction between general and limited partners in determining the 100-partner threshold (Reg. § 301.6011-3(d)(5)).

EXAMPLE

Partnership Q has 5 general and 90 limited partners on January 1 of the tax year. On April 1, 10 more limited partners acquire a partnership interest in Q. However, in May, the 10 newest partners sell their partnership interests to C, a corporation and one of the 90 limited partners. On December 31, Q has the same 95 partners as it had on January 1. It must still file electronically because it had 105 partners during the tax year.

Information Returns

Providers of certain information returns are required to file the returns electronically through the IRS Filing Information Returns Electronically (FIRE) Program. The information returns are handled by the IRS-Information Returns Branch (IRS-IRB).

The FIRE system is designed exclusively for the e-filing of:

- Form 1042-S, *Foreign Person's U.S. Source Income Subject to Withholding*
- Form 1097 series;
- Form 1098 series;
- Form 1099 series;
- Form 3921, *Exercise of an Incentive Stock Option Under Section 422(b);*
- Form 3922, *Transfer of Stock Acquired Through an Employee Stock Purchase Plan Under Section 423(c);*
- Form 5498 series;
- Form 8027, *Employer's Annual Information Return of Tip Income and Allocated Tips;*
- Form 8935, *Airline Payments Report;* and
- Form W-2G, *Certain Gambling Winnings.*

Persons required to file 250 or more of each type of information return (other than Form 8935) during the calendar year must file the returns electronically (Reg. § 301.6011-2).

Form W-2, *Wage and Tax Statement*, must be filed electronically if the 250-statement threshold is met. The form, however, is sent to the Social Security Administration and is electronically filed under the SSA's procedures.

The 250 threshold applies separately to each type of return or corrected return, and returns are not aggregated for purposes of determining the threshold (Reg. § 301.6011-2(b), (c)).

EXAMPLE

Star, Inc. is required to file 100 Forms 1099-B and 250 Forms 1099-INT. Only Forms 1099-INT must be filed electronically because the 250-return threshold is not met for Forms 1099-B.

The filing requirement applies to each type of reporting entity that has a separate employer identification number (usually an EIN).

EXAMPLE

MegaCorp has three branches. MegaCorp and each branch must file 100 Forms 1099-INT. If MegaCorp and the branches all use the same EIN, the aggregate total of forms is at least 250 and electronic filing is required.

PRACTICE POINTER

Each member of an affiliated group of corporations filing a consolidated return is a separate person for purposes of the threshold (Reg. § 301.6011-2(a)(3)).

Each year the IRS provides detailed standards for e-filing information returns. The current procedures for filing most information returns through the FIRE system are described in IRS Publication 1220, (Rev. Proc. 2010-26). The current procedures for filing Form 1042-S are in Publication 1187, *Specifications for Filing U.S. Source Income Subject to Withholding, Electronically* (Rev. Proc. 2011-33).

A person who wants to file electronic information returns must first submit Form 4419, *Application for Filing Returns Electronically (FIRE)*, at least 30 days before the returns are due.

Penalties and Hardship Waivers

The failure to comply with the mandatory e-filing rules can result in penalties, but the penalties may be avoided or the requirement may be waived in certain cases.

Penalties. A corporation or exempt organization that fails to e-file its return will be subject to failure to file penalties, unless the filer can establish that the failure to file was due to reasonable cause and not willful neglect (Reg. § 301.6011-5(c); Reg. §301.6033-4(c)).

Similarly, the failure to e-file partnership and other information returns may result in a penalty for failure to provide correct, complete and timely information returns, unless the failure is due to reasonable cause and not willful neglect (Reg. § 301.6011-2(f); Reg. § 301.6011-3(c)). This penalty is imposed only if the failure extends to returns that exceed the threshold requirements. The threshold is applied separately to each type of return, original returns and corrected returns (Code Sec. 6724(c); Reg. § 301.6721-1(a)).

> **EXAMPLE**
>
> Bellows Corp. is required to file 400 Forms 1099-DIV and files all of them on paper. Bellows is required to e-file the returns because the number of returns exceeds the 250- threshold requirement. The penalty applies only to 150 returns.

> **EXAMPLE**
>
> Bellows files 300 returns on Form 1099-DIV and later files 70 corrected Forms 1099-DIV. The corrected forms fall below the 250- threshold requirement and may be filed on paper or electronically.

Reasonable cause for failing to meet any of the mandatory e-filing requirements can be established if the filer shows that the requirements resulted in undue economic hardship. The filer must establish that it attempted to contract out electronic filing on a timely basis and that the cost was prohibitive (determined 45 days before the due date of the return, without extensions). The filer must also provide a minimum of two cost estimates and file paper returns (Reg. § 301.6724-1(c)(3)).

> **CAUTION**
>
> Generally, the waiver is available only once.

Hardship waiver. The e-filing requirement may be waived if compliance will cause an undue hardship (Reg. §§ 301.6011-2(c)(2), 301.6011-3(b); 301.6011-5(b); 301.6033-4(b)).

Corporations, exempt organizations, and partnership must request the waiver in writing. Each request will be approved or denied on the basis of the facts and circumstances, taking into consideration economic hardship and technical constraints. The statement must explain the steps taken to meet the requirement and why the steps were unsuccessful. The hardship must be described and the increased cost of e-filing compared with paper filing must be listed and supported. A request must also contain a statement of the steps that will be taken to ensure electronic filing in the future (Announcement 2002-3; Notice 2010-13).

Similarly, the e-filing requirement may be waived for information returns, with the principal factor in determining hardship being the increased cost of e-filing over paper filing (Reg. § 301.6011-2(c)(2)). To apply for the waiver, the filer must submit Form 8508, *Request for Waiver from Filing Information Returns Electronically*.

PRACTICE POINTER

Form 8508 requires the filer to provide two cost estimates from third parties for the cost of:

- Providing software, software upgrades, or programming for the current system; or
- Preparing returns.

The estimates must be current and not from a prior year.

STUDY QUESTION

> 7. The failure to meet the mandatory e-filing requirements will always result in penalties. *True or False?*

MANDATORY E-FILE FOR TAX RETURN PREPARERS

The Homeownership and Business Assistance Act of 2009 (P.L. 111-92) required specified tax return preparers to file individual income tax returns electronically, beginning in 2011 (Code Sec. 6011(e)(3); Reg. § 301.6011-7; Notice 2011-27). The mandate is an exception to the general rule that IRS regulations may not prohibit the filing of paper income tax returns by individuals, trusts or estates (Code Sec. 6011(e)(3)(C)).

Specified Return Preparers

A *specified tax return preparer* is any tax return preparer who reasonably expects to file 100 or more individual income tax returns in calendar year 2011 and 11 or more individual income tax returns in calendar years beginning after 2011 (Reg. § 301.6011-7(a)(3)).

COMMENT

The GAO recommended that Congress should replace the word *file* with broader language, such as *prepare or file* to expand the applicability of the e-filing mandate beyond preparers who file returns (*Electronic Tax Return Filing: Improvements Can Be Made Before Mandate Becomes Fully Implemented* (GAO-11-344), March 2011).

An individual income tax return is not limited to the Form 1040 series and includes:

- Form 1041 series of income tax returns for estates and trusts; and
- Form 990-T, *Exempt Organization Business Income Tax Return,* if the exempt organization is a trust subject to tax on unrelated business taxable income (Code Sec. 6011(e)(1)(C); Reg. § 301.6011-7(a)(2)).

All of the individual income tax returns of the tax return preparer or the members of a firm that are reasonably expected to be prepared and filed for the year are added together to determine whether the threshold is met (Reg. § 301.6011-7(d)).

Business projections, individual income tax filing history, and staffing decisions are factors that may indicate whether the preparer's belief is reasonable.

EXAMPLE

Joe Bennett is a solo practice divorce attorney. Joe estimates that he may be asked by only a few clients to prepare income tax returns for compensation. In calendar year 2012, Joe prepares 6 income tax returns. In 2013, Joe's practice doubles and he expects to file at least 12 individual income tax returns. Joe is not required to e-file the returns in 2012 because he reasonably expects to file 10 or fewer returns, and in fact does so. In 2013, Joe is required to e-file the returns because he reasonably expects to file more than 10 individual income tax returns.

COMMENT

Circular 230 was recently updated to provide that a tax return preparer who willfully fails to file returns electronically when required engages in disreputable conduct for which there are sanctions. A reasonable cause exception applies (Reg. § 10.51(a)(16)).

Exceptions to Mandatory Filing

Mandatory e-filing will not be required for taxpayers who choose to file a paper return, for preparers who request hardship waivers, and under certain administrative exceptions.

Taxpayers who choose to file paper returns. A tax return is not be considered filed and subject to the e-file mandate, if, on or before the return is filed, the tax return preparer obtains a hand-signed and dated statement from the taxpayer stating that the taxpayer chooses to file a paper return and that the taxpayer and not the tax return preparer will file the return with the IRS (Reg. § 301.6011-7(a)(4)).

Solely for calendar year 2011, a tax return preparer may prepare and *mail* an individual's income tax return in paper format to the IRS, but only if a hand-signed and dated statement indicating that this is the taxpayer's choice is obtained (Notice 2011-27).

Undue hardship waivers. The IRS may grant waivers of the e-filing requirement if there is an undue hardship (Reg. § 301.6011-7(c)). These waivers will ordinarily be granted only in rare circumstances and not for more than one calendar year.

> **COMMENT**
>
> A preparer may demonstrate that the additional cost of e-filing causes an undue economic hardship. The fact that the preparer does not have a computer or software or does not desire to obtain or use the equipment alone is not an undue hardship (Rev. Proc. 2011-25).

The request for an undue hardship waiver is made on Form 8944, *Preparer e-file Hardship Waiver Request.*

The IRS will send written notice of the approval or denial of the request. If the request is denied, the preparer can send a written request for reconsideration, but there is no further administrative or judicial review if reconsideration is denied.

Administrative exemptions. The IRS may provide administrative exemptions from the e-filing requirement for certain classes of specified tax return preparers and types of individual income tax returns.

> **PRACTICE POINTER**
>
> An *administrative exemption* is an automatic exemption (Notice 2011-26). Additionally, undue hardship waiver requests should not be made if the administrative exemption applies (Rev. Proc. 2011-25).

The current administrative exemptions for preparers cover three types of preparers, described in Table 3.

Table 3. Types of Administrative Exemptions

Type of Preparer	Requirements
Member of religious group	Religious group is conscientiously opposed to its members using electronic technology
Foreign preparer	Not a member of a firm eligible to e-file and applies for special PTIN for foreign preparers
Sanctioned preparer ineligible for IRS e-file program	Letter received enforcing sanction for at least part of the calendar year for which returns are filed

The current administrative exemptions extend to preparers who experience technical difficulties, in the following situations:

- Rejected returns for which the reject code or condition could not be resolved;
- Forms or schedules not supported by the preparer's software package; and
- A return or returns prepared by a specified tax return preparer or return preparer who experiences a short-term inability to e-file due to some other verifiable and documented technological problem.

Also covered by the administrative exemption are returns, required documentation and attachments that are not accepted electronically by the IRS. The following forms are currently not accepted electronically:

- Form 1040-NR, *U.S. Nonresident Alien Income Tax Return;*
- Form 1041-QFT, *U.S. Income Tax Return for Qualified Funeral Trusts;*
- Form 990-T, *Exempt Organization Business Income Tax Return;* and
- Form 1040X, *Amended U.S. Individual Income Tax Return,* and other amended individual income tax returns;
- Fiscal year Form 1040 individual income tax returns; and
- Fiscal year Form 1041 estate and trust income tax returns, ending during any month after June 30 of the current processing year.

Certain Forms 1041 are not accepted by IRS e-file, including a Form 1041 claiming a refund amount equal to or greater than $10 million or a Form 1041 with a dollar amount of over $99 billion.

Form 8948. Form 8948, *Preparer Explanation for Not Filing Electronically,* must be completed by a specified return preparer to explain why a paper return was filed. If the preparer applied for and received an undue hardship waiver, the waiver reference number and date of approval letter are entered. The administrative exemptions, other than the exemption for returns not currently accepted electronically by the IRS, must be listed.

The Form 8898 must be attached to the paper copy of the tax return prepared by the specified tax return preparer and furnished to the taxpayer.

STUDY QUESTION

> **8.** Which type of return preparer is eligible for an administrative exemption from e-filing?
>
>   **a.** Member of a religious group opposed to members using electronic technology
>   **b.** A preparer who does not have a computer or tax preparation software
>   **c.** A preparer who does not wish to use computer equipment to prepare returns

E-FILING IN 2011

In its annual report to Congress on the 2011 filing season, the Electronic Tax Administration Advisory Committee (ETAAC) reported that the IRS made steady progress in the filing season against the 80 percent goal. During 2011, there was a 6 percent increase in the filing of all major returns. The ETAAC estimated a 65.8 percent e-file rate for all major returns, driven by a full year individual filing rate of 77 percent. The rates for 2010 were 60 percent and 70 percent, respectively.

Filing Rates

The individual return filing rate increased approximately 12 percent from the number of returns filed from the previous season.

According to the ETAAC, four things will continue to drive growth in e-filing of individual returns:

- Mandated preparer-electronic filing requirement;
- Reduced e-file rejects;
- Promotion of e-filing computer self-prepared returns, as well as the reduction in associated barriers to e-filing; and
- IRS's decision to stop sending paper return packages.

The ETAAC also projected growth for other types of returns for 2011. Returns from corporations are projected to reach a 38 percent e-file rate for 2011 (compared to 34 percent for 2010), partnership returns are projected to reach a 37 percent e-file rate for 2011 (compared to 35 percent for 2010); and exempt organization returns are projected to reach 27 percent for 2011 (compared to 21 percent for 2010).

Additional Electronic Initiatives

The electronic filing of tax returns or e-file is only part of a broader effort to make sure that the majority of taxpayer and tax practitioner interactions with the tax administration system are handled electronically (IRS Oversight Board, *Electronic Filing 2010 Annual Report to Congress*).

Recent changes in the Electronic Federal Tax Payment System (EFTPS) and the process for obtaining a Preparer Taxpayer Identification Number (PTIN) are examples of these efforts.

EFTPS. The IRS is authorized to prescribe regulations for the development and implementation of an electronic funds transfer system to collect federal tax deposits (FTDs) (Code Sec. 6302(h)). The EFTPS is the system currently used by the Treasury to collect FTDs.

Depositors with aggregate annual FTDs that exceeded $200,000 were generally required to use EFTPS and other taxpayers could use Federal Tax Deposit coupons.

As part of the broad initiative to increase the number of electronic transactions in which taxpayers participate, the system of processing federal tax deposit coupons was discontinued beginning January 1, 2011. Small employers having quarterly employment tax deposit liabilities of less than $2,500 still have the option of remitting the taxes with their quarterly or annual return (T.D. 9507).

PTIN. Beginning after December 31, 2010, all tax return preparers were required to use a PTIN instead of their Social Security number as their identifying number. The PTIN is used to sign all returns, both paper and electronic. The IRS established an online PTIN application system on its website. The online system can be used to create a PTIN account, apply for the PTIN, pay the user fee, and receive the PTIN, all in the same session. The IRS launched the PTIN online application system in September 2010.

CHALLENGES FOR E-FILING IN THE FUTURE

The ETAAC identified several challenges to the advancement of electronic filing and made a number of recommendations to help reach this goal, including increasing employment tax e-file and reducing e-file rejects.

Tax Complexity, Budget Constraints and Taxpayer Expectations

Complex tax laws—as well as late-passed tax legislation—have an adverse impact on taxpayers, tax professionals, and software companies, according to the ETAAC. For example, tax legislation passed late in the year creates taxpayer anxiety and can prevent taxpayers from receiving planned refunds. Such legislation also impacts states and limits the time the IRS and software developers have to program and test return-generating systems.

Additionally, shrinking federal budgets present fiscal challenges and require the IRS to make tough tradeoffs. At the same time, taxpayers have high expectations when it comes to Internet functions and expect the same from the IRS when it comes to their tax returns. For example, taxpayers will question the inability of the IRS to report timely the status of a tax return's processing and why it has been delayed.

COMMENT

Return-free filing systems are now being seriously considered within the federal government for individual taxpayers with relatively simple returns. Both the United Kingdom and California have similar systems in place. Critics worry that such a system would increase compliance costs, and that "prepopulated tax returns" would make taxpayers more passive and less proactive in dealing with their tax situations. Yet with increasing pressure on Congress to "simplify the tax code," providing a simplified tax return process through prepopulated tax returns may be seen as part of an overall solution to complexity.

Employment Tax Returns

The ETAAC estimated that an additional 26 million returns must be electronically filed before the IRS can meet its 80 percent goal. The largest gap in e-filing is the filing of employment returns—primarily Form 940, *Employer's Annual Federal Employment (FUTA) Tax Return* and Form 941, *Employer's Quarterly Federal Tax Return*. The returns have a projected e-file rate of 24 percent and a volume gap of about 16 million returns.

The federal employment taxes filed with the IRS include:

- Income tax withholding;
- Social Security and Medicare tax withholding; and
- Federal unemployment taxes.

The returns contain no individual taxpayer information. Typically, information generated by the employer's payroll system is transcribed onto the form and mailed to the IRS.

Based on its survey of the employment return community, the ETAAC believes that to increase the e-filing rate, the e-file registration, filing, and payment process must be incredibly easy and convenient, given the current ease of paper filing these forms.

Additionally, the IRS will have to overcome misunderstandings in the filer community about filing employment tax returns electronically. Many filers are in-house preparers who support small business and are not members of any payroll or business organization. Many surveyed were unaware that the IRS accepted employment returns electronically and were concerned about increased liability if returns were e-filed.

E-File Rejects

The ETAAC regards the current 15 to 20 percent e-file reject rate to be a key barrier to continued e-file growth. The AGI/PIN signature method for identity proofing is one cause of the rejects. The ETAAC recommended that an IRS/industry working group be formed that would identify, review, and track actions to reduce e-file rejects and provide tools that allow for the validation of selected taxpayer identification information prior to final submission of the return for electronic filing.

STUDY QUESTIONS

9. Which type of entity return is estimated by the ETAAC to have the highest e-file rate for 2011?
   a. Exempt organization
   b. Partnership
   c. Corporation

10. Obstacles to instituting prepopulated tax returns include all of the following *except:*
    a. Their use might make taxpayers less proactive in reporting their tax situations
    b. They have not been tried by the states and other national tax e-filing systems
    c. They tend to complicate the tax code rather than simplify reporting

CONCLUSION

The IRS's goal is to have 80 percent of major returns e-filed by 2012. The extension of the mandatory e-filing requirements to preparers who file 11 or more individual returns should be of help in reaching this goal. Although there are many benefits to e-filing returns, the IRS faces challenges in reaching this goal. Reducing the number of e-file rejects and increasing the number of employment tax returns are also necessary for the IRS to meet its goal.

CPE NOTE: When you have completed your study and review of chapters 4–6, which comprise Module 2, you may wish to take the Quizzer for this Module.

For your convenience, you can also take this Quizzer online at **www.CCHGroup.com/TestingCenter**.

Navigating IRS Collection:
New Standards and Procedures

This chapter provides an overview of the IRS collection process, including the tools the IRS uses to collect delinquent tax liabilities and the options available to taxpayers who are unable to pay. This chapter also discusses some of the recent steps the IRS has taken to help taxpayers facing financial difficulties.

LEARNING OBJECTIVES

Upon completion of this chapter you will be able to:
- Understand the IRS collection process;
- Describe the methods and tools the IRS employs to collect unpaid taxes;
- Identify options that are available to taxpayers with outstanding tax liabilities; and
- Understand the changes the IRS has made in order to assist taxpayers affected by the troubled economy.

INTRODUCTION

The U.S. tax system relies on the voluntary compliance of federal internal revenue laws. Sometimes, however, taxpayers are unwilling or unable to pay tax due. As federal budget deficits reach record levels and the annual tax gap—the difference between the amount of tax that taxpayers owe and the amount that is actually paid—approaches $350 billion, tax collection has become increasingly important. However, as Americans continue to face challenging economic conditions the IRS faces the challenge of collecting taxes without exacerbating financial hardships.

This chapter overviews the IRS collection process and also details the options that are available at this time to taxpayers with delinquent tax liabilities. This chapter also discusses the recent changes the IRS has undertaken to help struggling taxpayers get a fresh start with their tax liabilities.

COLLECTION BASICS

Assessment

Assessment is the first step in the collection process. An *assessment* is a bookkeeping entry that records the liability of the taxpayer. An assessment is made when an IRS assessment officer signs Form 23C, *Assessment Certificate—Summary Record of Assessment.*

Most assessments are based on filed tax returns. These amounts are "self-assessed." Other assessments are based on determinations made by the IRS after an examination. Before assessing income, gift tax, and estate tax, the IRS generally must issue a Statutory Notice of Deficiency and allow the taxpayer to challenge the determination of the tax in the U.S. Tax Court. However, when deficiencies are attributable to mathematical or clerical errors, the IRS can assess the additional tax immediately without following the general deficiency procedures. In those cases, the IRS is only required to notify the taxpayer that additional tax is due and that the assessment has been or will be made, and explain the source of the error.

If the IRS believes that delay puts the collection of tax is in jeopardy after the taxpayer's return has been filed or come due, it may make a *jeopardy assessment* to immediately assess the tax. The jeopardy assessment procedures allow the IRS to bypass the time-consuming deficiency procedures and immediately levy against the taxpayer's property. The IRS may make a *termination assessment* when it finds that the taxpayer intends to suddenly leave the United States, remove or conceal property or perform any other act that will prejudice the normal tax collection process. A termination assessment allows the IRS to take immediate action to collect on a deficiency without complying with the ordinary waiting period.

Generally, the IRS must assess taxes within three years after the tax return is filed. However, there are several exceptions to the three-year limitations period;

- The normal period of limitations is extended to six years if an amount more than 25 percent of the gross income shown on the return is omitted; and
- If a taxpayer fails to file a return or files a false or fraudulent return with the intent to evade tax, there is no statute of limitations on assessment, and the IRS can assess and collect the tax at any time.

Collection Period

The IRS generally has 10 years from the time an assessment is made to collect the assessed liability, either through its administrative levy power or by initiating a court proceeding (Code Sec. 6502). The 10-year limitation period begins to run from the date of the underlying assessment. However, the statute of limitations on collection can be suspended in a number of ways. If a taxpayer files for bankruptcy, the collection period is suspended while the bankruptcy case is pending and for six months thereafter (Code Sec. 6503). The collection period is also suspended during the period the IRS is prohibited from levying to collect tax that is the subject of a pending offer in compromise or installment agreement (Code Sec. 6331(k)). Further, the IRS may ask a taxpayer to agree to extend the collection period in certain situations, including an agreement to extend the collection period in connection with an installment agreement.

COMMENT

Note that the 10-year collection period begins when the tax is assessed, not when the return reporting the liability is filed.

Notice and Demand

Within 60 days of a tax assessment, the Treasury Secretary must give notice of the assessment, the amount due, and demand for payment. This notice can be given to the taxpayer, left at the taxpayer's home or usual place of business, or sent to the taxpayer's last known address (Code Sec. 6303).

If the taxpayer does not respond to the initial demand for payment, the IRS typically sends additional notices. If there is no response to the subsequent notices, most cases are sent to the IRS's automated collection system (ACS) for action. ACS will attempt to contact the taxpayer by phone and by mail. ACS also has the power to initiate enforced collection action.

If the amount due is not collected by ACS, the case may be sent to a field revenue officer, who will contact the taxpayer directly and make additional demand for payment. If the taxpayer is unwilling or unable to pay the tax liability in full, the revenue officer will investigate the taxpayer's income and assets and determine whether to pursue enforced collection actions or consider the account uncollectable. If the account is collectable, the revenue officer may begin enforced collection through administrative collection actions such as levies and sales. The revenue officer can also refer the case for a lawsuit to reduce tax liabilities to judgment and to foreclose on the federal tax liens.

The IRS has numerous collection tools and powers at its disposal. It may:

- File a Notice of Federal Tax Lien to encumber a taxpayer's assets;
- Levy on the taxpayer's assets;
- Offset a taxpayer's overpayment of tax against an unpaid liability;
- Agree to a collection alternative, such as an installment agreement or offer in compromise; and
- Initiate a collection lawsuit against the taxpayer.

The IRS has significantly increased its use of liens and levies over the past year. During the 2010 fiscal year, the number of levies increased by 4 percent, and the number of liens issued by the collection field function and the automated collection system increased by 14 and 13 percent, respectively. Overall, the use of liens has increased by 74 percent since 2006. As a result, during the 2010 fiscal year, the IRS collected the most revenue on delinquent accounts in five years (Treasury Inspector General for Tax Administration Report, *Trends in Compliance Activities Through Fiscal Year 2010*, July 18, 2011 (Reference Number 2011-30-071)).

The IRS also has powerful resources to support its collection efforts. In addition to the internal information resources, the IRS can also use its summons power to gather information from taxpayers and third parties. The IRS can issue a summons to request books, records, papers, or other data that may be relevant to the collection of a tax liability, such as bank records, financial statements, property records, and records of property transactions.

STUDY QUESTIONS

1. The general three-year limitations period for assessment does **not** apply if:
   a. The taxpayer files for bankruptcy
   b. The taxpayer files a fraudulent return with the intention of tax evasion
   c. The taxpayer omits less than 25 percent of the gross income shown on the return

2. The first efforts to collect an unpaid tax liability are usually taken by the:
   a. Automated collection system
   b. Field revenue officer
   c. U.S. Tax Court

LIENS AND LEVIES

The federal tax lien and the administrative tax levy are the two principal tools the IRS uses to collect unpaid tax liabilities. The lien and levy are administrative collection tactics; neither requires any judicial action to become effective. Although they are closely related, they are used for different purposes and have different effects. A *lien* is a security claim against the taxpayer's property to secure the tax debt, whereas a *levy* is the actual seizure of property to satisfy the debt.

Federal Tax Liens

A federal tax lien arises after the IRS assesses the tax and issues a notice and demand for payment, but the taxpayer fails to pay the full amount demanded. After the IRS makes its demand, the taxpayer has ten days in which to pay (Code Sec. 6321). If the taxpayer fails to do so, the lien becomes effective as of the date of assessment.

A federal tax lien attaches to all of a taxpayer's property at the time the lien arises and all property acquired after the assessment date (Code Sec. 6321). Property includes anything that is subject to ownership, capable of transfer, and subject to jurisdiction and process by a court. State law determines whether a property interest exists; however, once a property interest has been identified, federal law determines whether the tax lien has validly attached. A state statute exempting certain property from the claims of creditors does not affect a federal tax lien, because only federal law can exempt property from a federal tax lien (Reg. § 301.6321-1).

A tax lien gives the IRS a security interest in all the taxpayer's property. It does not give the IRS a priority position relative to other creditors unless they have knowledge of the tax lien, which occurs when the IRS provides actual notice or files a Notice of Federal Tax Lien. Although a federal tax lien automatically attaches to all of a taxpayer's property, a Notice of Federal Tax Lien must be recorded to have priority over other creditors' liens. Until a tax lien is filed, it is not valid against competing claims of purchasers, holders of security interests, mechanic's lienors, and judgment lien creditors. Additionally, the lien does not have priority against certain other "superpriority" claims even if it is recorded.

To gain priority over other creditors, the IRS must file a Notice of Federal Tax Lien in the recording office designated by the state or government subdivision:

- For real property, this is the office designated by the state where the real property is located; and
- For personal property, it is the state-designated office where the taxpayer resides (Reg. § 301.6323(f)-1(d)(2)).

The IRS uses Form 668(Y)(c), *Notice of Federal Tax Lien*, for this purpose.

The IRS must notify the taxpayer in writing of the filing of a lien within five days of the filing. The notice must include;

- The amount of the unpaid tax;
- The right to request a hearing within 30 days after the five-day period;
- Administrative appeals procedures; and
- The provisions and procedures relating to release of liens.

Appeal procedures are discussed in greater detail later.

COMMENT

In 2010, the IRS filed 1,096,376 tax liens (*2010 IRS Data Book*).

Until recently, the IRS's policy was to file a Notice of Federal Tax Lien when a tax liability exceeded $5,000. As part of its "Fresh Start" initiative, the IRS has increased the threshold from $5,000 to $10,000. However, the IRS may still file liens to secure tax liabilities of less than $10,000 when circumstances warrant doing so.

Relief from Liens

Once a federal tax lien arises, it continues until the liability is satisfied or becomes unenforceable because the statutory collection period has expired. However, the lien may be released, withdrawn, or subordinated, and property may be discharged from it or certified that the lien does not apply to that property.

Release of a Federal Tax Lien

The release of a federal tax lien operates to completely extinguish the lien. The IRS must release a tax lien no later than 30 days after the day on which:

- The tax liability secured by the lien is fully satisfied;
- The tax liability becomes legally unenforceable; or
- The IRS accepts a bond for payment of the amount assessed plus interest, executed by a surety company that the Treasury Secretary has authorized to issue federal bonds (Code Sec. 6325).

Federal tax liens self-release when the statutory collection period expires. When a lien is self-releasing, the Notice of Federal Tax Lien itself is the release document. Taxpayers can also request a certificate of release by following the procedures prescribed in IRS Publication 1450, *Request for Release of Federal Tax Lien*.

Discharge of a Federal Tax Lien

While a release of federal tax lien operates to completely extinguish the lien, a discharge discharges only specific property to which the lien has attached. A discharge does not affect the lien on any other property to which the lien has attached.

The IRS may discharge property from its lien in the following situations:

- If the taxpayer's property remaining subject to the lien has a fair market value equal to at least twice the unpaid tax liability plus all the encumbrances that have priority over the federal tax lien;
- If the taxpayer or another person makes partial payment equal to the value of the government's interest in the property discharged;

- The IRS determines that the government's interest in the property has no value; or
- The property subject to the lien is sold and, by agreement with the IRS, the sale proceeds are held as a fund subject to the liens and claims of the United States in the same manner and priority as the liens and claims had with respect to the discharged property (Code Sec. 6235(b)).

Additionally, the IRS is required to issue a discharge if a third-party owner submits a proper request and either deposits money equal to the value of the lien on the property or furnishes a bond acceptable to the IRS (Code Sec. 6325(a)(2)).

Taxpayers can apply for a certificate of discharge by completing Form 14135, *Application for Certificate of Discharge of Federal Tax Lien*. Instructions for making the application can be found in IRS Publication 783.

> **COMMENT**
>
> Form 14135 requires taxpayer to include a professional appraisal and one additional informal valuation. In the past the IRS required taxpayers to submit two appraisals with the application.

> **COMMENT**
>
> Publication 783 recommends that the discharge application be submitted to the IRS at least 45 days before the desired closing date. In December 2008, the IRS announced that it was expediting the discharge process to make it easier for financially distressed homeowners to refinance or sell their homes (IRS News Release IR-2008-141).

Subordination of a Federal Tax Lien

In certain circumstances the IRS may agree to subordinate its lien to the interest of another creditor. The IRS has discretion to issue a certificate of subordination if the government is paid an amount equal to the amount by which the tax lien will be subordinated or if the IRS believes that the subordination will ultimately increase the amount realizable from the property in question.

Taxpayers can apply for a certificate of subordination by completing Form 14134, *Application for Certificate of Subordination of Federal Tax Lien*. Instructions for making the application are in IRS Publication 784.

COMMENT

Publication 784 recommends that the discharge application be submitted to the IRS at least 45 days before the transaction for which the subordination is needed. In December 2008, the IRS announced that it would be expediting the subordination process to make it easier for financially distressed homeowners to refinance or sell their homes (IRS News Release IR-2008-141, December 16, 2008).

Nonattachment of Federal Tax Lien

If the IRS determines that, because of confusion of names or otherwise, any person (other than the person against whom the tax was assessed) is or may be injured by the appearance that a notice of lien refers to such person, the IRS may issue a certificate of nonattachment stating that the lien does not attach to the property of such person (Code Sec. 6325(e)).

There is no standard form available for a request for nonattachment. For information required on an application, see IRS Publication 1024, *How to Prepare an Application for a Certificate of Nonattachment of Federal Tax Lien.*

Withdrawal of Notice

In certain circumstances, the IRS has the authority to withdraw a Notice of Federal Tax Lien. A Notice of Federal Tax Lien that is withdrawn is treated as if it had not been filed. Therefore, withdrawal of a notice of lien does not affect the underlying tax lien (Reg. § 301.6323(j)-1(a)); rather, it causes the IRS to give up any lien priority that had been obtained when the notice as filed.

The IRS may withdraw a Notice of Federal Tax Lien upon a determination that:

- The filing of the notice was premature or otherwise not in accord with administrative procedures;
- The taxpayer has entered an installment agreement to satisfy the liability for which the lien was imposed (and the installment agreement does not preclude the lien withdrawal);
- The withdrawal of the lien will facilitate collection of the liability for which the lien was imposed; or
- Withdrawal would be in the best interests of the taxpayer and of the United States (Code Sec. 6323(j)(1)).

At the written request of the taxpayer, the IRS must also make reasonable efforts to give notice of the withdrawal to:

- Credit reporting agencies;
- Financial institutions; and
- Creditors specified by the taxpayer (Code Sec. 6323(j)(2)).

As part of its initiative to help struggling taxpayers, the IRS recently announced a number of changes intended to make it easier for taxpayers to obtain lien withdrawals. The IRS will withdraw a lien notice at the taxpayer's request once the taxpayer's liability is paid in full. In order to speed the withdrawal process, the IRS will also streamline its internal procedures to allow collection personnel to withdraw the liens (IRS News Release IR-2011-20, February 24, 2011).

> **COMMENT**
>
> Taxpayer Advocate Nina Olson had criticized the IRS for its previous policy of not issuing notices of federal tax lien withdrawals after releasing tax liens. She noted that a lien that is released continues to be reflected on a taxpayer's credit record for seven years from the date of the release. However, a Notice of Federal Tax Lien that is withdrawn is treated as if it had not been filed and is removed from the taxpayer's credit record.

The IRS also announced that for taxpayers with unpaid assessments of $25,000 or less, the IRS will also allow lien withdrawals for taxpayers entering into a direct debit installment agreement or for taxpayers currently on a regular installment agreement who convert to a direct debit installment agreement. Additionally, the IRS will withdraw liens on existing direct debit installment agreements. Liens will be withdrawn after a probationary period demonstrating that direct debit payments will be honored (IRS News Release IR-2011-20, February 24, 2011). Installment agreements are discussed in greater detail below.

A taxpayer may request a tax lien withdrawal by filing Form 12277, *Application for Withdrawal of Filed Form 668(Y), Notice of Federal Tax Lien.*

LEVIES

The IRS is authorized to start procedures to levy on the property of any person liable to pay any tax who fails to do so within 10 days of notice and demand for payment (Code Sec. 6331).

> **COMMENT**
>
> Although the IRS is authorized to begin these procedures after 10 days of making notice and demand for payment, the process typically takes far longer.

Generally, the IRS may levy upon any property or property rights of a delinquent taxpayer other than those specifically exempted from levy. The IRS can seize real or personal proprty; seized personal property can be tangible or intangible. A lien is merely a security interest that protects the IRS's interest while the taxpayer remains in possession; but a levy allows the IRS to forcibly seize the property. A lien is not required to be placed upon a property before it is levied, although such a sequence is often the case.

These restrictions apply to the IRS's levy power:

- The IRS generally must get a court order to seize a taxpayer's principal residence; and
- Higher-level administrative approval is required before the IRS can seize an individual's business property (Code Sec. 6334(e)).
- Certain property is exempt from levy by statute, including:
  - Wearing apparel and schoolbooks, to the extent necessary for the taxpayer or members of the taxpayer's family,
  - Books and tools necessary for the taxpayer's trade, business, or profession up to an inflation-adjusted amount ($4,120 for 2011),
  - Fuel, provisions, furniture, and personal effects in the household, arms for personal use,
  - Livestock and poultry, up to an inflation adjusted amount ($8,370 for 2011);
  - Real property used by the taxpayer as a residence (whether or not a principal residence), and any nonrental property owned by the taxpayer but used by another person as a residence, if the amount of the levy does not exceed $5,000.

There are two types of levies: Continuous and noncontinuous. As a general rule, levies only attach to property and obligations in existence at the time of the levy. Therefore, most levies are noncontinuous. However, there are two exceptions to that rule:

- A levy on wages is continuous from the date of the levy until the levy is released; and
- The IRS can approve a continuous levy on up to 15 percent of certain specified payments made to or received by a taxpayer that are otherwise exempt.

COMMENT

Employees are often concerned about the effect an IRS levy may have on their employment. The Internal Revenue Manual notes that employers sometimes threaten to fire employees to avoid handling levies. The manual notes that firing an employee because of an IRS levy may be in violation of 15 U.S.C. § 1674, and may be punishable by a fine and imprisonment. IRS personnel are instructed to refer these cases to the Department of Labor (IRM 5.11.5.2).

Before the IRS can actually make a levy, it is required to provide the taxpayer with notice of intent to levy and notice that the taxpayer can appeal the proposed levy as under the collection due process (CDP) procedures (discussed later in this chapter). The notice of intent to levy and notice of a right to a hearing, also known as the "30-Day Notice" is in addition to the initial notice and demand for payment that the IRS is required to give after making an assessment.

In addition, prior to making a levy on property or rights to property that are to be sold, the IRS is required to make an investigation, including a verification of the taxpayer's liability, analysis of the costs of levy and sale compared to the fair market value of the property, a determination that the equity in the property is sufficient to yield net proceeds from a sale, and a thorough consideration of alternative collection methods.

COMMENT

The general levy requirements do not apply if the IRS finds that collection of the tax is in jeopardy. Instead, the IRS is allowed to levy on the taxpayer's property without giving prior notice of its intent to levy and the taxpayer's right to a hearing. Within five days of the jeopardy levy, the IRS must provide the taxpayer with a written statement of the information the IRS relied upon in making the jeopardy levy. Within 30 days after the receipt of the written statement or within 30 days of the end of the five-day period, the taxpayer can ask the IRS to review the jeopardy levy. The taxpayer may file suit within 90 days of the earlier of:

- The IRS's determination in response to the request for administrative review; or
- The 16th day after the written request for review was made.

Release of Levies

The IRS is required to release a levy if:
- The liability for which the levy was made is satisfied or becomes unenforceable through lapse of time;
- Release of the levy will facilitate collection of the tax liability;
- The taxpayer has entered into an installment agreement (unless the agreement prohibits releasing the levy, or releasing the levy would jeopardize the government's status as a secured creditor);
- The IRS determines that the levy is causing the taxpayer an economic hardship; or
- The fair market value of the property exceeds the tax liability and release of the levy on the property could be made without hindering the collection of the liability (Code Sec. 6343(a)(1); Reg. § 301.6343-1(b)).

As a practical matter, before it will consider releasing a levy, the IRS will request that the taxpayer file any missing tax returns and provide the appropriate collection information statements, Form 433-A, *Collection Information Statement for Wage Earners and Self-Employed Individuals*, and/or Form 433-B, *Collection Information Statement for Businesses*.

The IRS will release a levy based on economic hardship if the levy will cause an individual taxpayer to be unable to pay his or her reasonable basic living expenses. In determining a reasonable amount for basic living expenses, the IRS will consider any information provided by the taxpayer, including:

- The taxpayer's age, employment status and history, ability to earn, number of dependents, and status as a dependent;
- The amount reasonably necessary for food, clothing, housing, medical expenses, transportation, current tax payments, alimony, child support, or other court-ordered payments, and expenses necessary to the taxpayer's production of income;
- The cost of living in the taxpayer's geographic area;
- The amount of exempt property that is available to pay the taxpayer's expenses;
- Any extraordinary circumstances such as special education expenses, a medical catastrophe, or natural disaster; and
- Any other relevant factor that the taxpayer identifies.

Additionally, the taxpayer must act in good faith, and not falsify financial information, inflate actual expenses or costs, or fail to make full disclosure of assets.

COMMENT

Because *economic hardship* is defined as the inability to meet reasonable basic living expenses, it applies only to individuals.

COMMENT

Although the taxpayer must provide information proving undue economic hardship, the Tax Court has held that Reg. § 301.6343-1(b)(4) requires the IRS to release a levy that creates an economic hardship, regardless of a taxpayer's noncompliance with filing requirements. Neither case law nor the tax code or regulations condition the release of a levy upon compliance with filing and payment requirements when there is an economic hardship (**K.A. Vinatieri**, 133 TC No. 16).

In most cases, the IRS is required to make a determination and release a levy promptly. The IRS must release a levy on the salary or wages of a taxpayer "as soon as practicable" after the IRS and the taxpayer agree that the tax is not collectable.

As part of its efforts to help struggling taxpayers the IRS announced that it will speed the delivery of levy releases by easing requirements on taxpayers who request expedited levy releases for hardship reasons. Taxpayers seeking expedited releases for levies to an employer or bank should contact the IRS at the number shown on the notice of levy to discuss available options. Taxpayers should be prepared to provide the IRS with the fax number of the bank or employer processing the levy (IRS News Release IR-2009-2, January 6, 2009).

STUDY QUESTIONS

3. A federal tax lien is extinguished when:
   a. A release of federal tax lien is issued
   b. A subordination of federal tax lien is issued
   c. Property is discharged from the tax lien

4. The IRS may *not* levy:
   a. Any real property the taxpayer uses as a principal or second residence, provided the levy is for $5,000 or less
   b. Any amount of livestock and poultry
   c. Business or trade books and tools worth any amount

COLLECTION ALTERNATIVES

Offers in Compromise

A *compromise* is an agreement between the taxpayer and the IRS that settles a tax liability for payment of less than the full amount owed (Code Sec. 7122). Most *offers in compromise* are submitted during the collection process, by taxpayers who are experiencing financial difficulty. If the IRS accepts the offer, tax liens are removed and enforced collection is avoided.

The IRS will accept an offer in compromise in three situations:

- Doubt as to collectability—if it is unlikely that the IRS can collect the tax liability in full;
- Doubt as to liability—if there is a legitimate dispute as to the amount the taxpayer owes; and
- Effective tax administration—if collection of the full amount of unpaid tax liability would cause the taxpayer economic hardship, or based on other compelling public policy or equity considerations (Reg. § 301.7122-1(b)).

An offer in compromise can be made by almost any taxpayer, including an individual and a taxable entity such as a trust, estate, or corporation. However, nonindividual entities cannot make an offer in compromised based on hardship grounds. Because *economic hardship* is defined as the inability to meet reasonable basic living expenses, it applies only to individuals.

COMMENT

In 2010, the IRS accepted approximately 13,886 offers in compromise—the most offers the IRS has accepted since 2006. Nevertheless, the IRS has faced criticism for not accepting more offers. Taxpayer Advocate Nina Olson, in her 2010 annual report to Congress, asserted that the offer in compromise program is underused and noted that in 2010 the IRS accepted only 1 offer for every 290 taxpayers having delinquent accounts.

Doubt as to Collectibility

The IRS generally accepts an offer in compromise based on doubt as to collectibility if:
- It is unlikely that the tax liability can be collected in full; and
- The offer reasonably reflects the taxpayer's *reasonable collection potential* (RCP), which is the amount the IRS could collect through all available means.

The IRS determines a taxpayer's RCP based on the information presented in financial statements required to be submitted with the taxpayer's offer, the Form 433-A, *Collection Information Statement for Wage Earners and Self-Employed Individuals*, and/or Form 433-B, *Collection Information Statement for Businesses*. RCP generally has four components:
- The amount collectable from the taxpayer's realizable equity in assets;
- The amount collectable from the taxpayer's future income;
- The amount the IRS could expect to collect from third parties through administrative or judicial action; and
- Assets and/or income that are available to the taxpayer, but are beyond the reach of the government.

For purposes of calculating an offer amount, a taxpayer's income includes gross monthly income, less allowable expenses. For individual taxpayers, expenses are generally only allowable if they are necessary expenses. A *necessary expense* is one that is necessary to provide for the health, welfare, and/or production of income for a taxpayer and his or her family. Allowable expenses are based on the IRS's Collection Financial Standards, which establish national and local expense standards for housing, household expenses, food, clothing, transportation, and health care. For purposes of determining an individual's ability to pay, the national and local standards normally represent the maximum amounts that the IRS will allow for living expenses. However, the IRS will allow more than the standard amount if failing to do so will cause the taxpayer economic hardship. For example, a taxpayer with physical disabilities or an unusually large family may have housing costs in excess of the local standard.

> **COMMENT**
>
> The Collection Financial Standards are available on the IRS website, at **http://www.irs.gov/individuals/article/0,,id=96543,00.html.**

Expenses that do not meet the necessary expense test are considered conditional expenses, and are generally only allowed in limited cases.

Future income. The determination of a taxpayer's future income is based on an estimate of the taxpayer's ability to pay for a specific number of months into the future. Generally, the amount is calculated by taking the projected gross monthly income, less allowable expenses, and multiplying the difference by the applicable number of months. The number of months used in the calculation of future income depends on the proposed payment terms of the offer. If the offer will be paid in 5 months or less, future income is projected based on the amount the taxpayer could pay over 48 months. If the offer will be paid in more than 5 months, future income is projected based on the amount the taxpayer could pay over 60 months.

As part of its effort to assist taxpayers facing financial difficulties, in March 2010 the IRS announced that it would be exercising more flexibility in considering offers in compromise. Specifically, the IRS announced that it would consider a taxpayer's current income and potential for future income when negotiating an offer in compromise. Previously, when the IRS evaluated an offer from an unemployed or underemployed taxpayer, the income calculation was based on an average that included income in prior years. This new policy gives the IRS greater flexibility in evaluating offers from unemployed taxpayers (IRS News Release IR-2010-29, March 10, 2010).

Valuation. For offer purposes, assets are valued at *net realizable equity*, which is generally the quick sale value of the asset, less amounts owed to secured lien holders with priority over the IRS's federal tax liens. *Quick sale value* is an estimate of the price a seller could expect to receive for an asset if forced to sell in a short period of time, usually 90 days or less. The IRS generally calculates quick sale value as 80 percent of fair market value. However, a higher or lower percentage may be applied when appropriate, depending on the type of asset and current market conditions.

For example, if a taxpayer owns a home in an area where real estate is selling slowly and well below listing prices, the IRS may agree to use a percentage lower than 80 percent.

For real estate, the IRS first establishes the fair market value of the property, using the recent purchase price or an existing contract to sell, recent appraisals, real estate tax assessments, market comparables, or insurance replacement cost. Once fair market value is established, an appropriate reduction of value for offer purposes must be determined.

COMMENT

As part of its initiative to assist taxpayers facing financial difficulties, the IRS announced that it is offering additional review of home values for offers when real estate valuations may not be accurate (IRS News Release IR-2010-29, March 10, 2010). The IRS has since incorporated these changes into the Internal Revenue Manual (IRM 8.23.3.3.2.3).

COMMENT

The decision to accept or reject an offer based on doubt as to collectibility is usually based on whether the amount offered reflects the taxpayer's RCP. However, even if a taxpayer's offer does reflect RCP, the IRS may still reject it based on public policy reasons or if acceptance would not be in the best interests of the government.

Special circumstances. The IRS will also consider an offer based upon doubt as to collectibility with special circumstances, which is something of a hybrid between an offer based upon doubt as to collectibility and an offer based upon effective tax administration due to economic hardship. As with a regular doubt as to collectibility offer, the taxpayer must demonstrate that he or she cannot fully pay the tax due. However, the IRS will accept an amount less than the taxpayer's RCP if paying the full RCP would cause the taxpayer economic hardship. *Economic hardship* and *special circumstances* are defined as they are for purposes of offers based upon effective tax administration, and include advanced age, illness, or other factors that may affect a taxpayer's ability to pay the full RCP amount.

Offers in compromise based on doubt as to collectibility and effective tax administration must be submitted on Form 656, *Offer in Compromise*. Taxpayers must pay a user fee of $150 for each offer in compromise submitted, unless the offer is based solely on doubt as to liability or filed by a low-income taxpayer. Taxpayers submitting offers based on doubt as to collectibility or effective tax administration must also make partial payments with their offers. For offers in compromise based on doubt as to collectibility or effective tax administration, taxpayers must submit collection information statements with their offers (Form 433-A, *Collection Information Statement for Wage Earners and Self-Employed Individuals* or Form 433-B, *Collection Information Statement for Businesses*).

For offers in compromise based upon doubt as to collectibility or effective tax administration, taxpayers have two payment options:

- A required 20 percent of the total offer to be paid with the offer and the remaining balance paid in five or fewer payments upon acceptance of the offer; or
- Payment of the offer amount in installments that extend for more than five months.

Under the latter option, the taxpayer submitting the offer must submit the first payment with the offer and continue making subsequent payments under the terms proposed while the IRS is evaluating the offer. For offers in compromise based upon doubt as to liability, taxpayers do not have the option to propose payment terms. The offer amount must be paid within 90 days of written notification that the offer has been accepted.

> **COMMENT**
>
> These payment options reflect a slight change in offer procedures that went into effect when the IRS released an updated Form 656, *Offer in Compromise*, in March 2011. The previous version of Form 656 offered three different payment options.

Doubt as to Liability

A taxpayer may make an offer in compromise based on doubt as to liability, which exists where there is a genuine dispute as to the existence or amount of the correct tax liability under the law. Doubt as to liability does not exist where the liability has been established by a final court decision or judgment concerning the existence or amount of the liability (Reg. §301.7122-1(b)(1)).

> **COMMENT**
>
> Because doubt as to liability requires a legitimate dispute regarding an assessed tax liability, it is rarely used as a ground for compromise. However, doubt as to liability offers can be used to contest certain liabilities, such as the trust fund recovery penalty under Code Sec. 6672 and matters involving an innocent spouse.

The taxpayer files a doubt as to liability offer on Form 656-L, *Offer in Compromise (Doubt as to Liability)*. In evaluating an offer based on doubt as to liability, the IRS is not concerned with the taxpayer's ability to pay; therefore, the taxpayer does not have to file a collection information statement. Instead, the taxpayer must submit documentation and other relevant evidence to support doubts as to liability. The IRS will determine the extent of any doubt by evaluating the supporting evidence and circumstances. An offer to compromise based on doubt as to liability is generally acceptable if it reasonably reflects the amount the IRS would expect to collect through litigation (Rev. Proc. 2003-71).

Effective Tax Administration

If there is no doubt as to liability for a tax or doubt concerning the collectibility of a tax, the IRS may still accept an offer in compromise based upon effective tax administration. An offer based on effective tax administration is unique in that the taxpayer making the offer does not dispute that the amount of the liability is correct and acknowledges that the IRS could collect the full amount owed. The IRS may compromise the liability in such cases if there are exceptional circumstances that warrant doing so. There are two general types of effective tax administration offers: those based on economic hardship and those based upon equity or public policy (Reg. § 301.7122-1(b)(3)).

Economic hardship. The IRS may compromise a tax liability to promote effective tax administration when it determines that it could collect the full amount of the liability, but doing so would cause the taxpayer economic hardship. The standard for determining economic hardship for this purpose is similar to the standard the IRS uses to determine whether a levy is causing an economic hardship. For this purpose, economic hardship exists when collection of the full tax liability would leave the taxpayer unable to pay reasonable basic living expenses (Reg. § 301.7122-1(b)(3) (i); Reg. § 301.6343-1(d)). An offer in compromise based on economic hardship is generally acceptable when the amount offered reflects the amount the IRS can collect without causing the taxpayer economic hardship (Rev. Proc. 2003-71).

> **EXAMPLE**
>
> Larry Hampton has a $100,000 tax liability and a RCP of $125,000. In order to avoid economic hardship, it is determined that Larry will need $75,000. The remaining $50,000 will be considered the acceptable offer amount (IRM 5.8.11.4.3).

> **CAUTION**
>
> Because economic hardship is the inability to meet reasonable basic living expenses, it applies only to individuals (including sole proprietorships). Corporations, partnerships, and other nonindividual entities are not eligible for effective tax administration offers based on economic hardship.

Basic living expenses provide for the health, welfare, and production of income of the taxpayer and the taxpayer's family; thus, they vary according to the unique circumstances of the individual taxpayer. The IRS uses national and local standard expense amounts in determining taxpayer's basic living expenses, unless the taxpayer provides reasonable substantiation that a standard amount is inadequate. In addition to the basic living expenses, the IRS considers the taxpayer's age and employment status; the number, age, and health of the taxpayers dependents; the cost of living in the taxpayer's area; extraordinary circumstances such as special education expenses, a medical catastrophe, or natural disaster; and any other relevant factors.

> **COMMENT**
>
> National standards apply to food, clothing, and certain other expenses. Local standards apply to housing, utilities, and transportation costs. The national standard for food, clothing, and other items range from $534 monthly for a single individual to $1,377 for a family of four. For each additional person above four, taxpayers may add $262 to the four-person allowance.

Equity or public policy. If there are no grounds for compromise based on doubt as to collectibility or liability, or to promote effective tax administration based on economic hardship, the IRS may compromise a tax liability based on compelling public policy or equity considerations identified by the taxpayer. The IRS accepts an offer on these grounds where, due to exceptional circumstances, collection of the full amount owed would undermine public confidence that the tax laws are being administered in a fair and equitable manner. A taxpayer submitting an offer based on public policy or equitable grounds is expected to demonstrate circumstances that justify compromising the liability, even though a taxpayer in a similar circumstances may have paid his or her liability in full (Reg. § 301.7122-1(b)(3)(ii). For instance. a case may be compromised on these grounds if a taxpayer incurred a liability as a result of following erroneous advice or instructions from the IRS, or because of a processing error or delay by the IRS. An acceptable offer would be expected to restore the taxpayer to the same position as if the error or delay had not occurred (IRM 5.8.11.4.3).

COMMENT

The IRS assumes that Congress imposes tax liabilities only when it determines it is fair to do so. Therefore, the IRS rarely accepts compromises on these grounds. The IRS will not compromise a tax liability on equitable or public policy grounds because the imposition of a particular tax law provision is unjust or inequitable. For example, the IRS properly rejected an offer in compromise from married taxpayers who had significant alternative minimum tax (AMT) liability arising from their exercise of an incentive stock option on stock that then fell in value. The fact that their tax bill was much higher than the value of the stock they received was not a reason for the IRS to accept their offers. Whether or not the AMT is unfair is a question for Congress, not the IRS or the courts (*Speltz v Commr*, CA-8, 2006-2 USTC ¶50,403).

The decision to accept or reject an offer in compromise is left to the discretion of the Secretary of the Treasury. Each offer in compromise that is properly submitted to the IRS undergoes a thorough review process, during which the IRS usually requests additional information and documentation in order to determine whether the offer should be accepted or rejected.

Streamlined Program

In 2010, the IRS implemented a "streamlined" offer in compromise program. In investigating these offers, the IRS makes fewer requests for additional financial information, relying instead on internal research, and when additional information is needed, it is requested by phone. Further, the IRS is more flexible in allowable expenses and future income calculations in considering taxpayers' ability to pay. The streamlined offer in compromise program is open to taxpayers with annual incomes up to $100,000 and tax liabilities of less than $50,000 (Interim Guidance Memorandum SBSE-05-0511-026, May 13, 2011).

COMMENT

The streamlined offer in compromise program was previously open only to taxpayers with liabilities of less than $25,000. The expansion of the program was announced in February 2011 as part of the IRS's recent initiative to help taxpayers facing financial difficulties (IRS News Release IR-2011-20, February 24, 2011).

Defaults

An offer that is accepted by the IRS becomes binding and is enforceable as a contract, according to its terms. If the taxpayer fails to meet the terms and conditions of the offer, the offer will be considered in default and terminated, and the IRS may attempt to collect the unpaid balance of the offer or the unpaid balance of the original liability. However, as part of its efforts to assist taxpayers facing financial difficulties, the IRS has announced that it will be flexible with previously compliant taxpayers that have difficulty paying (IRS News Release IR-2009-2, January 6, 2009; IRS News Release IR-2010-29, March 10, 2010).

STUDY QUESTIONS

5. For an offer in compromise based on doubt as to collectibility, an individual's reasonable collection potential (RCP) calculation excludes:
   a. Necessary expenses
   b. Asset equity
   c. Assets beyond the government's reach

6. A $150 user fee to submit an offer in compromise applies to:
   a. Low-income taxpayers
   b. An offer based on doubt as to liability
   c. An offer based on doubt as to collectibility

INSTALLMENT AGREEMENTS

An *installment agreement* is an agreement that allows for a tax liability to be paid over time through scheduled periodic payments. The IRS is authorized to enter into an installment agreement if it determines that the agreement will facilitate full or partial collection of the liability (Code Sec. 6159(a)).

Generally, four types of installment agreements provide for the full payment of taxes over time:
- Guaranteed installment agreements;
- Streamlined installment agreements;
- In-business trust fund express agreements; and
- Installment agreements requiring financial analysis.

Guaranteed Installment Agreements

A guaranteed, or mandatory, installment agreement is available for the payment of tax liabilities of $10,000 or less, exclusive of interest, penalties, additions to tax, and any other additional amounts, provided that the liability can be paid within three years and during the preceding five years, the taxpayer (and spouse if filing jointly) has filed all required income tax returns, paid all required taxes as shown on the returns, and has not entered into an installment agreement to pay any income tax. The taxpayer must also agree to comply with the tax laws while the agreement is in effect.

> **CAUTION**
>
> Guaranteed installment agreements are only available to individuals. Businesses and other entities are not entitled to a guaranteed installment agreement, regardless of the amount of the liability.

Taxpayers seeking a guaranteed installment agreement are not required to submit a *Collection Information Statement* (Form 433-A, 433-B or 433-F) or otherwise disclose information about their ability to pay their outstanding tax liabilities.

Streamlined Installment Agreements

Taxpayers who do not qualify for a guaranteed installment agreement, but whose tax liabilities are less than $25,000, may qualify for a streamlined installment agreement. A streamlined installment agreement will generally be granted if a taxpayer's assessed tax, penalties, and interest total $25,000 or less, and can be paid in full within five years.

> **COMMENT**
>
> These agreements are "streamlined" because the IRS will grant them without requiring taxpayers to submit collection information statements or otherwise disclose information about their ability to pay their outstanding tax liabilities.

> **COMMENT**
>
> A taxpayer with assessed liabilities in excess of $25,000 may still qualify for a streamlined installment agreement if the taxpayer is able to make payments that reduce the balance due to streamlined range.

Unlike guaranteed installment agreements, streamlined installment agreements are available for both individuals and businesses. However, in-business taxpayers may only seek a streamlined installment agreement for income tax liabilities.

In-business Trust Fund Express Agreements

An in-business trust fund express installment agreement is available to business taxpayers with trust fund liabilities such as employment tax liabilities, provided that the total balance due does not exceed $25,000 and can be paid within 24 months or before the expiration of the collection statute of limitations, whichever is earlier. No financial statement is required, and the IRS does not determine any trust fund recovery penalty.

> **COMMENT**
>
> In-business trust fund express agreements were previously available to business taxpayers having tax liabilities of $10,000 or less. The IRS recently increased raised the dollar limit from $10,000 to $25,000 in order to make the program available to more taxpayers. However, businesses entering into these agreements are required to enroll in a direct debit installment agreement (IRS News Release IR-2011-20, February 24, 2011).

Installment Agreements Requiring Financial Analysis

The last type of agreement is for taxpayers who do not qualify for a guaranteed, streamlined, or in-business trust fund express installment agreement, typically because their total tax liabilities exceed $25,000. The IRS requires these taxpayers to submit a collection information statement, detailing their income, expenses, and assets. There are special considerations for in-business taxpayers that do not qualify for in-business trust fund express agreements.

Requests for regular installment agreements are evaluated on a case-by-case basis and are accepted only if the IRS determines that the taxpayer is unable to fully or partially satisfy a balance due, and that an installment agreement will facilitate the collection of the debt. The IRS generally does not grant an installment agreement if liabilities can be fully or partially satisfied by liquidating the taxpayer's assets, unless there are factors such as the taxpayer's advanced age, ill-health, or other special circumstances. Absent any special factors, taxpayers are required to make full or partial payment using available assets, such as available equity in real or personal property, before the IRS will grant an installment agreement.

The Form 433, *Collection Information Statement,* is used to determine the taxpayer's ability to pay the liability in full or in part from assets and disposable income (gross income less allowable expenses). The installment agreement must reflect the taxpayer's ability to pay on a monthly basis. This amount is equal to the taxpayer's gross monthly income less allowable monthly expenses, which must meet the necessary expense test discussed above regarding offers in compromise. Expenses that do not meet this test are conditional expenses that generally are not allowed unless they meet certain exceptions.

As with offers in compromise, allowable expenses for installment agreements are based on the IRS's Collection Financial Standards. The IRS will allow more than the standard amount if failing to do so will cause the taxpayer economic hardship; however, the taxpayer must verify the necessary amount of the expense.

Even if there is no risk of causing economic hardship, necessary expenses in excess of the standard amount may still be allowed under a "one-year rule," which allows an individual taxpayer up to one year to modify or eliminate excessive necessary expenses. Further, all expenses (both excess necessary expenses and conditional expenses) may be allowed under a "five-year rule" if the following conditions are met:

- The taxpayer establishes that he or she can stay current with all tax filing and payment requirements;
- The total tax liability, including projected accruals of penalties and interest, can be paid within five years; and
- The expense amounts are reasonable.

If a business taxpayer is in compliance with current tax obligations, and has the ability to remain current while paying the delinquent tax liabilities and ongoing operating expenses, the IRS considers an installment agreement based on the taxpayer's ability to pay. If the collection information statements indicate that the taxpayer has the ability to pay the balance due from current income and/or assets, the IRS will not grant an installment agreement. If the Form 433 shows that the taxpayer can sell or borrow against equity in assets, the IRS may request that the taxpayer do so, if appropriate.

> **COMMENT**
>
> The IRS does not categorize a business taxpayer's expenses as necessary or conditional, as it does an individual's expenses. Although the IRS may review the business's Form 433-B and determine that a particular expense is not allowable, a business taxpayer has more room for negotiation.

Partial Payment Installment Agreements

Under a typical installment agreement, the IRS and a taxpayer enter into an agreement for the taxpayer to pay a liability in full over a period of time. However, when a taxpayer is unable to pay an outstanding liability in full under general installment agreement guidelines, the IRS may enter into a *partial payment installment agreement* that does not provide for full payment of the liability within the statutory period for collection.

> **COMMENT**
>
> Although a partial payment installment agreement does not provide for the full payment of a tax liability, it does not reduce the amount of taxes, interest, or penalties owed (Reg. § 301.6159-1(c)(1)(ii). As with any installment agreement, however, the penalties for failure to pay may accrue at a reduced rate.

A taxpayer seeking a partial payment installment agreement must submit a collection information statement detailing the taxpayer's ability to pay. The IRS takes a stricter approach to its analysis of income and expenses in determining eligibility for a partial payment agreement than for typical installment agreements. Conditional expenses are not allowed for partial payment installment agreements; only necessary expenses are permitted.

Requesting an Installment Agreement

Taxpayers can request an installment agreement by mailing their request to the IRS. Any written request that identifies the taxpayer by name and taxpayer identification number, the tax liability at issue and proposes a payment amount is accepted as a request. As a practical matter, however, written requests should be made using the prescribed forms, Form 9465, *Installment Agreement Request,* and Form 433-D, *Installment Agreement.*

An Online Payment Agreement application is available on the IRS website, **http://www.irs.gov.** Eligible taxpayers and their authorized representatives can apply, and if qualified, receive immediate notification that the installment agreement was approved. The application allows users to pay a balance due in full, request an extension of up to 120 days to pay the balance due in full, or enter into an installment agreement.

Taxpayers who use the online payment agreement application to arrange an installment agreement can set up a:

- Direct debit installment agreement;
- Payroll deduction installment agreement; or
- Regular installment agreement for making monthly payments directly to the IRS.

Generally, a taxpayer who enters into an installment agreement must pay a nonrefundable user fee of $105, payable by check, money order, credit card, or payroll deduction. A reduced fee of $52 applies when a taxpayer enters into a direct debit installment agreement, in which payments are made by electronic funds withdrawal from a checking account (Reg. § 300.1). For low-income taxpayers, the fee is $43, regardless of the method of payment. A *low-income taxpayer* for this purpose is an individual whose income is at or below 250 percent of the dollar amount established by U.S. Department of Health and Human Services (HHS) poverty guidelines (Reg. § 300.1(b) (2)). An additional fee of $45 applies for restructuring or reinstating an installment agreement after a default.

Taxpayers have several options for making monthly installment agreement payments. Payments may be made by any of the following:

- Check or money order;
- Direct debit from a checking account;
- Payroll deduction;

- Electronic Federal Tax Payment System (EFTPS); or
- Credit card.

By entering into an installment agreement, taxpayers agree to meet certain terms and conditions. Most importantly, each installment payment must be made in full and on time. All payments must be received by the IRS by the due date each month. Unlike most tax filing and payment requirements, the timely mailing rule does not apply to payments made under an installment agreement. Therefore, taxpayers making payments by check or money order should send their payments well in advance of the due date.

> **COMMENT**
>
> The IRS has announced that it is taking steps to help financially distressed taxpayers, including added flexibility for missed payments on installment agreements. The IRS may allow a missed payment before placing an installment agreement in default. Although this is not a new policy, the IRS has not openly publicized it in the past (IRS News Release IR-2010-29, March 10, 2010; IRS News Release IR-2009-2, January 6, 2010; IRM 5.19.1.5.5.20).

The IRS may (but is not required to) withdraw a notice of lien if an installment agreement is in effect (Code Sec. 6323(j)(2)(B)). However, the IRS has issued interim guidance expanding its lien withdrawal policy and setting forth the procedures under which a lien will be withdrawn when a taxpayer has entered into a direct debit installment agreement (Memorandum SBSE-05-0411-036, April 7, 2011).

EXTENSION OF TIME TO PAY

If a taxpayer is able to pay a tax liability in full but needs some additional time to obtain the funds, a short-term extension of time to pay a tax liability may be available as an alternative to an installment agreement. For taxpayers whose cases are in the notice stage or are being handled by the IRS Automated Collection System (ACS), the IRS can generally authorize an extension of time to pay delinquent liabilities in full, without requiring taxpayers to submit collection information statements (Form 433-A, Form 433-B, or Form 433-F). An extension can be granted on assessed or preassessed balances due for individual and business taxpayers, regardless of the dollar amount. The maximum extension is 120 days, or 60 days if the taxpayer's account is being handled by the ACS (IRM 5.19.1.5.4).

> **PLANNING POINTER**
>
> An extension of time to pay can be a useful tool for a taxpayer who will be able to pay a balance due within a relatively short period of time but is temporarily short of funds. This is particularly true for a taxpayer who is ineligible for a guaranteed or streamlined installment agreement, but does not want to provide the IRS with the financial statement that is required for regular installment agreements.

An extension of time to pay is not an installment agreement; therefore, the taxpayer does not have to pay a user fee (IRM 5.19.1.5.3.4(11)). However, it is important to note that interest and penalties for failure to pay will accrue until the tax is paid in full.

STUDY QUESTIONS

7. A partial payment installment agreement:
   a. Eliminates the penalties for failure to pay
   b. Is an installment agreement under which the underlying liability may not be fully paid
   c. Automatically withdraws the taxpayer's notice of lien

8. An extension of time to pay a tax liability in full does not apply to business taxpayers. *True or False?*

COLLECTION APPEALS

In many cases, taxpayers have the right to administratively appeal IRS collection actions to the IRS Office of Appeals. The Office of Appeals is an independent division of the IRS and acts as an informal forum for the resolution of tax disputes. Its mission is to resolve tax controversies without litigation, on a basis that is fair and impartial to both the government and the taxpayer, and in a manner that enhances voluntary compliance and public confidence in the integrity and efficiency of the IRS.

There are three main types of collection appeals:
- Collection Due Process (CDP) appeals;
- Appeals in an equivalent hearing; and
- Appeals under the IRS Collection Appeals Program (CAP).

Taxpayers also have certain rights to appeal other IRS actions and decisions, including the assessment of the trust fund recovery penalty, the rejection of an offer in compromise, the denial of a request for penalty abatement, and jeopardy levies.

Collection Due Process Hearings

The CDP hearing provisions give taxpayers an opportunity for an independent review by the IRS Appeals Office to ensure that a levy on the taxpayer's property or filing of a Notice of Federal Tax Lien is warranted and appropriate.

The IRS generally must notify taxpayers of their rights to CDP hearings when it files a notice of federal lien with respect to an unpaid liability, or prior to levying on a taxpayer's property to collect an unpaid liability. The IRS generally issues either a Notice of Federal Tax Lien Filing and Your Right to a Hearing Under IRC 6320 (Lien Notice); or a Final Notice— Notice of Intent to Levy and Notice of Your Right to Hearing (levy notice) (Code Secs. 6320 and. 6330). In either case, the taxpayer may appeal the collection action by making a written request within 30 days after receiving the notice.

A taxpayer may request a CDP hearing by submitting Form 12153, *Request for a Collection Due Process or Equivalent Hearing*. The request for a CDP hearing must state the reason or reasons why the taxpayer disagrees with the IRS's collection action and identify the taxpayer's proposed collection alternative, such as an installment agreement, installment agreement, or, in the case of a lien filing, lien subordination.

The request for a CDP hearing must be sent to the address indicated on the CDP notice, and must be postmarked within

- The 30-day period that commences the day after the end of the five-business-day period within which the IRS is required to provide the taxpayer with notice of the filing of the Notice of Federal Tax Lien; or
- 30 days after the date of the levy notice.

CAUTION

The IRS can disregard a request for a hearing if it determines that the application is frivolous. It can treat the portion of the application that is considered frivolous as if it were never submitted and that portion is not subject to any further administrative or judicial review (Code Sec. 6330(g)). Further, a $5,000 penalty can be imposed on taxpayers making frivolous tax submissions (Code Sec. 6702).

A taxpayer's timely request for a CDP hearing suspends all collection action and the periods of limitation for collection, criminal prosecution, and civil suit. The suspension period begins on the date the IRS receives the taxpayer's written request for a hearing, and continues until the determination resulting from the CDP hearing becomes final, or the taxpayer's request is withdrawn.

A CDP hearing must be conducted by an impartial Appeals employee or officer who has no prior involvement with the unpaid tax. CDP hearings are conducted informally, and are generally conducted by telephone or correspondence. However, a taxpayer who presents relevant, nonfrivolous reasons for disagreement with a proposed collection action is ordinarily offered an opportunity for a face-to-face conference.

Appeals considers the following matters raised by a taxpayer at a CDP hearing:

- The validity, sufficiency, and timeliness of the CDP notice and the request for the CDP hearing;
- Any relevant issue relating to the unpaid tax;
- Appropriate spousal defenses;
- Challenges by the taxpayer to the appropriateness of the collection action;
- Any offers for collection alternatives; and
- Whether the proposed collection action balances the need for the efficient collection of taxes with the taxpayer's legitimate concern that the collection action be no more intrusive than necessary (Code Sec. 6330(c)(2)(A)).

A taxpayer can only dispute the underlying tax liability in a CDP hearing if he or she did not receive a notice of deficiency or otherwise have a prior opportunity to dispute the liability.

Following the hearing, the Appeals Office issues a notice of determination setting forth its decision and advising the taxpayer of the right to seek judicial review of the determination in the Tax Court.

Equivalent Hearings

A taxpayer that files an untimely request for a CDP hearing nevertheless has the right to request a similar administrative appeals hearing, called an "equivalent hearing." Appeals considers the same issues that it would have considered at a CDP hearing and follows the same procedures in arriving at its decision. Following the equivalent hearing, Appeals issues a Decision Letter, which generally contains the same information as a Notice of Determination.

However, unlike a CDP hearing determination, the decision of Appeals following an equivalent hearing is final, and cannot be appealed to the Tax Court. Additionally, collection action and the statute of limitations for collection are not automatically suspended during the period of the equivalent hearing, as they are during CDP hearings.

A taxpayer may request an equivalent hearing by submitting Form 12153 to the IRS at the address shown on the lien or levy notice. The taxpayer must check the box indicating an equivalent hearing request on Line 7 of Form 12153.

Collection Appeals Program

As an alternative to a Collection Due Process hearing, taxpayers have the option to appeal certain collection actions under the IRS Collection Appeals Program (CAP). The CAP procedure is available under a greater range of circumstances than CDP appeals. Unlike a CDP appeal, which can only be requested after the IRS issues a Notice of Federal Tax Lien Filing or a Final Notice of Intent to Levy, a taxpayer may request a CAP hearing before or after the IRS files a Notice of Federal Tax Lien or levies property, or to protest the rejection of a proposed installment agreement or the termination of an existing installment agreement. However, a CAP appeal offers taxpayers fewer options. Taxpayers cannot challenge the existence or amount of a tax liability in a CAP case. Additionally, Appeals' decisions are final following a CAP conference; taxpayers cannot appeal an adverse decision to the Tax Court.

Prior to initiating a CAP appeal, a taxpayer is generally required to contact a collection manager to discuss the collection action at issue. If the taxpayer is unable to reach a favorable outcome with the manager, the case is forwarded to Appeals for review, and the taxpayer is not required to submit an appeal request in writing. If the taxpayer has been contacted by a revenue officer, the taxpayer must request a conference with a collection manager prior to submitting a CAP request. A taxpayer who is unable to resolve the disagreement with the manager may submit a request for Appeals consideration, preferably by completing Form 9423, *Collection Appeal Request*, and submitting it to the collection office. A request for an appeal of a lien, levy, or seizure must submitted within two business days after the date of the conference with the collection manager, or the IRS will resume collection action (IRS Publication 1660, *Collection Appeal Rights*).

COMMENT

No conference is required before appealing the termination or rejection of an installment agreement because the right to appeal is established by statute (Code Sec. 7122).

After the taxpayer requests a CAP appeal, IRS Appeals holds a conference with the taxpayer and reviews the disputed action based on law, regulations, policy, and procedures, considering all of the relevant facts and circumstances. CAP conferences, like collection due process conferences, are conducted very informally, typically by telephone.

Appeals decisions are binding on the taxpayer and the IRS, with certain limited exceptions. For instance, the default of an installment agreement granted by Appeals releases the IRS from the terms of the agreement. The taxpayer's failure to fully disclose any material information or any material misrepresentation of fact also makes any agreement, such as a delay in lien or levy, voidable.

STUDY QUESTIONS

> **9.** A taxpayer can appeal to the Tax Court following an adverse decision in which of the following:
>
>   **a.** An equivalent hearing
>   **b.** A Collection Due Process hearing
>   **c.** A Collection Appeals Program hearing
>
> **10.** If a taxpayer wishes to appeal a lien, levy, or seizure under the CAP rules, if he or she does not request an appeal before a scheduled conference with an IRS collection manager, the IRS will resume its collection action. ***True or False?***

CONCLUSION

Although the IRS has recently taken steps to make the collections process easier for delinquent taxpayers facing financial difficulties, taxpayers and practitioners have reason to remain wary. The IRS's collection powers and resources make it unlike any other creditor. However, taxpayers have a number of options for resolving their unpaid liabilities and avoiding enforced collection.

MODULE 3: CHANGING CIRCUMSTANCES — CHAPTER 8

Exempt Organizations: More Transparency, More Rules

Changes and modifications in the methods and requirements related to the federal government's oversight of tax-exempt organizations have increased both in scope and frequency lately, with that trend promising to continue into the foreseeable future. This chapter provides updates on this recent government oversight with respect to exempt organizations, with particular focus on several areas in which Congress or the courts have been especially active.

LEARNING OBJECTIVES

Upon completion of this chapter you will be able to:

- Explain the requirements to become a qualified nonprofit health insurance issuer;
- Distinguish between the nonprofit promotion of lines of business and for-profit business activities;
- Identify and explain the various required elements to be contained in a written community health needs assessment;
- Determine whether specific activities of credit unions constitute the conduct of unrelated business subject to tax; and
- Describe the procedures by which a small organization may apply for a retroactive reinstatement of exempt status, lost for failure to file an e-postcard for three consecutive years.

INTRODUCTION

The nonprofit sector continues to grow rapidly, despite facing a number of substantial issues including funding concerns in a weak economy, increasingly complex governance requirements from funding sources, and shifting reporting requirements—all of which increase the difficulty in managing tax-exempt organizations. Concern has continued to grow over the appropriateness of exempt status for some types of organizations, even as Congress has created new types of exempt organizations to help deal with some of society's ills. And with increasing complexities comes the need for greater transparency.

HEALTH CARE REFORM AND NONPROFIT HEALTH INSURANCE ISSUERS

The *Patient Protection and Affordable Care Act* (P.L. 111-148) and the *Health Care and Education Reconciliation Act* (P.L. 111-152), which were both enacted in March of 2010, together constitute the Obama Administration's signature health care reform legislation. These two laws jointly were designed to reform of the private health insurance industry and public health insurance programs, to improve coverage for those with preexisting conditions, expand access to care for more than 30 million Americans, and reduce the long-term costs of the United States health care system.

Health Insurance Exchanges

Among the numerous mandates established by these pieces of legislation, the Patient Protection Act included the establishment of health insurance exchanges designed to provide a mechanism for both individuals and certain employers to buy lower-cost health insurance as part of a purchasing pool. Employers with not more than 100 employees and individuals with incomes between 113 and 400 percent of the federal poverty level will be eligible to participate in the exchanges once they become operational. The exchanges should be operational by January 1, 2014. States will be permitted to allow employers with more the 100 employees to participate in the exchanges beginning January 1, 2018.

CO-OP Program

In this regard, the legislation requires the Secretary of Health and Human Services (HHS) to establish a Consumer Operated and Oriented Plan (CO-OP) program under which grants and loans may be made to assist in the creation (or expansion) of qualified nonprofit health insurance issuers. These nonprofits will offer qualified health plans through the American Health Benefit Exchanges and Small Business Health Options Program (SHOP) Exchanges within the states in which they are licensed.

Tax-exempt status under Code Sec. 501(a) has been made available to qualified nonprofit health insurance issuers that receive grants or loans under the CO-OP program. The CO-OP program has been designed to encourage the creation of qualified nonprofit health insurance issuers that will offer qualified health plans to individuals in the states in which the issuers are licensed to offer such insurance plans. Any such qualified nonprofit health insurance issuer must give notice to the Secretary of the Treasury (in a manner to be described by regulation) that it is applying for recognition of exempt status under Code Sec. 501(c)(29).

> **COMMENT**
>
> Only a qualified nonprofit health insurance issuer that receives a loan or grant under the CO-OP program may apply to the IRS to be recognized as an organization described in Code Sec. 501(c)(29) and exempt from tax under Code Sec. 501(a). An issuer will qualify for the exemption from income tax only as long as it complies with:
>
> - The rules specified in the Patient Protection Act and the Internal Revenue Code and regulations; and
> - The terms of its loan or grant under the CO-OP program.
>
> If an organization loses its exempt status, it will be subject to federal income tax, including all of the provisions of Subchapter L of the Internal Revenue Code if it qualifies as an insurance company.

A *qualified nonprofit health insurance issuer* is an organization that meets the following criteria:
- It is organized under state law as a nonprofit, member corporation;
- Substantially all of the organization's activities consist of the issuance of qualified health plans in the individual and small group markets in each state in which the organization is licensed to issue such plans; and
- The organization must meet all the other requirement of Act Sec. 1322(c) of the Patient Protection Act.

Barred from being considered a qualified nonprofit health insurance issuer is:
- Any organization, related entity, or predecessor of either an organization or related entity that was a health insurance issuer on July 16, 2009, or
- Any organization that is sponsored by a state or local government, any political subdivision thereof, or any instrumentality of such government or political subdivision.

In addition, certain governance requirements are imposed on qualified nonprofit health insurance issuers. Unless an organization meets these governance requirements, it will not be treated as meeting the definition:
- The governance of the organization must be subject to a majority vote of its members;
- The organization's governing documents must incorporate ethics and conflict of interest standards protecting against insurance industry involvement and interference; and
- The organization must operate with a strong customer focus, including timeliness, responsiveness, and accountability to its members.

This last governance requirement regarding having a strong customer focus will be described in fuller detail when regulations specifically on this issue are issued by the Secretary of the Treasury.

Federal and State Requirements for Qualified Nonprofit Health Insurance Issuers

Application of federal rules. Like most tax-exempt organizations, qualified nonprofit health insurance issuers must:

- Not participate in, or intervene in (including the publishing or distributing of statements), any political campaign either on behalf of or in opposition to any candidate for public office;
- Not engage in any substantial activities involving the carrying on of propaganda or otherwise attempting to influence legislation; and
- Not permit any portion of their net earnings to inure to the benefit of any private shareholder or individual.

Exceptions to inurement of profits. The prohibition against inurement will not apply to an issuer when all the profits of the issuer are required to be used to lower the premiums, improve the benefits, or advance other programs designed to improve the quality of the health care delivered to its members.

> **COMMENT**
>
> The tax on excess benefit transactions under Code Sec. 4958 applies to Code Sec. 501(c)(29) organizations in the same manner as it applies to organizations that are exempt under Code Secs. 501(c)(3) and 501(c)(4). Notice 2011-23, discussed below, clarifies that the excise tax is payable by the disqualified person on each excess benefit transaction between the applicable tax-exempt organization and the disqualified person. Code Sec. 4958 also imposes an excise tax on organization managers who knowingly participate in an excess benefit transaction, unless such participation was not willful and due to some reasonable cause.

Reinsurance contracts. As part of the transition to the health insurance system developed by Congress, each state must either establish or enter into contracts with reinsurance entities to carry out the reinsurance program. These state programs must be maintained to collect payments and make payments to the health insurance issuers that cover high-risk individuals in the individual market during the three-year period beginning January 1, 2014. States are permitted to have more than one such applicable reinsurance entity, and states are also permitted to enter into agreements under which reinsurance entities may carry out such programs on a multistate basis for the states entering into the agreement.

State-level requirements. Certain requirements are also imposed on qualified nonprofit health insurance issuers at the state level. A qualified nonprofit health insurance issuer must meet all of the requirements that other issuers of qualified health plans are required to meet in the state in which the organization offers qualified health plans, including:

- Solvency and licensure requirements;
- Rules on payments to providers;
- Compliance with network adequacy rules, rate and form filing rules; and
- Any applicable state premium assessment rules.

Also, an organization may not offer any health plan in any state until that state has in effect (or the Secretary of the Treasury has implemented for that state) certain health insurance market reforms that were required by the *Public Health Service Act* (Title XXVII, part A).

An organization that becomes a qualified nonprofit health insurance issuer under Code Sec. 529(c)(29) must include the following information on its returns filed pursuant to Code Sec. 6033(m):

- The amount of reserves on hand; and
- The amount of reserves required by each state in which the issuer is licensed to issue qualified health plans.

Notice 2011-23

The IRS has issued Notice 2011-23 to clarify these requirements. In addition, Notice 2011-23 requires any organization that has either filed or intends to file an application for exemption under Code Sec. 501(c)(29) to file Form 990, *Return of Organization Exempt from Income Tax,* for all applicable tax years that end before the organization receives a determination letter. The organization must indicate on its Form 990 that it is filing that form in the belief that it qualifies as a qualified nonprofit health insurance issuer under Code Sec. 501(c)(29) and is, therefore, exempt from income tax under Code Sec. 501(a), but that the IRS has not yet recognized its exemption.

Notice 2011-23 states that the IRS intends to publish a revenue procedure detailing how a qualified issuer should apply to be recognized as a Code Sec. 501(c)(29) organization. First, a qualified issuer must enter into an agreement with HHS. Only thereafter may a qualified issuer submit its request for recognition of exempt status to the IRS, but the IRS will not accept any such applications until after the revenue procedure has been published.

The revenue procedure is also expected to address the effective date of exemptions that are granted to qualified issuers. According to Notice 2011-23, this date is expected to be the latter of the date of the organization's formation or March 23, 2010 (the date of enactment for the Patient Protection Act), provided that the qualified issuer's purposes and activities have been consistent with the requirements for exemption under Code Sec. 501(c)(29) since that date.

> **COMMENT**
>
> In an ongoing effort to encourage qualified nonprofit health insurance issuers to be up and running by the time the American Health Benefit Exchanges and Small Business Health Options Program (SHOP) Exchanges launch in 2014, federal officials announced $3.8 billion in loan funding for these nonprofit organizations on Monday, July 18, 2011.

Funding Issues

Given that these exchanges do not launch until 2014, one concern is that the current enthusiasm for deficit and spending reductions in Congress could result in a loss of funding for the CO-OP program. Should this occur, when health insurance consumers go to one of the new exchanges in 2014 they will only be able to chose from the same insurance options that would otherwise be available. And without the option of qualified nonprofit health insurance issuers on the exchanges, there would be no lower-cost health insurance options available for consumers to select.

There have been numerous legislative proposals to undermine the health care reform law since it was enacted. Most have taken the form of eliminating government funding for specific elements of the overall health care reform scheme. Currently, there are no legislative proposals aimed specifically at the CO-OP program except for a proposal to repeal the Patient Protection Act in its entirety, which is highly unlikely to receive much consideration.

STUDY QUESTIONS

1. Qualified health plans created or expanded by the CO-OP program will be offered through all of the following organizations by states **except:**

   a. American Health Benefit Exchanges

   b. Patient Protection Act Exchanges

   c. Small Business Health Options Program (SHOP) Exchanges

2. Reinsurance contracts

   a. Will be granted to one entity per state

   b. Will carry out the reinsurance program under state contracts beginning January 1, 2014

   c. Will be applied within a single state only

BUSINESS LEAGUES: DISTINGUISHING FOR-PROFIT FROM NONPROFIT

A *business league* is an association of persons having a common business interest. Its purpose is to promote that common interest and not to engage in a regular business of a kind ordinarily carried on for profit. Being an organization of the general class of exempt organization (under Code Sec. 501(c)(6)) that includes chambers of commerce and boards of trade, its activities should be directed to the improvement of business conditions of one or more lines of business as distinguished from the performance of particular services for individual persons.

> **COMMENT**
>
> The exemption from income tax for business leagues under Code Sec. 501(c)(6) also covers professional football leagues that otherwise meet the requirements of Reg. § 1.501(c)(6)-1, whether or not the football league administers a pension fund for its football players.

To qualify for exemption under Code Sec. 501(c)(6) and Reg. § 1.501(c)(6)-1, an organization must:

- Be a membership organization with a significant level of membership support;
- Be an association of "persons" having some common business interest, and the purpose of that association is to promote such common business purpose;
- Conduct activities directed to the improvement of business conditions for one or more lines of business;
- Not conduct activities that include the performance of particular services for individual persons;
- Not be organized for profit;
- Not engage in a regular business of the kind ordinarily considered carried on for profit—even if the business is operated on a cooperative basis or produces only sufficient income to be self-sustaining; and
- Allow no part of the organization's net earnings to inure to the benefit of any private shareholder or other individual person.

It is essential that an organization meet all of the above requirements to qualify under Code Sec. 501(c)(6), so careful analysis must be done when seeking to establish a business league. These characteristics are highly interrelated, and if the IRS has concerns regarding any of these characteristics, it is highly probable that the IRS will raise issues regarding other characteristics.

Qualifying for Tax-Exempt Status

A key in qualifying for tax-exempt status for any organization is that the organization be organized and operated for one of the primary purposes for which exemptions may be granted under the provisions of the Internal Revenue Code. For business leagues, that purpose must be regarding a common business interest among its members and serving or promoting a business purpose for its members.

COMMENT

Conceptually, this can be a difficult distinction for many who view all business activities as being (at their core) for the purpose of generating profit. But operating a successful business generally involves far more than merely getting customers to "cough up some cash," and business leagues can be very helpful to their members in these areas without conducting activities that constitute engaging in business activities or the performance of services of the kinds normally carried on to produce a profit.

Case Law for Business Leagues

For purposes of this exemption, the concept of business is construed very broadly and encompasses virtually any and all occupations and "embraces everything about which a person can be employed" (*Associated Industries of Cleveland,* 7 TC 1449). It includes merchants and tradespeople, businesspeople and professionals, and cooperatives and nonprofits. In one case, a group made up of the wives of the members of a business league formed their own business league for the purpose of advancing their husbands' profession (Rev. Rul. 67-343, 1967-2 CB 198).

Examples such as this last one can unfortunately sometimes make it appear that it is quite simple to organize and operate a tax-exempt business league, but many organizations have discovered that—although being members of a business league can have many benefits—it is crucial to understand the limits of what the business league can do, and what activities the members must undertake for themselves.

EXAMPLE

A nonprofit organization whose members represented a wide range of business types, and which used various types of computer systems in those businesses, was organized and operated for the purpose of assisting its members to utilize computer technology efficiently. The organization qualified as a business league exempt under Code Sec. 501(c)(6).

EXAMPLE

An organization that provided conferences and seminars to its members on operational and technical problems with business computer systems did not qualify as a business league under Code Sec. 501(c)(6) because it primarily promoted the use of computers by a single manufacturer. Reg. § 1.501(c)(6)-1 requires that a business league promote a common business interest of an association of persons, but in this case it was the interest of a particular computer manufacturer that was principally promoted.

This is illustrated by a recent court decision (***Bluetooth SIG Inc.,*** 2010-2 USTC ¶50,510). Bluetooth technology has become a commonplace element of Americans' electronic lives during the last few years, existing in mobile phones, laptop computers, wireless headsets, personal digital assistants (PDAs), gaming systems, etc. Because this technology has become relatively ubiquitous in recent years, it is easy to think of it as representative of the wireless communication industry. But would an association with the purpose of promoting uniform practices in connection with Bluetooth technology be eligible for exempt status under Code Sec. 501(c)(6)?

No, according to the Court of Appeals for the Ninth Federal Judicial Circuit. Although incidental activities that fall outside the definition of a business league will not, of themselves, prevent an organization from tax-exempt status as a business league, the association owned and marketed the wireless networking protocol and directly owned the trademark and patent for the Bluetooth brand. As such, the association provided nonincidental services to a particular member. The association's activities did not benefit all or even most members of either the wireless communication industry or the consumer electronics industry. To the contrary, the business interests of the association were advanced specifically at the expense of other members of those industries. The promotional activities were not designed to promote the products or services of the industry as a whole, but rather to endorse the Bluetooth brand and trademark only. Such competitive practices are contrary to the cooperative nature that is a key element of the basis for granting exempt status to business leagues.

The association argued that because Bluetooth technology exists in a wide range of different types of electronic equipment manufactured by an array of differing consumer electronics manufacturers, a separate industry of "Bluetooth-enabled products" exists, and that the association served to promote this industry. However, because the manufacturers could not avail themselves of this technology without first becoming members of the association, no meaningful differentiation between the for-profit business and the association existed.

STUDY QUESTIONS

---

3. As long as they meet the requirements of Code Sec. 501(c)(6), professionals and nonprofits are eligible to form tax-exempt business leagues. ***True or False?***

4. The Ninth Federal Judicial Circuit Court of Appeals ruled that the business league representing Bluetooth-brand interests should not be a tax-exempt organization because:

    a. Bluetooth technology was limited to a single product line

    b. There was no substantial difference between the for-profit business and the Bluetooth association

    c. Business leagues may only be formed by tradespeople or brick-and-mortar businesses

---

COMMUNITY HEALTH NEEDS ASSESSMENTS FOR NONPROFIT HOSPITALS

Code Sec. 501(c)(3) Facilities

Charitable organizations, i.e., organizations described in Code Sec. 501(c)(3), generally are exempt from federal income tax, are eligible to receive tax-deductible contributions, have access to tax-exempt financing through state and local governments, and generally are exempt from state and local taxes. A charitable organization must operate primarily in pursuit of one or more tax-exempt purposes constituting the basis of its tax exemption.

The Internal Revenue Code specifies such purposes as:

- Religious;
- Charitable;
- Scientific;
- Educational;
- Literary;
- Testing for public safety;
- Fostering international amateur sports competition; or
- The prevention of cruelty to children or animals.

In general, an organization is organized and operated for charitable purposes if it provides relief for the poor and distressed or the underprivileged.

The tax code does not provide a per se exemption for hospitals. Rather, a hospital qualifies for exemption if it is organized and operated for a charitable purpose and otherwise meets the requirements of Code Sec. 501(c)(3). The promotion of health has been recognized by the IRS as a charitable purpose that is beneficial to the community as a whole. It includes not only the establishment or maintenance of charitable hospitals, but also clinics, homes for the aged, and other providers of health care.

Determining Whether a Hospital Is Charitable

Since 1969, the IRS has applied a "community benefit" standard for determining whether a hospital is charitable. According to Rev. Rul. 69-545, community benefit can include, for example:

- Maintaining an emergency room open to all persons regardless of ability to pay;
- Having an independent board of trustees composed of representatives of the community;
- Operating with an open medical staff policy, with privileges available to all qualifying physicians;
- Providing charity care; and
- Using surplus funds to improve the quality of patient care, expand facilities, and advance medical training, education, and research.

Since 2009, hospitals generally have been required to submit information on community benefit on their annual information returns filed with the IRS. The *Patient Protection and Affordable Care Act of 2010* (P.L. 111-148) added Code Sec. 501(r) establishing four new requirements applicable to Code Sec. 501(c)(3) hospitals. The new requirements are in addition to, and not in lieu of, the requirements otherwise applicable to an organization described in Code Sec. 501(c)(3). These additional requirements generally apply to any Code Sec. 501(c)(3) organization that operates at least one hospital facility, and an organization is required to comply with the following requirements with respect to each hospital facility operated by such organization.

For these purposes, a *hospital facility* generally includes:

- Any facility that is, or is required to be, licensed, registered, or similarly recognized by a state as a hospital; and
- Any other facility or organization the Secretary of the Treasury determines has the provision of hospital care as its principal purpose.

COMMENT

The addition of these requirements reflects concerns that have arisen in recent years about whether nonprofit hospitals are providing adequate public benefits—particularly in their local community—to justify their tax-exempt status. Because not-for-profit status impacts not just federal, state, and municipal income taxes but also property and sales taxes, the exempt status of sizable hospitals can result in cash-strapped local economies receiving far less in tax revenues than they would for facilities without exempt status. Presumably this is a fair tradeoff if the communities are receiving substantial nonmonetary benefits, but in an era of tight government budgets, the question of whether the communities are actually receiving those countervailing benefits naturally arises.

Implementation for community health needs assessment. *First,* each charitable hospital facility is required to conduct a community health needs assessment at least once every three tax years and adopt an implementation strategy to meet the community needs identified through such an assessment. The assessment process must take into account input from persons who represent the broad interests of the community served by the hospital, including those with special knowledge or expertise of public health issues. Each hospital facility is required to make the assessment widely available.

Written financial assistance policy for patients. *Second,* each hospital facility is required to adopt, implement, and widely publicize a written financial assistance policy. The financial assistance policy must indicate the eligibility criteria for financial assistance and whether such assistance includes free or discounted care. For patients eligible for discounted care, the policy must indicate the basis for calculating the amounts that will be billed to such patients. The policy must also indicate how to apply for such assistance.

If a hospital does not have a separate billing and collections policy, the financial assistance policy must also indicate what actions the hospital may take in the event of nonpayment, including collections action and reporting to credit agencies. In addition, each hospital facility is required to adopt and implement a written policy to provide, without discrimination, emergency medical treatment to individuals regardless of their eligibility under the financial assistance policy.

Equal billing. *Third,* each hospital facility is permitted to bill patients who qualify for financial assistance no more than the amount generally billed to insured patients. A hospital facility may not use gross charges (i.e., standardized "chargemaster" rates) when billing individuals who qualify for financial assistance. Those who qualify for financial assistance should be billed based on either the best, or an average of the three best, negotiated commercial rates, or the Medicare rates.

Collection actions. *Fourth,* a hospital facility (or its affiliates) may not undertake certain extraordinary collection actions—even if those actions are otherwise permitted by law—against a patient without first making reasonable efforts to:

- Inform the patient about the hospital's financial assistance policy, and
- Determine whether the patient is eligible for assistance under the policy.

Such extraordinary collection actions would include lawsuits, liens on residences, arrests, body attachments, or other similar collection processes.

For these purposes, reasonable efforts by the hospital should include notification by the hospital of its financial assistance policy upon admission, and in written and oral communications with the patient regarding the patient's bill, including invoices and telephone calls, before collection action or reporting to credit rating agencies is initiated. Further guidance regarding what constitutes reasonable attempts is expected from the IRS.

Disclosures. In addition to these four requirements, a hospital must disclose on its annual information return (Form 990 and related schedules) how it is addressing the needs that were identified in the community health needs assessment and, if all identified needs are not addressed, the reasons why (e.g., lack of financial or human resources). Each hospital organization that is required to complete a community health needs assessment must file with its annual information return a copy of its audited financial statements (or, in the case of an organization the financial statements of which are included in a consolidated financial statement with other organizations, such consolidated financial statements).

> **COMMENT**
>
> The Secretary of the Treasury will review at least once every three years the community benefit activities of each hospital organization to which Code Sec. 501(r) applies.

Excise tax. If a hospital organization meets the additional requirements of Code Sec. 501(r) but fails to meet the community health needs assessment requirements under Code Sec. 501(r)(3), an excise tax is imposed on the hospital. The tax on the organization is $50,000 for any applicable tax year. For example, if a facility does not complete a community health needs assessment in tax year one, two, or three, it is subject to the penalty in year three. If it then fails to complete a community health needs assessment in year four, it is subject to another penalty in year four (for failing to satisfy the requirement during the three-year period beginning with tax year two and ending with tax year four).

The IRS has yet to issue proposed regulations under Code Sec. 501(r), but the IRS has issued guidance (Notice 2011-52) addressing the community health needs assessment requirement and related obligations for the purpose of allowing hospital organizations to begin conducting these assessments and implementing strategies to meet community health needs. The assessment requirements are effective for tax years beginning after March 23, 2012, so hospital organizations—especially those with multiple facilities—might use this delayed effective date to organize and plan how they are going to conduct their assessments.

COMMENT

The Treasury Department and the IRS intend that future guidance regarding any categories of organizations that provide hospital care as their principal exempt function or purpose will only apply prospectively, once finalized. Therefore, only organizations operating state-licensed hospital facilities will be considered hospital organizations that must satisfy the community health needs assessment requirements prior to the effective date of future guidance—presumably final regulations under Code Sec. 501(r). This means that of the two part definition of a hospital facility, above, the IRS will only consider the first part ("any facility that is, or is required to be, licensed, registered, or similarly recognized by a state as a hospital") and not the second portion ("any other facility or organization the Secretary of the Treasury determines has the provision of hospital care as its principal purpose") because the IRS and Treasury do not intend to exercise the determination authority contained in this second part until final guidance is released. The IRS anticipates the guidance contained in Notice 2011-52 will match what will be contained in the regulations under Code Sec. 501(r) when they are proposed.

A hospital organization's completed community health needs assessment would consist of a written report including, at a minimum, the following five areas of information:

- A description of the community served by the hospital facility and how the scope was determined;
- A description of the process and methods used to conduct the assessment, plus any gaps in the information gathered that impact the organization's ability to assess the community needs;
- A description of how the hospital organization used input from persons representing the interests of the community, including
  - How and when such persons were consulted,
  - Identifying any organizations that were also consulted,
  - Listing any community leaders or representatives consulted, and
  - Noting anyone consulted who has special knowledge or expertise in public health;
- A prioritized description of all of the community health needs identified through the assessment, and a description of the process and criteria used in prioritizing such health needs; and
- A description of the existing health care facilities and other resources within the community available to meet the community health needs identified through the assessment.

The community input requirement described in the third point, above, requires the assessment to take into account input from:

- Persons with special knowledge of or expertise in public health;
- Federal, tribal, regional, state, or local health or other departments or agencies that possess current data or other information relevant to the health needs of the community served by the hospital facility; and
- Leaders, representatives, or members of medically underserved, low-income and minority populations, and populations with chronic disease needs, that exist in the community.

The hospital organization may and normally should also seek the input of other persons located within the community served by the hospital facility, but consulting persons in the three categories above constitute the minimum that will satisfy this requirement.

STUDY QUESTIONS

5. A standard established by the IRS in 1969 to determine whether a hospital is charitable is the:

  a. Public health standard

  b. Community benefit standard

  c. Patient protection standard

6. Imposing liens on residences and arresting patients who fail to pay for hospital services are prohibited for Code Sec. 501(c)(3) charitable hospitals as:

  a. Extraordinary collection actions

  b. Nonpayment consequence procedures

  c. Restitution practices

7. Charitable hospitals have until their tax year beginning after ____ to begin conducting community health needs assessments and other reporting requirements to substantiate their tax-exempt purpose for the Secretary of the Treasury.

  a. December 1, 2011

  b. January 15, 2012

  c. March 23, 2012

The assessment will only be considered complete when it is made widely available to the public. To satisfy this requirement, the hospital facility must post the written report on its website or on the website of the hospital organization that operates the facility. The report must be readily accessible, in a format that exactly reproduces the image of the report when downloaded, and available without the payment of a fee. In addition, the assessment must be available to the public until such date as a subsequent assessment for that hospital facility is made widely available to the public.

Notice 2011-52 also contains numerous points of clarification regarding community health needs assessments and 501(r) hospitals, including:

- A hospital facility located outside the United States will not be considered a state-licensed facility for purposes of Code Sec. 501(r) because "state" includes only the 50 states plus the District of Columbia, but not any U.S. possession or territory or foreign country;
- A 501(r) hospital organization includes state-licensed hospital facilities operated through a disregarded entity or a joint venture, a limited liability company, or any other entity treated as a partnership for federal tax purposes; and
- A hospital organization that operates more than one hospital facility must conduct a community health needs assessment for each hospital facility it operates. Hospital organizations my collaborate with other organizations when conducting such assessments, as well as when developing implementation strategies, but hospital organizations operating multiple hospital facilities must document separately the assessment and implementation strategy for each of it hospital facilities.

STUDY QUESTIONS

8. A multihospital system may include all of the hospitals it administers in its needs assessment and reporting as long as the demographics of their patient populations are the same socioeconomically and ethnically. *True or False?*

CREDIT UNIONS AND THE TAX ON UNRELATED BUSINESS

Credit unions were first established in Germany. They are designed to be cooperative financial institutions that are owned by their members, controlled by a board of directors derived from that membership, and operated to assist their members financially by providing credit at beneficial rates and promoting thrift amongst their membership.

U.S. Tax-Exempt Status

In the United States, credit unions without capital stock, organized and operated for mutual purposes and without profit, are exempt from income taxation under Code Secs. 501(a) and 501(c)(14). Therefore, credit unions are occasionally referred to as 501(c)(14) organizations. The exemption from income tax is provided because the purpose of the credit union is to operate to serve its members' interests, and not to maximize its profits. For this reason, credit unions generally have only individuals (rather than businesses) as members. Membership in credit unions includes more than 40 percent of the U.S. population that holds some type of financial account.

For many years, major banks have complained that many credit unions were unfairly competing in areas that were too commercial to be appropriate for tax-exempt organizations, and that in doing so, those credit unions were operating outside the realm of activities for which they were granted exempt status. If true, this situation would make any such credit unions unfair competitors to the banks because the credit unions would be competing in the same commercial arena with no liability for taxes on their income. Some banks even tried lobbying for repeal of the tax-exempt category for credit unions under Code Sec. 501(c)(14).

Process of Analyzing Operations of Credit Unions

Congress has shown no real interest in, nor taken any steps toward, repealing Code Sec. 501(c)(14). The IRS, however, has in recent years released numerous technical advice memoranda (TAMs) finding individual credit unions liable for tax on income from their substantial unrelated business activities: the *unrelated business income tax,* or UBIT.

Purposes of the credit unions. The TAMs are remarkably similar. They start by describing the principal purposes of the credit unions (those purposes for which they receive their exempt status) as:

- The promotion of thrift, and
- To provide low-cost credit for their members through mutual nonprofit operations.

STUDY QUESTION

> **9.** Credit unions are liable for tax if they:
>
> **a.** Charge the same interest on loans to their members as individuals could find at banks
> **b.** Have unrelated business income
> **c.** Offer the same interest rates on savings as do banks

Comparison of conduct with purposes. The IRS then analyzes the activities conducted by the credit unions to determine whether their various activities were substantially related to their principal purposes. When the activities are not substantially related to their principal purposes, the activities are unrelated business activities that may be subject to the UBIT on such activities under Code Sec. 511.

In these TAMs, the IRS determined that a great number of the activities conducted by these credit unions were not substantially related to either of their two principal purposes. The IRS frequently applied factors from *Alabama Central Credit Union* (86-2 USTC ¶9658, 646 FSupp 1199) in determining that the credit unions' activities were not substantially related, and that the amounts received from these activities were therefore *unrelated business taxable income (UBTI)*.

As stated in *Alabama Central Credit Union*:

> A primary legislative purpose for enacting the unrelated business income tax was to eliminate the unfair competitive advantage of exempt organizations. This legislative objective of preventing unfair competition included the objective of preventing exempt organizations from expanding their operations with tax-free profits, while their taxpaying competitors could expand only with profits remaining after taxes (*C.F. Mueller Co. v. Commissioner*, 73-1 USTC ¶9460, 479 F.2d 678).

Tax consequences. To date, the IRS has chosen the intermediate sanction of imposing the tax on unrelated business activities under Code Sec. 511 on these credit unions rather than considering the more drastic approach of revoking their exempt status, but presumably revocation is a possibility when sufficiently substantial and prolonged unrelated business activities are present.

The income of an exempt organization is subject to UBIT imposed by Code Sec. 511 *only* if two conditions are present:

- The income must be from a trade or business that is regularly carried on by the organization; and
- The trade or business must not be substantially related—aside from the need of the organization for funds or the use of profits—to the organization's exercise or performance of the purposes or functions on which its exemption is based.

Excluded from the definition of *unrelated trade or business* are any trade or business activities:

- In which substantially all of the work in carrying on the trade or business is performed for the organization without compensation;
- Carried on by a Code Sec. 501(c)(3) organization or by a governmental college or university (as described in Code Sec. 511(a)(2)(B)) primarily for the convenience of the organization's members, students, patients, officers or employees;
- That consist of selling merchandise, substantially all of which has been received by the organization as gifts or contributions; and
- Of a local employees' association, organized before May 27, 1969, for the purpose of selling items to members that are normally sold through vending machines, food-dispensing facilities, or snack bars, if the sales are for the convenience of the members and made at their usual place of employment.

In these TAMs, tax-exempt credit unions were subject to UBIT with respect to funds derived from the sale of:

- Financial management services;
- Accidental death and disability (AD&D) insurance;
- Credit life and credit disability insurance;
- Group life insurance;
- Group health insurance;
- Group cancer insurance;
- Stand-alone cancer insurance;
- Dental insurance;
- Guaranteed auto protection (GAP) insurance;
- Car warranties (not tied to car purchase loans); and
- The operation of a car-buying service.

Such sales did not benefit the credit unions' memberships as a whole (except through the production of income), and the sales were not related to the obtaining of credit or a loan, nor were there any provisions in the insurance that would guarantee that insurance payouts would be used for the repayment of members' outstanding loans.

> **COMMENT**
>
> Certainly, the preceding list should not be considered an exhaustive list of potential unrelated business possibilities for a credit union.

However, not all of the activities in question in these TAMs were outside the scope of the credit unions' exempt purposes. For example, the sale of collateral protection insurance (CPI) did not result in unrelated business income. The CPI protected the credit unions as lenders against damage to the collateral during periods in which borrowers failed to maintain their own insurance on collateral property. Therefore, the sale of CPI insurance in conjunction with member loans was substantially related to the credit unions' exempt purposes. In addition, the sale of checks by the credit unions to their members was determined to support the credit unions' exempt purposes, because the checks allowed members to access their funds held on deposit, which is a central function of a credit union. Also, the interchange income derived from credit card and debit card (or checkcard) programs were financial services income substantially related to the credit unions' exempt purposes. Therefore, any net income from interchange fees for debit or credit card usage, as well as fees from member usage of ATM terminals, was not subject to unrelated business income tax.

COMMENT

Because these credit unions conducted substantial business activities that were not related to their principal purposes, they have risked being considered as not operating for the exempt purposes. This is a considerable risk because an organization will not continue to be regarded as exempt if more than an insubstantial part of its activities fail to be in furtherance of its exempt purposes.

EXAMPLE

A credit union, exempt from tax under Code Sec. 501(c)(14), operates a financial services program that offers for sale to its members annuities, mutual funds and insurance (including accidental death and disability insurance, cancer insurance, and dental insurance). The operation of a financial services program is not substantially related to the credit union's principal purpose of promoting thrift and providing low cost credit to its members, and therefore the credit union would be liable for UBIT on its income derived from the financial services program.

EXAMPLE

A credit union, exempt from tax under Code Sec. 501(c)(14), provides members with either debit or credit cards, and operates a series of automatic teller machines in area shopping malls available for use to the general public. The income from interchange fees related to member usage of their debit/credit cards, as well as member usage of ATM terminals, is substantially related to the credit union's principal purpose of promoting thrift and providing low cost credit to its members, and therefore the credit union would not be liable for UBIT on any such income. However, the fees charged for nonmember ATM usage are primarily for the purpose of generating income, not substantially related to accomplishing the credit union's exempt purposes, and therefore subject to UBIT.

STUDY QUESTIONS

10. Which of the following is *not* an activity of credit unions that has triggered the unrelated business income tax?

    a. Activities carried on for the convenience of members

    b. Offers of group life insurance

    c. Operation of a car-buying service

---

11. Interchange income derived from credit and debit card programs of credit unions was not subject to unrelated business income tax because:

    a. Every member had the opportunity to apply for obtaining the credit or debit cards

    b. The programs were financial services income substantially related to the exempt purposes of the credit unions

    c. The credit unions were required to outsource management of the card services to unrelated banks

---

QUALIFYING TO FILE AND REINSTATEMENT AS A SMALL EXEMPT ORGANIZATION

Organizations that are exempt from income tax under Code Sec. 501(a) generally must file an annual information return; the tax exemption does not excuse organizations from annual filing. In fact, organizations that claim such exempt status prior to actually being granted such status must also file annual information returns during the period in which the organizations; applications for exemption are pending with the IRS.

Form 990 Filing Requirements

The IRS released a revised version of Form 990, *Return of Organization Exempt From Income Tax,* for use beginning with tax year 2008 (filed in 2009), as well as instructions for the updated form. There are three basic versions of this form:

- Form 990, *Return of Organization Exempt From Income Tax;*
- Form 990-EZ, *Short Form Return of Exempt Organizations;* and
- Form 990-N, *Electronic Notice for Tax-Exempt Organizations Not Required to File Form 990 or 990-EZ.*

COMMENT

Private foundations, so labeled because their funding comes primarily from a small group of private sources (as opposed to a public charity's funding derived from the general public), have their own version: Form 990-PF, *Return of Private Foundation or Section 4947(a)(1) Nonexempt Charitable Trust Treated as a Private Foundation.*

Versions of Form 990 must be filed by:

- Organizations that are tax exempt under Code Sec. 501(c);
- Political organizations that are exempt under Code Sec. 527; and
- Charitable trusts as described in Code Sec. 4947(a)(1).

There is a very limited list of exempt organizations that are not required to file any version of Form 990, including:

- Churches and religion-affiliated organizations;
- State institutions exempt from income tax under Code Sec. 115; and
- Organizations created by an Act of Congress as instrumentalities of the United States, as described in either Code Sec. 501(a)(1) or 501(l).

The thresholds that delineate which exempt organizations file which of the three basic versions of Form 990 are set forth by the IRS. The IRS has reduced the thresholds related to Form 990 and Form 990-EZ in recent years:

- For 2008, the threshold allowing a filing of Form 990-EZ was gross receipts of less than $1 million and total assets of less than $2.5 million.
- For 2009, this threshold was reduced to gross receipts of less than $500,000 and total assets of less than $1 million; and
- For 2010, tax-exempt organizations with gross receipts of less than $200,000 and total assets of less than $500,000 could file Form 990-EZ; exempt organizations at or above these limits had to file Form 990. The IRS has given no indication that it is likely to adjust these thresholds any further for 2011.

COMMENT

The IRS recently released a new one-page form—Form 8940, *Request for Miscellaneous Determination* (issued June 2011)—that tax-exempt organizations should use to request determinations (other than initial exemption applications) about their tax-exempt status. Included among the nine types of requests that may be made using the form is a request for an exemption from Form 990 filing requirements.

Qualifying for Status as a Small Exempt Organization

Prior to the passage of the *Pension Protection Act of 2006*, exempt organizations with gross receipts of less than $25,000 were generally not required to file annual information returns. However, by adding Code Sec. 6033(i), Congress began requiring exempt organizations with gross receipts of less than $25,000 to file electronic information notices for annual periods beginning after 2006. Subsequently, the IRS raised the $25,000 filing threshold to $50,000 for tax years beginning on or after January 1, 2010.

These small organizations, which are extremely numerous, may now file Form 990-N, *Electronic Notice for Tax-Exempt Organizations Not Required to File Form 990 or 990-EZ*, unless they voluntarily chose to file either Form 990 or 990-EZ. This latter form is frequently referred to—even by the IRS—as an e-postcard. Therefore, those small tax-exempt organizations whose annual gross receipts are normally $50,000 or less ($25,000 for tax years ending after December 31, 2007, and before December 31, 2010) should electronically submit Form 990-N every year by the 15th day of the fifth month of the organization's tax year. The form must be completed and submitted electronically; there is no paper version of Form 990-N.

The e-postcard requires the following basic items of information:

- The employer identification number (EIN) or taxpayer identification number (TIN);
- The organization's legal name and mailing address;
- A list of any other names the organization uses publicly;
- The name and address of the organization's principal officer;
- The organization's web site address (if it has one);
- Confirmation that the organization's annual gross receipts are normally not more than $50,000 ($25,000 for tax years beginning before January 1, 2010); and
- A statement that the organization has terminated or is terminating (going out of business), if applicable.

Although most small tax-exempt organizations must file the e-postcard, certain organizations are either exempted from this requirement or barred from filing Form 990-N because they are required to file an alternate form. The exempted/barred group includes:

- Organizations that are included in the group return of a parent organization;
- Churches, their integrated auxiliaries, and conventions or associations of churches;
- Private foundations (which are required to file Form 990-PF);
- Most Code Sec. 509(a)(3) supporting organizations (which are required to file Form 990 or Form 990-EZ); and
- Political organizations exempt under Code Sec. 527 (required to file Form 990 or Form 990-EZ).

Submitting a Form 990-N (e-postcard) is not the equivalent of filing an information return, and, as a result, does not trigger the limitations period under Code Sec. 6501(g)(2). Similarly, failing to file a Form 990-N does not trigger the monetary penalty under Code Sec. 6652(c)(1(E). However, the failure to file for three consecutive years will result in the revocation of the organization's tax-exempt status (see Code Sec. 6033(j)).

In order to be eligible to file Form 990-N, *Electronic Notice for Tax-Exempt Organizations Not Required to File Form 990 or 990-EZ,* an organization must have annual gross receipts that are "normally not more than $50,000" ($25,000 for tax years ending after December 31, 2007, and before December 31, 2010). The "normally not more than" language seemed rather imprecise, so the IRS has released guidance in Rev. Proc. 2011-15 to clarify the meaning of this expression, including how it may be applied during the early years of a small tax-exempt organization's existence:

- An organization that has been in existence for one year or less will be considered to have annual gross receipts normally not more than $50,000 if the organization's actual gross receipts, including amounts pledged by donors, are $75,000 or less during its first taxable year;
- An organization that has been in existence for more than one year but less than three years will be considered to have annual gross receipts normally not more than $50,000 if the organization's actual gross receipts for its first two taxable years are $60,000 or less; and
- An organization that has been in existence for three years or more will be considered to have annual gross receipts normally not more than $50,000 if the organization's average annual gross receipts for the immediately preceding three tax years—including the tax year for which the return is filed—are $50,000 or less.

These rules and guidance also apply to foreign organizations and United States possession organizations that are exempt from the U.S. federal income tax under Code Sec. 501(a) if:

- The organization does not receive more than $50,000 in annual receipts from sources within the United States; and
- The organization has no significant activity, such as lobbying and political activity, or operating a trade or business (but not including investment activity), within the United States.

COMMENT

Every tax-exempt organization, regardless of size, must file Form 990-T, *Exempt Organization Business Income Tax Return,* for any year in which it has $1,000 or more in unrelated business taxable income. Therefore, even if an organization has insufficient income to require it to file a Form 990 or Form 990-EZ return, it must still file Form 990-T if the organization earns sufficient gross unrelated business income.

STUDY QUESTIONS

12. A type of Form 990 must be filed annually by each of the following *except:*

   a. Private foundations
   b. Political organizations exempt under Code Sec. 527
   c. Churches

---

13. The IRS considers entities to be small exempt organizations if their annual gross receipts are no more than:

   a. $50,000

   b. $75,000

   c. $200,000

Reinstatement as a Small Exempt Organization

As stated above, submitting a Form 990-N (e-postcard) is not the equivalent of filing an information return, does not trigger the limitations period under Code Sec. 6501(g)(2), and failing to file it does not trigger the monetary penalty under Code Sec. 6652(c)(1)(E). However, the failure to file for three consecutive years will result in the revocation of the organization's tax-exempt status (see Code Sec. 6033(j)). Since Congress began requiring exempt organizations with gross receipts of less than $25,000 to file electronic information notices for annual periods beginning after 2006 ($50,000 for tax years beginning on or after January 1, 2010), the earliest that a small exempt organization could have its exempt status revoked for failure to file required Forms 990-N was during 2010.

> **COMMENT**
>
> The IRS announced that approximately 275,000 organizations lost their exempt status during 2010 for failing to file Form 990-N for three consecutive years. Because of the large number of such small organizations, and the fact that they often struggle with funding and governance issues, many of these organizations may have become defunct during this period.

Transitional relief. The IRS has provided transitional relief permitting retroactive reinstatement of the tax-exempt status of a small exempt organization that has had it exemption automatically revoked for failing to file Form 990-N. To regain exempt status after it is revoked for this reason, Notice 2011-44 makes clear that the organization is required by Code Sec. 6033(j)(2) to apply for reinstatement – even if the organization was not originally required to apply for exemption.

Application requirements. An organization wishing to have its exempt status reinstated must apply using whichever standard application form any other applicant would use to apply for tax-exempt status:

■ Form 1023 for organizations applying for exempt status under Code Sec. 501(c)(3); or

■ Form 1024 for organizations applying for exempt status under other subsections.

An organization seeking to have its exempt status reinstated *retroactively* must also show reasonable cause for its consecutive filing failures. This is accomplished by submitting with its application a written request for retroactive instatement. However, there are two different sets of requirements for submitting a retroactive reinstatement request, depending on the status of the organization at the time it makes such a request. The IRS recognizes that, although some small exempt organizations may have become defunct over the years in question, others will have been more successful and no longer qualify for small organization status by the time the organization submits its reinstatement request.

As described in Notice 2011-43, a small organization requesting retroactive reinstatement must attach a statement establishing it had reasonable cause for failing to file Form 990-N because it met the following three criteria:

- The organization was not required to file an annual return (Form 990 or Form 990-EZ) for tax years beginning prior to 2007;
- The organization was eligible in each of its tax years beginning in 2007, 2008, and 2009 to file Form 990-N; and
- On or before December 31, 2012, the organization submits to the IRS a properly completed and executed application for reinstatement of its exempt status.

The organization needs to print "Notice 2011-43" on the top of the application form (Form 1023 or Form 1024) it submits.

As described in Notice 2011-44, an organization that formerly was a small exempt organization and is requesting retroactive reinstatement of its exempt status must also attach certain statements to its application. The request must include:

- A written statement with facts supporting its claim of reasonable cause for failing to file required returns or notices for three consecutive years;
- A written statement describing the safeguards the organization has implemented to ensure that there will be no future failures to file required returns;
- Evidence to substantiate all material aspects of the above statements;
- Properly completed and executed Forms 990-EZ for all years during and after the three-year period that the organization was eligible to file Form 990-N but failed to file either that form or an annual return; and
- An original declaration, dated and signed under penalties of perjury by an officer, director, trustee, or other official who is authorized to sign for the organization.

The organization needs to print "Automatically Revoked" both on the top of the application form and on the envelope in which the application is sent.

Also, a formerly small organization applying for retroactive reinstatement of exempt status must submit such application and supporting statements within 15 months of the later of the date of the revocation letter or the posting of the organization's name on the IRS's revocation list.

COMPLIANCE POINTER

The original declaration described above should read as follows:

I, _____(name), _____(title) declare, under penalties of perjury, that I am authorized to sign this request for retroactive reinstatement on behalf of [name of organization], and I further declare that I have examined this request for retroactive reinstatement, including the written explanation of all the facts and information pertaining to the claim for reasonable cause and the evidence to substantiate the claim for reasonable cause, and to the best of my knowledge and belief, this request is true, correct, and complete.

EXAMPLE

A group of members from a local church congregation decided to establish a charitable shop in which low income members of their community could obtain good quality, used dress clothing for the purpose of helping such individuals present themselves better at job interviews, thereby helping them land better jobs and assisting them at working their way out of poverty. The shop was operated by volunteers who did not have experience operating a business, and because they paid no salaries and took in only enough money to cover the shop's overhead expenses, they did not believe they needed to do any kind of filing with the IRS beyond an initial filing of Form 1023. However, after three years the organization received a letter from the IRS stating that they were losing their exempt status.

To apply for retroactive reinstatement, the organization must refile a Form 1023 with "Notice 2011-43" written across the top. Together with Form 1023, the organization must file a Form 990-N for each of the three years it failed to file, a written statement with facts supporting its claim of reasonable cause for failing to file for three consecutive years, a written statement describing what steps the organization has taken to ensure that the required returns will be timely filed in the future, all available evidence in support of these two written statements, and an original declaration (as described in the Compliance Tip, above) dated and signed under penalty of perjury by an official authorized to sign for the organization.

The IRS has also provided a reduced fee for applications for retroactive reinstatement, applicable to small organizations that normally have annual gross receipts of not more than $50,000 in their most recently completed tax year and are otherwise eligible for the transitional relief described in Notice 2011-43. Thus, this reduced fee only applies to small organizations that lost their tax-exempt status for failing to file e-postcards for tax years beginning in 2007, 2008, and 2009, and continue to meet the financial limitations to be considered a small organization. The reduced fee is $100 and is effective for applications postmarked no later than December 31, 2012 (see Rev. Proc. 2011-36).

STUDY QUESTIONS

14. What is the major consequence for small exempt organizations that fail to file an e-postcard for three consecutive tax years?
    a. The Code Sec. 6652(c)(1)(E) monetary penalty is imposed
    b. The organization's tax-exempt status is revoked
    c. The IRS required an audit of the organizations' financial statements for each of the three years

15. For retroactive reinstatement of a small organization's exempt status, the entity must complete and execute an application for reinstatement to the IRS on or before:
    a. December 31, 2011
    b. April 15, 2012
    c. December 31, 2012

CONCLUSION

The IRS is responsible for ensuring that organizations are not abusing the tax exemptions, but it is also responsible for providing exempt organizations with clear guidance and details regarding the specific compliance requirements each of the many varieties of exempt organization must follow. Legislative changes to the tax code provisions keep the IRS busy on one hand, whereas ever-inventive individuals and organizations challenge the IRS oversight abilities on the other hand. Constant attention to change is essential for any practitioner in the exempt organizations area.

CPE NOTE: When you have completed your study and review of chapters 7–8, which comprise Module 3, you may wish to take the Quizzer for this Module.

For your convenience, you can also take this Quizzer online at **www.CCHGroup.com/TestingCenter**.

Answers to Study Questions

MODULE 1 — CHAPTER 1

1. a. *Incorrect.* The exemption from the AMT is set to decrease after 2011.
b. *Correct.* The limitation on itemized deductions reverts after 2012, not 2011.
c. *Incorrect.* The exclusion for unemployment payments expired in 2010.

2. a. *Correct.* The exemption increased for 2010 to $47,450 for individuals and $72,450 for joint filers and surviving spouses. For 2011 the exemptions are $48,450 and $74,450, respectively. In 2012 the exemption drops to $33,750 and $45,000 unless Congress "repatches" the AMT.
b. *Incorrect.* In 2012 the exemption is due to drop to $33,750 for unmarried taxpayers and $45,000 for joint filers.
c. *Incorrect.* The exemption is not the same for 2010 and 2011 returns, and it is lowered for 2012 unless Congress acts to "repatch" the AMT.

3. a. *Incorrect.* The adoption credit is not set to increase for 2012.
b. *Correct.* In 2012 the inflation-adjusted credit is set to decrease by $520 ($13,170 – $12,650).
c. *Incorrect.* The adoption credit is set to change in 2012 but is not being eliminated.

4. a. *Correct.* Although receipts and substantiation of values of noncash donations are required, the 2010 Tax Relief Act did not eliminate all deductions for these contributions.
b. *Incorrect.* The 2010 Tax Relief Act extended these provisions through 2011.
c. *Incorrect.* Tax-free distributions to charity from IRAs of up to $100,000 per taxpayer will expire after 2011.

5. True. *Correct.* These dates apply to 100 percent bonus depreciation; different rules for property acquisition apply to the 50 percent depreciation.
False. *Incorrect.* Unlike the 100 percent bonus depreciation that considers the date accrual-basis taxpayers incur the cost of property, the 50 percent rate considers when they take physical possession of the property.

6. a. *Incorrect.* Such a decrease is not in the provisions of the 2010 Tax Relief Act.

b. *Correct.* A Section 179 deduction for qualified real property may not be carried forward to tax years beginning after 2011.

c. *Incorrect.* Section 1250 expensing differs from rules applied to Section 1245 property.

7. a. *Incorrect.* The deduction applies to computer equipment and software donated to all levels of educational institutions.

b. *Correct.* The deductibility issues of contributions to Code Sec. 527 groups were not changed by the 2010 Tax Relief Act.

c. *Incorrect.* Businesses may claim the enhanced deduction for food donations through the end of 2011.

8. True. *Correct.* Through 2011, RICs are treated as qualified investment entities under FIRPTA.

False. *Incorrect.* The 2010 Tax Relief Act extended the inclusion of RICs in the definition under Code Sec. 897.

9. a. *Incorrect.* The AGI threshold is higher to reduce or even eliminate the personal exemption starting in 2013 when the EGTRRA sunset occurs.

b. *Correct.* The exemption amount will be reduced by 2 percent for each $2,500, or fraction thereof, by which the AGI exceeds the $122,500 threshold amount.

c. *Incorrect.* A lower AGI threshold applies to the personal exemption phaseout scheduled to begin in 2013.

10. a. *Incorrect.* Although a zero percent GST rate applied in 2010 transfers, the rate for 2011 and 2012 is set to exceed 28 percent.

b. *Correct.* After a zero percent rate applying in 2010, the GST rate is set to become 35 percent for transfers in 2011 and 2012.

c. *Incorrect.* The 2010 Tax Relief Act set lower rates for 2011 and 2012, although a zero percent rate applied in 2010.

MODULE 1 — CHAPTER 2

1. a. *Correct.* The continuity of current coverage applies to grandfathered plans, which were in existence on March 23, 2010.

b. *Incorrect.* Starting in 2010, children ineligible for employer-sponsored coverage can be covered up to age 26 under their parents' family coverage, even if the children are not dependents.

c. *Incorrect.* Grandfathered plans are not covered by the discrimination provisions under PPACAA.

2. a. *Incorrect.* SIMPLE cafeteria plans do not have to include employees having less than one year of service with the employer.
b. *Correct.* The plan must cover employees having more than one year of service with the employer, are not nonresident aliens, and have worked with the employer for at least 1,000 hours during the previous year.
c. *Incorrect.* Nonresident aliens do not have to be covered by the SIMPLE cafeteria plan.

3. a. *Incorrect.* Such coverage may continue without penalty, especially for grandfathered plans.
b. *Correct.* Such plans include employee-only coverage costing at least $10,200 and family coverage of at least $27,500.
c. *Incorrect.* Under PPACA, applicable large employers, not insurers, are required to report the value of employer-provided health insurance to their employees.

4. a. *Incorrect.* The Due Process Clause is not central to the individual mandate issue, being applied more often to nexus considerations.
b. *Correct.* The suits allege that the mandate exceeds Congress' power to regulate commerce.
c. *Incorrect.* The individual mandate generally is not considered a First Amendment freedom issue.

5. True. *Correct.* The health care reform package imposes the 3.8 percent unearned income Medicare contributions tax on passive activity income, which will make it less attractive for taxpayers.
False. *Incorrect.* Gains and income from a passive activity, as well as interest, dividends, rents, and royalties, will be subject to the unearned income Medicare contributions tax beginning in 2013.

6. a. *Incorrect.* The new small employer tax credit was not added to the existing work opportunity credit.
b. *Correct.* The new small employer tax credit was added to the general business credit.
c. *Incorrect.* The new small employer tax credit was not made part of the empowerment zone and renewal community employment credit.

7. a. *Correct.* Also considered minimum essential coverage are government-sponsored programs and eligible individual market plans.
b. *Incorrect.* Disability insurance is considered an excepted benefit, not minimum essential coverage.
c. *Incorrect.* Long-term care, nursing home coverage, and home health care are all considered excepted benefits, not included in minimum essential coverage.

8. a. *Correct.* **The exchanges must offer qualified plans of essential health benefits by 2014.**
b. *Incorrect.* The deadline for establishing state exchanges is a different year.
c. *Incorrect.* The implementation date for exchanges to offer essential health benefits packages is a later year.

9. True. *Correct.* **The credit reduces the benefit of employer-sponsored health benefits as well.**
False. *Incorrect.* The credit offers a strong incentive for employers to offer affordable group plans.

10. a. *Correct.* **Because the Treasury Department pays the advance amount, the taxpayer can repay the excess to the department on his or her federal tax return.**
b. *Incorrect.* There is no planned carryover.
c. *Incorrect.* The taxpayer is not required to file an amended tax return to submit the excess received.

MODULE 1 — CHAPTER 3

1. a. *Incorrect.* Depreciable computer software purchased at a brick and mortar store is off-the-shelf computer software and qualifies for bonus depreciation.
b. *Correct.* **A listed property that is used 50 percent or less for business in the year that it is placed in service must be depreciated using the MACRS alternative depreciation system (ADS). Bonus depreciation does not apply to mandatory ADS property. A pick-up truck is a listed property ("property used for transportation") even if it is not subject to the luxury car depreciation caps because it has a gross vehicle weight rating in excess of 6,000 pounds.**
c. *Incorrect.* Bonus depreciation applies to MACRS recovery property with a recovery period of 20 years or fewer.

2. a. *Correct.* **The cost of an asset is reduced by any amount expensed under Code Sec. 179 and then multiplied by the applicable bonus rate.**
b. *Incorrect.* The basis reduction for an energy grant is 50 percent. This is the same reduction that applies if the energy credit was taken.
c. *Incorrect.* Bonus depreciation is computed before the regular first-year depreciation deduction. The regular first-year deduction does not affect the amount of the bonus deduction.

3. a. *Correct.* **Property acquired after September 8, 2010, and placed in service before January 1, 2012, qualifies for the 100 percent bonus rate. Property placed in service in 2012 qualifies for a 50 percent rate.**

b. Incorrect. The 100 percent rate also applies to property placed in service after September 8, 2010.

c. Incorrect. Property acquired before September 9, 2010, does not qualify for bonus depreciation at the 100 percent rate.

4. a. Incorrect. The placed-in-service date and the acquisition date are not necessarily the same date.

b. Incorrect. Property is deemed acquired by a cash-basis taxpayer when the property is paid for.

c. Correct. Solely for purposes of the 100 percent rate, property is acquired when paid for by a cash-basis taxpayer or incurred by an accrual-basis taxpayer. The general rules for determining the year of a tax deduction as set forth in Code Sec. 461 and its regulations apply for this purpose. Generally, for purposes of the 50 percent rate, property is acquired when physical possession is taken.

5. a. Incorrect. Property that is not long production property must be placed in service before January 1, 2012, in order to qualify for the 100 percent rate.

b. Correct. The extended-placed-in service deadline for longer production property to qualify for the 100 percent rate is January 1, 2013.

c. Incorrect. January 1, 2014, is the extended placed-in-service deadline that applies to longer production property for purposes of the 50 percent bonus rate.

6. True. Incorrect. Unless a technical correction reverses the qualification, 2012 progress expenditures on longer production property may claim the 100 percent rate if the property is placed in service before January 1, 2013.

False. Correct. 2012 progress expenditures on longer production property qualify for the 100 percent rate if placed in service before January 1, 2013, unless a technical correction to the contrary is enacted.

7. a. Incorrect. If a binding written contract for the acquisition of longer production property is entered into after 2007 and before 2013, the acquisition date requirement for the 50 percent rate is deemed satisfied.

b. Incorrect. The written binding contract must be entered into before January 1, 2012, in order for the 100 percent acquisition date requirement to be considered satisfied.

c. Correct. Even if a property with a longer production period is not actually acquired before the January 1, 2012, acquisition date deadline for the 100 percent rate, the deadline will be treated as satisfied if a binding written contract for the acquisition was entered into after September 8, 2010, and before January 1, 2012.

8. a. Incorrect. A self-constructed asset is not considered acquired for bonus depreciation purposes when it is placed in service. However, if the asset qualifies for bonus depreciation, the bonus deduction is claimed in the tax year that it is placed in service.

b. Correct. A self-constructed asset is considered acquired when construction begins. Construction begins when a safe harbor test is satisfied (if elected) or work of a significant physical nature begins.

c. Incorrect. The date that construction of an asset ends is not of consequence in determining the acquisition date for bonus depreciation purposes. Generally, construction of an asset will be finished in the same tax year that it is placed in service. The bonus allowance is claimed in the tax year that a qualifying asset is placed in service.

9. a. Incorrect. The safe harbor is satisfied by paying or incurring a specified amount of construction costs, excluding certain types of preliminary costs, but 5 percent is the incorrect threshold.

b. Correct. When a taxpayer self-constructs a property and elects the safe harbor, an asset is considered acquired on the date that more than 10 percent of the construction costs are paid (cash-basis taxpayer) or incurred (accrual-basis taxpayer), without regard to certain preliminary costs.

c. Incorrect. A self-constructed asset is deemed acquired on the date that work of a significant physical nature begins if the safe-harbor method is not elected.

10. a. Incorrect. The 100 percent rate cannot apply to components of self-constructed property that is not placed in service in 2011 (2012 if the self-constructed property is longer production property) even if the components separately meet the 100 percent rate acquisition date and placed-in-service date requirements. Assuming the self-constructed property is placed in service in 2012 (2013 for longer production property) the self-constructed property and its components can only qualify for a 50 percent bonus rate.

b. Correct. If the only reason that a self-constructed property does not qualify for the 100 percent bonus rate is that construction began before September 9, 2010, a component of the self-constructed property will qualify for the 100 percent rate if the component was acquired after September 8, 2010, or construction of the component began after September 8, 2010, provided that the self-constructed property is placed in service before January 1, 2012 (before January 1, 2013, if the self-constructed property is property with a longer production period).

c. Incorrect. If a taxpayer begins construction on a property before 2008, neither the property nor any of its components can qualify for bonus depreciation.

11. a. *Incorrect.* Bonus depreciation is allowed in full for alternative minimum tax purposes.
b. *Incorrect.* The IRS has clarified that bonus depreciation may be claimed on a retail improvement property or restaurant property that is also a qualified leasehold improvement property.
c. *Correct.* The basis of property is not reduced by the amount of bonus depreciation claimed, whether at the 50 percent or 100 percent rate, when determining whether more than 40 percent of the basis of depreciable property placed was placed in service in the last quarter of the tax year. This treatment is in contrast to the Section 179 deduction, which does reduce basis for this purpose.

12. True. *Incorrect.* The election is only available for the 2010 tax year if the taxpayer uses the calendar year.
False. *Correct.* The election to claim a 50 percent rate in lieu of a 100 percent rate only applies to a tax year that includes September 8, 2010. Thus, a calendar tax year taxpayer may only make the election for the 2010 tax year.

13. a. *Incorrect.* A taxpayer cannot elect the safe harbor by filing an amended 2010 return. The correct amount of safe-harbor depreciation has already been claimed in the year that the vehicle was placed in service even though the safe harbor was not issued until many 2010 returns were filed.
b. *Correct.* A taxpayer elects the safe-harbor method by computing depreciation on the vehicle in the second tax year of its recovery period as if a 50 percent rate applied in the year that it was placed in service.
c. *Incorrect.* A taxpayer who elects the safe-harbor method may claim depreciation in amount that would be allowed as if a 50 percent bonus rate originally applied to the vehicle.

14. a. *Correct.* The election to expense qualified real property applies to tax years beginning in 2010 and 2011. No election can be made for a tax year beginning in 2012.
b. *Incorrect.* The portion of a Section 179 carryforward attributable to an election to expense qualified real property may not be carried forward to a tax year beginning in 2012 or thereafter.
c. *Incorrect.* The maximum amount of qualified real property that may be expensed is limited to $250,000. Any amount expensed reduces the $500,000 annual limit.

15. a. *Incorrect.* Bonus depreciation and the Section 179 allowance may be claimed in full for AMT purposes. No AMT is required.

b. *Correct.* **The bonus allowance and Section 179 allowance are both treated as depreciation deductions for depreciation recapture purposes. In the case of Section 1245 property, the entire amount is subject to recapture to the extent of gain. In the case of Section 1250, the Section 179 or bonus deduction in excess of straight-line depreciation that could have been claimed through the year of disposition is subject to ordinary income recapture.**

c. *Incorrect.* Bonus depreciation does not apply to used property on account of the original use requirement. The Section 179 deduction may be claimed on used or new property.

MODULE 2 — CHAPTER 4

1. a. *Correct.* **Health care coverage costs are for the employees' information. Information on the W-2 is also filed with the Social Security Administration.**

b. *Incorrect.* Workers' compensation and similar types of coverage described in Code Sec 9832(c)(1) are excluded from W-2 reporting.

c. *Incorrect.* Because coverage to pay for a specified disease or illness has not deduction under Code Sec. 162(1), and it is thus not included on the Form W-2.

2. a. *Incorrect.* The *de minimis* exception for third-party settlement organization has higher dollar and frequency thresholds.

b. *Incorrect.* Third-party settlement organizations have different monetary and volume thresholds for filing returns of network transactions.

c. *Correct.* **The *de minimis* exception excludes reporting requirements if the third-party settlement organization's aggregate payments to that payee do not exceed $20,000 or the number of transactions is less than 200.**

3. a. *Incorrect.* The credit card organization, such as MasterCard or Visa, merely directs the transfer of funds through the issuing bank to debit the issuing bank and credit funds to the merchant or service provider's bank.

b. *Correct.* **Code Sec. 6050W information reporting requirements reflect that the merchant acquiring bank is best suited to file the information return to the provider.**

c. *Incorrect.* The card issuing bank receives transfer instructions from the credit card organization to debit funds on the issuing bank's account at another bank. The issuing bank is not involved in then settling the transaction.

4. True. *Correct.* **The foreign address exclusion enables the payment settlement agency not to file an information return if the payee has given the agency documentation substantiating it as a foreign person.**

False. *Incorrect.* The payment settlement agency may rely on previously supplied documentation that the participating payee is not a U.S. person.

5. True. *Correct.* **The amended Code Sec. 3406 requires reportable amounts paid to participating payees to have backup withholding beginning on January 1, 2012.**
False. *Incorrect.* The *Housing and Economic Recovery Act of 2008* amended Code Sec. 3406 to include this rule for backup withholding because payment settlement agencies are better situated to manage the withholding.

6. a. *Correct.* **New Code Sec. 6045A and 6045B stipulate that such information be included on broker returns.**
b. *Incorrect.* Certain exempt foreign persons are also exempted from the reporting requirements.
c. *Incorrect.* Such information about the securities is extraneous to the information brokers and their clients use in determining gains and losses.

7. a. *Correct.* **The adjusted basis in the hands of the donor is simpler to determine for gifts of securities, whereas unless the broker can ascertain the fair market value of the securities at the decedent's death, the broker must treat the securities as uncovered.**
b. *Incorrect.* The donor's adjusted, not original, value is used for gifts of securities, and the value on the date of receipt of the securities by the recipient is not used in the calculation.
c. *Incorrect.* Except for RIC and DRP stock, the broker uses the same reporting method for either type of securities transfer—usually FIFO, unless the customer applies for lot relief.

8. a. *Incorrect.* U.S. residents are required to file an FBAR.
b. *Incorrect.* If the value of foreign accounts exceeds $10,000 on June 30 of each calendar year, citizens, corporations, LLCs, and U.S. trusts must file Form TD F 90-22.1.
c. *Correct.* **If the foreign account is valued at less than $10,000 or was created under foreign law, the FBAR form is not required.**

9. True. *Incorrect.* With few exceptions, employees having signature authority but no underlying financial interest in their employers' foreign financial accounts are not exempt from the reporting requirements.
False. *Correct.* **FinCEN declined to exempt such employees from FBAR's reporting requirement.**

10. a. Incorrect. The FATCA withholding and reporting requirements take effect after the end of 2011.

b. Correct. FATCA withholding and reporting rules will apply to payments made after December 31, 2012, with preliminary guidance from the IRS provided in Notice 2010-60.

c. Incorrect. The effective date of the new requirements is earlier than 2014. The IRST has issued interim guidance for the rules in Notice 2010-60.

MODULE 2 — CHAPTER 5

1. a. Incorrect. The IRS stated that the number of taxpayers who prepared their own returns did not decline.

b. Incorrect. During that span of years, the IRS stated that the number of taxpayers preparing their own returns without outside assistance changed considerably.

c. Correct. The number of taxpayers preparing their own returns during that period fell by more than two-thirds, and for the 2008 tax year, paid tax return preparers completed more than 87 million federal returns.

2. a. Incorrect. Responses totaling 98 percent favored instituting ethics standards for paid return preparers.

b. Correct. Expanding peer reviews to all preparers (CPA members of the AICPA currently participate in peer reviews) is not a provision of Notice 2009-60.

c. Incorrect. Minimum testing requirements for paid return preparers were recommended by 90 percent of those responding to the notice.

3. a. Incorrect. Mandatory testing of paid preparers applies only to those who are not CPAs, EAs, attorneys, or otherwise exempt from testing. Testing is expected to begin in late 2011.

b. Correct. Paid preparers were required to obtain and use Preparer Tax Identification Numbers (PTINs) at the beginning of 2011 unless they had religious objections to obtaining Social Security numbers or were foreign preparers or otherwise exempt.

c. Incorrect. Mandatory continuing education is expected to begin in 2012 for paid preparers who are not CPAs, EAs, attorneys, or otherwise exempt from continuing education (whereas their professional associations and state statutes may have separate continuing education requirements).

4. a. Incorrect. Seniority is not the determinant of which preparer lists his or her PTIN on the return.

b. Correct. The only PTIN listed is that of the signing return preparer, the rules for that individual are unaffected by the PTIN requirement.

c. Incorrect. Only one PTIN is given for the return, regardless of how many preparers were involved in completing the return.

5. a. Incorrect. The ERPA practitioner designation, specializing in plan compliance and Form 5500 filings, was not created by the final Circular 230 regulations of June 2011.
b. Correct. The June 2011 final regulations created the designation registered tax return preparer as well as extending Circular 230 provisions to all return preparers.
c. Incorrect. The enrolled agent (EA) designation was not created in the June 2011 final regulations for Circular 230.

6. True. Incorrect. The CPA designation is conferred only on persons duly licensed to practice as a certified public accountant in the United States (by successfully completing the CPA examination by the jurisdiction of the practice).
False. Correct. Issuance of a license to practice accountancy issued in, or by, a non-U.S. jurisdiction confers no certification to claim the CPA designation in the United States.

7. a. Incorrect. Business return preparers are not the top priority in implementing the competency testing of preparers.
b. Correct. The designation will initially limit administration of the competency examination to those preparing individual tax returns.
c. Incorrect. The target of initial competency testing is those preparing certain types of returns, not the status of the preparer.

8. a. Correct. The final Circular 230 regulations delete the limited practice exception as it relates to unenrolled preparers. The IRS removed the limited practice authorization for unenrolled preparers; they will have to become registered tax return preparers or seek another recognized designation.
b. Incorrect. Because unenrolled preparers will need to become registered tax return preparers or seek another designation, the IRS did not permanently retain the limited practice exception in the final Circular 230 regulations.
c. Incorrect. The final Circular 230 regulations do not extend the limited practice exception for one year.

9. a. Incorrect. According to the IRS, the focus of the compliance check under Circular 230 will be whether the preparer has filed all required returns.
b. Incorrect. The compliance check will examine whether the individual paid or arranged to have paid any federal tax debts.

c. Correct. The suitability check, not the compliance check, will inquire about any conduct that would justify suspension or disbarment of the registered tax preparer.

10. a. Incorrect. The registered tax return preparer will be issued a registration certificate or card by the IRS to show he or she has obtained the designation.
b. Correct. Individuals designated as registered tax return preparers do not need to have their work supervised by CPA, EAs or attorneys. However, registered tax return preparers will have to successfully complete a competency exam and continuing education requirements.
c. Incorrect. Registered tax return preparers, like other preparers, must have a current and valid PTIN to practice before the IRS.

11. a. Correct. Individuals who are certified return preparers under state law, who are not CPAs, EAs, or attorneys, and who prepare certain federal returns for compensation must complete IRS competency testing and continuing education requirements. All unenrolled preparers, including state-certified preparers, who are not CPAs, EAs, or attorneys, must obtain the designation registered tax return preparer or another designation.
b. Incorrect. Certification under state law, without any further credentials, is insufficient under current IRS rules to ensure a competency level that would eliminate testing or continuing education.
c. Incorrect. The IRS has not "grandfathered" any unenrolled preparers, including preparers who are state-certified, from competency testing and continuing education.

12. True. Correct. The LPAs in states that do not equate their status equal to that of CPAs will be required to successfully complete the competency test under Circular 230.
False. Incorrect. In states that grant LPAs the same rights and privileges as CPAs, the LPAs will not be required to pass the competency test to become registered tax return preparers. In those states that do not confer equal treatment of CPAs and LPAs, the LPAs will be required to become registered tax return preparers or obtain other credentials under Circular 230.

13. a. Correct. Covered returns are required to be e-filed by paid preparers, with certain exceptions.
b. Incorrect. These forms were exceptions to the electronic filing requirements that became effective January 1, 2011.
c. Incorrect. Form 8508, *Request for Waiver From Filing Information Returns Electronically*, is not required to be e-filed.

14. a. *Correct.* **If a firm files 100 returns or more in 2011, and expects to file at least 11 returns in 2012 and subsequent years, e-filing is required.**
b. *Incorrect.* The e-filing thresholds were different for the electronic filing mandate under the 2009 Worker Act.
c. *Incorrect.* Lower thresholds apply for 2011 and 2012 returns in the attempt to encourage firms and individuals to e-file federal returns.

15. True. *Incorrect.* As long as the preparer attaches Form 8948, *Preparer Explanation for Not Filing Electronically,* to the client's paper return, the client may mail his or her return on paper.
False. *Correct.* **In 2012 a client of a specified tax return preparer may request independently to file a paper return using the mail, and the preparer must attach Form 8948, *Preparer Explanation for Not Filing Electronically,* to the client's return.**

MODULE 2 — CHAPTER 6

1. a. *Incorrect.* The IRS requires Authorized e-file Providers to ensure the security of taxpayer information, but the IRS does not provide the specific requirement for establishing a comprehensive information security program.
b. *Correct.* **The Federal Trade Commission's Safeguard Rule requires companies that collect personal information from their customers to develop a security program. The rules were implemented in response to the *Gramm-Leach Bliley Act* (P.L. 106-102) .**
c. *Incorrect.* Reporting agents are Authorized e-file Providers that typically act as agents for electronic employments tax filings and deposits.

2. True. *Correct.* **The penalties apply to all categories of Authorized e-file Providers, and the definition includes persons providing auxiliary services as well.**
False. *Incorrect.* All categories of Authorized e-file Providers are subject to civil and criminal penalties, and the definition of *tax return preparer* applies to auxiliary service providers who make unauthorized disclosures of tax return information

3. a. *Incorrect.* Taxpayers use the Self-Select method when they prepare their own returns and select their own PINs.
b. *Correct.* **The taxpayer authorizes the preparer to enter or generate a PIN on the individual's behalf.**
c. *Incorrect.* Under the Form 8453 signature method, business, not individual, taxpayers have their returns signed by an authorized tax return signer of their entity type.

4. a. *Correct*. Form 8453 is used by the authorized signer for the entity, giving it the same legal effect as if the taxpayer had physically signed the form.
b. *Incorrect*. A corporate officer uses Form 8879-C when the corporate return is filed using an ERO and the corporate officer signs the return with a PIN.
c. *Incorrect*. Modernized e-File is an electronic filing system intended to replace the current IRS e-file system in October 2012.

5. a. *Correct*. The ISP processes the tax information and either forwards the information to a Transmitter or returns the information back to the taxpayer for online filing.
b. *Incorrect*. The Software Developer creates the tax software but does not accept completed electronic return information.
c. *Incorrect*. The Reporting Agent manages e-filing of employment tax returns and federal tax deposits, but it does not manage individual returns.

6. a. *Incorrect*. The IRS has instructed nonresident aliens who file using Form 1040-NR not to use e-filing.
b. *Correct*. Taxpayers having adjusted gross incomes that qualify for use of the Free File program may use brand name tax preparation software to e-file their returns for free through the IRS website.
c. *Incorrect*. Fiscal year individual taxpayers may not use e-filing.

7. True. *Incorrect*. If it can be proven that the failure to e-file was due to reasonable cause (such as economic hardship), no penalty is imposed.
False. *Correct*. The penalties for failure to comply with the mandatory e-filing requirement may be avoided if it is established that the failure was due to reasonable cause and not willful neglect.

8. a. *Correct*. The preparer may obtain an administrative exemption if his or her religious organization is conscientiously opposed to use of electronic technology.
b. *Incorrect*. Lack of a computer or preparation software is not an undue hardship that would afford the preparer an administrative exemption from e-filing.
c. *Incorrect*. Merely preferring not to use a computer and software to develop returns is not sufficient grounds for an administrative exemption from e-filing.

9. a. *Incorrect*. E-filing by exempt organizations is expected to reach 27 percent of returns in 2011, which is the lowest rate among the entity types shown.

b. *Incorrect.* For 2011, partnerships are expected to have a 37 percent e-file rate, which is not the highest among the entity types shown.

c. *Correct.* The corporate e-file rate is projected to reach 38 percent of returns for 2011, up from 34 percent for the 2010 tax year.

10. a. *Correct.* A concern among critics of return-free filing systems and prepopulated electronic forms is that taxpayers might become passive in entering data on returns.

b. *Incorrect.* California and the United Kingdom currently employ similar systems.

c. *Incorrect.* Congress is under pressure to use prepopulated returns as part of an overall solution to the complexity of the U.S. tax code.

MODULE 3 — CHAPTER 7

1. a. *Incorrect.* Bankruptcy does not affect the three-year limitation on the IRS assessment period.

b. *Correct.* There is no statute of limitations if the taxpayer does not file a return or files a fraudulent return.

c. *Incorrect.* The normal limitations apply when the omission is 25 percent or less of the income listed. The period lengthens to six years if the omission is greater than 25 percent.

2. a. *Correct.* The IRS's efforts to collect unpaid liabilities usually begin with the automated collection system. The automated collection system can become involved at an earlier step in the collection process. The ACS may also take enforced collection actions and make collectability determinations.

b. *Incorrect.* Amounts not collected by the ACS are referred to field revenue officers who apply numerous collection tools and powers.

c. *Incorrect.* Although the Tax Court has the authority to review certain IRS collection decisions, the Tax Court does not itself collect tax liabilities.

3. a. *Correct.* The release completely extinguishes the lien.

b. *Incorrect.* The subordination does not eliminate the entire lien.

c. *Incorrect.* The tax lien continues to attach to property that has not been discharged from the lien.

4. a. *Correct.* Also restricted from levy is the taxpayer's nonrental property used by another person as a residence if the levy is for $5,000 or less. A judge's approval is required for a principal residence.

b. *Incorrect.* The cap for the levy restriction is $8,370 for 2011.

c. *Incorrect.* The restriction allows only $4,120 in trade, business, or professional books and tools in 2011 for exclusion from levy.

5. a. Correct. Such expenses encompass expenses providing for the health, welfare, and/or production of income for the taxpayer and family.
b. Incorrect. Asset equity is part of the reasonable collection potential (RCP) calculation of the offer amount.
c. Incorrect. Such assets are included in the reasonable collection potential (RCP) calculation that sets the offer amount.

6. a. Incorrect. Low-income taxpayers are not required to pay the user fee.
b. Incorrect. Offers that question the taxpayer's liability are not subject to the user fee.
c. Correct. Such offers must include the user fee and required partial payments with the Form 656.

7. a. Incorrect. Installment agreements do not eliminate the failure to pay penalties, but this type of agreement may reduce the rate of the penalty's accrual.
b. Correct. This type of agreement may be appropriate when a taxpayer has some ability to pay, but cannot pay the full amount owed within the remaining collection period.
c. Incorrect. The IRS may, but is not required to, withdraw the notice of lien when an installment agreement is in effect.

8. True. Incorrect. Both individual and business taxpayers may obtain an extension of time to pay their tax liabilities in full.
False. Correct. Individual and business taxpayers may be granted a 120-day maximum extension, but just 60 days if the account is already being handled by the ACS.

9. a. Incorrect. An IRS Appeals Office decision following an equivalent hearing is final and cannot be appealed to the Tax Court.
b. Correct. A taxpayer may seek judicial review of an adverse CDP determination in the Tax Court.
c. Incorrect. An IRS Appeals Office decision following a CAP conference is final, can cannot be appealed to the Tax Court.

10. True. Incorrect. The request for a CAP appeal is not required to be submitted prior to the conference with the collection manager. Only if the taxpayer is unable to reach a resolution with the collection manager should the request for a CAP appeal be made, by submitting Form 9423 within two days after the manager conference .
False. Correct. The appeal request must submitted within two days following the conference with the collection manager.

MODULE 3 — CHAPTER 8

1. a. *Incorrect.* The CO-OP program will provide grants and loan available though American Health Benefit Exchanges.
b. *Correct.* **The *Patient Protection and Affordable Care Act* and *Health Care and Education Reconciliation Act* are the two acts enacted as the health care reform legislation that mandated formation of the CO-OP program, but the laws did not create the state programs.**
c. *Incorrect.* SHOP Exchanges are nonprofits through which the CO-OP program will offers qualified health plans.

2. a. *Incorrect.* States will be allowed to have more than one reinsurance entity to collect and make payments to health insurance issuers for high-risk individuals.
b. *Correct.* **The three-year transition period begins January 1, 2014, during which payments will be managed under state programs for high-risk individuals.**
c. *Incorrect.* Reinsurance entities may carry out multistate programs.

3. True. *Correct.* **Business leagues are not limited to formation by businesspeople and tradespeople, and even professionals such as physicians and staff of nonprofit organizations may form tax-exempt business leagues.**
False. *Incorrect.* Profitability is not the determinant of what type of occupation may form a business league. Cooperatives, nonprofits, and professional organizations may form business leagues.

4. a. *Incorrect.* Bluetooth technology exists in multiple types of electronic equipment.
b. *Correct.* **Manufacturers could not employ the Bluetooth technology without becoming members of the association, so the differentiation between the two was meaningless.**
c. *Incorrect.* Having a brick-and-mortar facility is not a prerequisite for forming a business league.

5. a. *Incorrect.* Knowledge of public health issues is a quality required for the community health needs assessment that charitable hospitals must conduct but is not the name of the standard to qualify hospitals as tax-exempt entities.
b. *Correct.* **Rev. Rul. 69-545 outlined ways a charitable hospital can demonstrate its community benefit, such as having an emergency department available regardless of patients' ability to pay and providing charity care.**

c. Incorrect. Although there is no patient protection standard to measure a hospital's charitable intent, the *Patient Protection and Affordable Care Act of 2010* added new requirements hospitals must meet to qualify as tax-exempt Code Sec. 501(c))(3) facilities.

6. a. Correct. Such collection practices are prohibited as one of the four requirements established by the *Patient Protection and Affordable Care Act of 2010* for Code Sec. 501(c)(3) facilities.
b. Incorrect. The *Patient Protection and Affordable Care Act of 2010* classifies practices such as liens, lawsuits, and attachments for nonpayment as prohibited for charitable hospitals, which must describe their approach to nonpayment in a financial assistance policy.
c. Incorrect. The *Patient Protection and Affordable Care Act of 2010* stipulated the types of procedures charitable hospitals could practice when patients fail to pay for services, but the actions are not described as restitution.

7. a. Incorrect. The IRS allowed more time for the assessments and reporting by Code Sec. 501(c)(3) health care facilities so they can plan how to address the new requirements.
b. Incorrect. The new assessment and reporting obligations do not take effect in 2011.
c. Correct. The IRS outlined charitable hospital reporting obligations in Notice 2011-52, which provides this delayed effective date so hospital organizations can plan how to conduct their assessments.

8. True. Incorrect. Under Code Sec. 501(r), each hospital must use input from its own community representatives, complete a separate needs assessment, and prepare and post its report, although facilities may collaborate in developing implementation strategies and a reporting mechanism.
False. Correct. Each hospital must conduct its own community health needs assessment and written reports, as well as post the results in each respective facility, although the facilities could plan their implementation strategies together.

9. a. Incorrect. Credit unions are not bound to offer loans at lower interest rates than do banks, but one of their major purposes is to assist their members with beneficial loan rates.
b. Correct. Revenues of an exempt organization such as a credit union is taxable if they arise from an unrelated business regularly carried on by the organization, which triggers UBIT.
c. Incorrect. Offering beneficial interest rates on savings is one of the reasons credit unions are formed, but they are not required to do so under Code Sec. 501(c)(14).

10. a. *Correct.* Activities conducted by a Code Sec. 501(c)(3) organization or a governmental college or university primarily for the convenience of members are excluded from being classified as unrelated trade or business activities.
b. *Correct.* Sales of group life, health, and cancer insurance have been subject to UBIT.
c. *Incorrect.* A car-buying service was subject to UBIT; it did not benefit the credit union's membership as a whole.

11. a. *Incorrect.* Whether all members could apply for the cards was not the determining factor in avoiding UBIT on the income.
b. *Correct.* No UBIT applied to the net income for interchange fees as well as charges from member usage of ATM machines.
c. *Incorrect.* The credit unions were not required to contract with banks to offer credit or debit cards without paying UBIT.

12. a. *Incorrect.* Private foundations must file Form 990-PF, *Return of Private Foundation or Section 4947(a)(1) Nonexempt Charitable Trust Treated as a Private Foundation*.
b. *Incorrect.* Political organizations must file a version of Form 990.
c. *Correct.* Churches and religion-affiliated organizations are exempt from filing Form 990.

13. a. *Correct.* The IRS raised the filing threshold for small exempt organizations that wish to use Form 990-N (the e-postcard) to $50,000 for tax years beginning in 2010 and thereafter.
b. *Incorrect.* The IRS uses a different maximum annual threshold to qualify as a small exempt organization.
c. *Incorrect.* The ceiling for gross receipts of small exempt organizations wishing to file the e-postcard (Form 990-N) for 2011 is much lower.

14. a. *Incorrect.* No monetary penalty is imposed for failing to file Form 990-N (the e-postcard).
b. *Correct.* For failing to file, the small exempt organization loses its tax-exempt status, which may be regained by following the steps for retroactive reinstatement.
c. *Incorrect.* The IRS does not audit the organization, but for it to be retroactively reinstated as tax exempt, the entity must substantiate all their reasons for failing to file, and demonstrate that the organization submitted annual information returns for years during and after the three-year period.

15. a. *Incorrect.* The deadline for applying for reinstatement of tax-exempt status is not until 2012 for organizations that lost their status in 2010.

b. *Incorrect.* The deadline for applying for retroactive reinstatement using Form 1023 or Form 1024 is a different date.

c. *Correct.* Small organizations may apply for retroactive reinstatement of their tax-exempt status on or before December 31, 2012.

TOP FEDERAL TAX ISSUES FOR 2012 CPE COURSE

Index

TOP FEDERAL TAX ISSUES FOR 2012 CPE COURSE

CPE Quizzer Instructions

The CPE Quizzer is divided into three Modules. There is a processing fee for each Quizzer Module submitted for grading. Successful completion of Module 1 is recommended for **7 CPE Credits.*** Successful completion of Module 2 is recommended for **7 CPE Credits.*** Successful completion of Module 3 is recommended for **5 CPE Credits.*** You can complete and submit one Module at a time or all Modules at once for a total of **19 CPE Credits.***

To obtain CPE credit, return your completed Answer Sheet for each Quizzer Module to **CCH Continuing Education Department, 4025 W. Peterson Ave., Chicago, IL 60646**, or fax it to (773) 866-3084. Each Quizzer Answer Sheet will be graded and a CPE Certificate of Completion awarded for achieving a grade of 70 percent or greater. The Quizzer Answer Sheets are located after the Quizzer questions for this Course.

Express Grading: Processing time for your Answer Sheet is generally 8-12 business days. If you are trying to meet a reporting deadline, our Express Grading Service is available for an additional $19 per Module. To use this service, please check the "Express Grading" box on your Answer Sheet and provide your CCH account or credit card number **and your fax number.** CCH will fax your results and a Certificate of Completion (upon achieving a passing grade) to you by 5:00 p.m. the business day following our receipt of your Answer Sheet. **If you mail your Answer Sheet for Express Grading, please write "ATTN: CPE OVERNIGHT" on the envelope.** NOTE: CCH will not Federal Express Quizzer results under any circumstances.

NEW ONLINE GRADING gives you immediate 24/7 grading with instant results and no Express Grading Fee.

The **CCH Testing Center** website gives you and others in your firm easy, free access to CCH print Courses and allows you to complete your CPE Quizzers online for immediate results. Plus, the **My Courses** feature provides convenient storage for your CPE Course Certificates and completed Quizzers.

Go to **CCHGroup.com/TestingCenter** to complete your Quizzer online.

---

* Recommended CPE credit is based on a 50-minute hour. Participants earning credits for states that require self-study to be based on a 100-minute hour will receive ½ the CPE credits for successful completion of this course. Because CPE requirements vary from state to state and among different licensing agencies, please contact your CPE governing body for information on your CPE requirements and the applicability of a particular course for your requirements.

Date of Completion: The date of completion on your Certificate will be the date that you put on your Answer Sheet. However, you must submit your Answer Sheet to CCH for grading within two weeks of completing it.

Expiration Date: December 31, 2012

Evaluation: To help us provide you with the best possible products, please take a moment to fill out the Course Evaluation located at the back of this Course and return it with your Quizzer Answer Sheets.

CCH is registered with the National Association of State Boards of Accountancy (NASBA) as a sponsor of continuing professional education on the National Registry of CPE Sponsors. State boards of accountancy have final authority on the acceptance of individual courses for CPE credit. Complaints regarding registered sponsors may be addressed to the National Registry of CPE Sponsors, 150 Fourth Avenue North, Suite 700, Nashville, TN 37219-2417. Web site: www.nasba.org.

CCH is registered with the National Association of State Boards of Accountancy (NASBA) as a Quality Assurance Service (QAS) sponsor of continuing professional education. State boards of accountancy have final authority on the acceptance of individual courses for CPE credit. Complaints regarding registered sponsors may be addressed to NASBA, 150 Fourth Avenue North, Suite 700, Nashville, TN 37219-2417. Web site: www.nasba.org.

CCH has been approved by the California Tax Education Council to offer courses that provide federal and state credit towards the annual "continuing education" requirement imposed by the State of California. A listing of additional requirements to register as a tax preparer may be obtained by contacting CTEC at P.O. Box 2890, Sacramento, CA, 95812-2890, toll-free by phone at (877) 850-2832, or on the Internet at www.ctec.org.

Processing Fee:	Recommended CPE:	Recommended CFP:
$84.00 for Module 1	7 hours for Module 1	3 hours for Module 1
$84.00 for Module 2	7 hours for Module 2	3 hours for Module 2
$60.00 for Module 3	5 hours for Module 3	2 hours for Module 3
$228.00 for all Modules	19 hours for all Modules	8 hours for all Modules
CTEC Course Number:	**CTEC Federal Hours:**	**CTEC California Hours:**
1075-CE-9841 for Module 1	3 hours for Module 1	N/A for Module 1
1075-CE-9838 for Module 2	3 hours for Module 2	N/A for Module 2
1075-CE-9842 for Module 3	2 hours for Module 3	N/A for Module 3
	8 hours for all Modules	N/A for all Modules

One **complimentary copy** of this course is provided with certain copies of CCH Federal Taxation publications. Additional copies of this course may be ordered for $39.00 each by calling 1-800-248-3248 (ask for product 0-4457-500).

Quizzer Questions: Module 1

1. The payroll tax holiday period that was to expire after 2011 has been recommended for extension through 2012 in the:

   a. *American Jobs Act*
   b. *Tax Relief, Unemployment Insurance Reauthorization, and Job Creation Act of 2010*
   c. *American Recovery and Reinvestment Act of 2009*

2. The 2010 Tax Relief Act extended the election to take an itemized deduction for state and local income taxes paid through the year:

   a. 2010
   b. 2011
   c. 2012

3. The maximum 2011 above-the-line deduction for qualified education expenses is:

   a. $2,000
   b. $4,000
   c. $5,000

4. An extra deduction that allows businesses to write off 100 percent of depreciable property costs in the year placed in service is called:

   a. First-year depreciation
   b. Accelerated depreciation
   c. Bonus depreciation

5. The higher limits for Code Sec. 179 expensing scheduled to expire after 2011 enable taxpayers to elect:

   a. To use bonus depreciation instead if the property is not qualifying
   b. To treat costs for qualifying property as expenses rather than capital expenditures
   c. To elect in which tax year the cost of the property can be deducted

6. The 100 percent income exclusion for stock acquired before January 1, 2012 applies to qualifying small business stock:

   a. Of S corporations and professional corporations
   b. Of C corporations having gross assets not exceeding $50 million
   c. Of any corporation as long as the shares are preferred stock

7. The EGTRRA provisions extended until the end of 2012 that enable married couples filing jointly to claim twice the basic standard deduction of single taxpayers are known as:

   a. Marriage penalty relief
   b. Spousal deduction
   c. Defense of marriage provisions

8. For 2011 and 2012, the maximum estate tax rate is:

   a. 0
   b. 25 percent
   c. 35 percent

9. Many of the provisions that are set to expire after 2012 were enacted as part of the *Economic Growth and Tax Relief Reconciliation Act of 2001* and the *Jobs and Growth Tax Relief Reconciliation Act of 2003*. *True or False?*

10. The health care reform package increases Medicare taxes for employers although the pay of higher-income individuals is not taxed additionally. *True or False?*

11. Which of the following is *not* one of the years in which major provisions of the health care reform package take effect?

    a. 2014
    b. 2016
    c. 2018

12. New and nongrandfathered health care plans must *now* comply with all of the following reform requirements *except:*

    a. No prior authorization is required for emergency services
    b. Paying an applicable large employer payment if the employer has more than 50 full-time equivalent employees
    c. They must not make employees pay cost-sharing for preventive services

13. By establishing a SIMPLE cafeteria plan, small employers can meet the health plan nondiscrimination requirements if the companies have fewer than:

    a. 10 employees
    b. 50 employees
    c. 100 employees

14. Grandfathered health plans lose their status if they:

    a. Increase employee copayments by any amount
    b. Raise deductibles on employee coverage by a significant amount
    c. Change their plan to increase benefits

15. The $2,000 "all-employee" insurance penalty for employers due to commence in 2014 applies only to employers of at least:

    a. 10 employees
    b. 25 employees
    c. 50 employees

16. Which health care exchange level offers participants 80 percent essential benefits coverage?

    a. Silver
    b. Gold
    c. Platinum

17. Generally, employer-sponsored health plans that existed as of March 23, 2010 are grandfathered from requirements of the *Patient Protection and Affordable Care Act of 2010*. This means employees can keep their coverage unless their employer loses the grandfather status. *True or False?*

18. The 3.8 percent unearned income Medicare contributions tax and 0.9 percent additional hospital insurance tax imposed starting in 2013 both apply to unearned income. *True or False?*

19. After 2013, the small employer tax credit will apply only to health insurance small employers purchase through a state-established insurance exchange. *True or False?*

20. For 2014, the individual mandate penalty will equal $250 or 3 percent of income. *True of False?*

21. Which of the following assets does **not** qualify for bonus depreciation?

   a. Property that must be depreciated using the MACRS alternative depreciation system

   b. MACRS recovery property with a depreciation period of 20 years or fewer

   c. Qualified leasehold improvement property

22. The bonus deduction is computed after the cost of an asset is reduced by any amount expensed under Code Sec. 179 and the amount of basis adjustments for tax credits such as the energy credit. **True or False?**

23. In order for the 100 percent bonus rate to apply, the original use of an asset must begin with the taxpayer:

   a. After December 31, 2007

   b. After September 8, 2010

   c. After December 31, 2010

24. The 100 percent bonus depreciation rate applies to qualifying property:

   a. Acquired after December 31, 2007, and placed in service before January 1, 2012

   b. Acquired after December 31, 2009, and placed in service before January 1, 2012

   c. Acquired after September 8, 2010, and placed in service before January 1, 2012

25. Property eligible for the 100 percent bonus rate is considered acquired when:

   a. Possession of the property is taken by the taxpayer

   b. The property is placed in service by the taxpayer

   c. The taxpayer pays for the property if the taxpayer uses the cash basis or incurs the cost of the property if the taxpayer uses the accrual basis

26. Property with a longer production period:

   a. Must be placed in service before January 1, 2013, in order to qualify for bonus depreciation at the 100 percent rate

   b. Must have a production period exceeding three years

   c. Must have a cost exceeding $5 million

27. Longer production property subject to a written, binding acquisition contract meets the acquisition date requirement applicable to the 100 percent bonus rate if the contract was entered into:

   a. After December 31, 2007, and before January 1, 2014
   b. After December 31, 2007, and before January 1, 2013
   c. After September 8, 2010, and before January 1, 2012

28. For purposes of the election to claim 100 percent bonus depreciation on a component of a self-constructed property, a *component* is any part used in the manufacture, construction, or production of the larger self-constructed property. The definition applies regardless of whether the component is the same as an asset for depreciation purposes or the same as the unit of property for purposes of other tax code sections. ***True or False?***

29. If a taxpayer begins constructing a machine on January 1, 2010, and places the machine in service on December 1, 2011:

   a. The machine and its components qualify for bonus depreciation at a 100 percent rate
   b. The taxpayer must make the component election in order for components of the machine acquired after September 8, 2010, to qualify for bonus depreciation at the 100 percent rate, whereas the remainder of the machine qualifies for bonus depreciation at the 50 percent rate
   c. Neither the machine nor its components qualifies for bonus depreciation

30. The bonus depreciation deduction:

   a. May be claimed on qualified retail improvement property and qualified restaurant property only if such property is also qualified leasehold improvement property
   b. Is not subject to ordinary income depreciation recapture
   c. May not be claimed on the carryover basis of property received in a like-kind exchange

31. A taxpayer may elect 50 percent bonus depreciation in place of 100 percent bonus depreciation for any class of property:

   a. Placed in service after September 8, 2010, and before January 1, 2012
   b. Other than the MACRS 5-year property class
   c. Placed in service in a tax year that includes September 9, 2010

32. If a taxpayer claims 100 percent bonus depreciation on a passenger automobile that is subject to the Code Sec. 280F depreciation caps and does not elect the safe harbor method, the depreciation deduction claimed on the taxpayer's return for each of the second through sixth years of the vehicle's depreciation period is equal to:

   a. The amount of the Code Sec. 280F annual cap that applies for the year
   b. $0
   c. $11,060

33. For a tax year beginning in 2010 or 2011, the maximum Section 179 deduction is equal to:

   a. $250,000
   b. $500,000
   c. $2 million

34. The election to expense qualified real property under Section 179:

   a. Applies to qualified leasehold improvements, qualified retail improvements, and qualified restaurant property placed in service in a tax year that begins in 2010 or 2011
   b. Is limited to $500,000 of qualified real property
   c. Was repealed because qualified real property is eligible for 100 percent bonus depreciation

35. The bonus deduction and Section 179 deduction:

   a. May be claimed on new or used property
   b. Are treated as depreciation deductions for recapture purposes
   c. Are subject to a taxable income limitation

Quizzer Questions: Module 2

36. Employers must report to their employees the cost of which of the following insurance types beginning for tax year 2012?

   a. Accidental death or dismemberment insurance
   b. Nonintegrated dental and vision insurance
   c. Employer-sponsored health insurance

37. In situations in which two or more persons qualify as payment settlement entities for any reportable payment transaction:

   a. Only the payment settlement entity that in fact makes the payment in settlement is obligated to report the payment
   b. The payment settlement entity that is obligated to make the report may absolve itself of liability by designating another qualifying entity to satisfy the reporting obligation
   c. The payment settlement entity that is obligated to make the report may not designate another qualifying entity to satisfy the reporting obligation

38. For each participating payee in a payment card transaction, reporting is required by gross amount in:

   a. The aggregate for the year
   b. The aggregate for the month and year
   c. The aggregate for the week, month, and year

39. Which of the following may qualify as a third-party payment network?

   a. A health care network
   b. An electronic payment facilitator
   c. An automated clearing house

40. For the foreign address exclusion to be considered as a participating payee:

   a. Foreign offices of U.S. domestic corporations are U.S. payors or middlemen
   b. Participating payees are excluded as long as they have foreign addresses
   c. State and federal governments, as well as their political subdivisions, are not U.S. payors or middlemen

41. Under the new broker reporting rules, stock in a dividend reinvestment program (DRP) is becoming a covered entity as of:

    a. January 1, 2011
    b. January 1, 2012
    c. January 1, 2013

42. Special broker reporting rules apply to each of the following *except:*

    a. RIC stock
    b. Wash sales
    c. Stock rights

43. The default method for reporting the basis of corporate stock is:

    a. The average basis method
    b. First-in, first-out (FIFO) method
    c. Specific identification method

44. Which of the following account types must file FBAR forms under the final Treasury regulations?

    a. Hedge fund accounts
    b. Private equity accounts
    c. Pension and welfare funds

45. The civil penalties for a *non-willful* failure to comply with the FBAR requirements include fines of:

    a. Up to $5,000
    b. Up to $10,000
    c. Up to $25,000

46. According to the IRS, the majority of paid federal income tax return preparers are:

    a. CPAs
    b. Unenrolled return preparers
    c. Tax law attorneys

47. As of October 2011, competency testing and continuing education for paid return preparers who are not CPAs, EAs, or attorneys is required under the:

    a. *American Recovery and Reinvestment Act of 2009*
    b. 2008 Taxpayer Bill of Rights
    c. Final Circular 230 regulations

48. The age requirement for obtaining a Preparer Tax Identification Number (PTIN) is

   a. 21
   b. 18
   c. There is no age requirement

49. Enrolled retirement plan agents may *not* represent taxpayers on:

   a. Matters related to Form 5500 filings
   b. Actuarial issues
   c. The Employee Plans Master program

50. Registered tax return preparers may *not* represent taxpayers before:

   a. Revenue agents
   b. Taxpayer Advocate Service
   c. IRS Appeals

51. Which of the following paid preparers must complete the IRS competency examination and continuing education requirements to obtain the designation registered tax return preparer or seek another designation?

   a. Unenrolled return preparers
   b. Enrolled agents
   c. CPAs

52. All preparers (unless specifically excluded) who prepare federal returns for compensation must have a Preparer Tax Identification Number (PTIN):

   a. Beginning January 1, 2011
   b. Beginning January 1, 2012
   c. Beginning January 1, 2013

53. Approved IRS hardship waivers to mandatory e-filing by specified tax return preparers are valid:

   a. For 30 days
   b. For one calendar year
   c. For two calendar years

54. Which of the following is *not* considered an IRS administrative exemption from mandatory e-filing for specified tax return preparers?

    a. Lack of a computer and tax preparation software
    b. Lack of eligibility due to having an IRS sanction
    c. Lack of a Social Security number of the specified return preparer because he or she is foreign

55. What is *not* a purpose of IRS in-person visits to return preparers?

    a. Verifying compliance with record retention requirements
    b. Distributing compact disks containing IRS Publication 1437 procedures for the e-file program
    c. Assessing preparer penalties when violations are found

56. Non-Form 1040 series preparers are exempt from IRS competency testing and continuing education. *True or False?*

57. A Preparer Tax Identification Number (PTIN) is the same as an Electronic Filing Identification Number (EFIN). *True or False?*

58. Final Circular 230 regulations extend the rules of practice before the IRS to all preparers who prepare federal returns for compensation. *True or False?*

59. Final Circular 230 regulations extend the practitioner privilege under Code Sec. 7525 to protect communications between a registered tax return preparer and a taxpayer. *True or False?*

60. Preparers who are state-certified preparers are automatically exempt from IRS competency testing and continuing education requirements. *True or False?*

61. The IRS developed a strategic plan to promote electronic filing and to strive toward a goal of e-filing 80 percent of tax and information returns as a result of the:

    a. *Homeownership and Business Assistance Act of 2009*
    b. *The IRS Restructuring and Reform Act of 1998*
    c. *e-Postcard Act of 2010*

62. Each of the following is a benefit of e-filing *except:*

   a. Voluntary, rather than mandated, participation in the program for all taxpayers

   b. Submission of increased information that can raise enforcement revenue

   c. Lower cost of processing returns for the IRS

63. Which of the following is *not* a category of Authorized e-file Provider?

   a. Transmitter

   b. Software Developer

   c. Modernized e-File System Provider

64. Taxpayers who prepare their own returns use the _____ e-signature process for signing returns and the Declaration of Taxpayer.

   a. Authorized tax return signer

   b. Self-Select PIN method

   c. Practitioner PIN method

65. The Volunteer Income Tax Assistance (VITA) program is directed to help taxpayers who:

   a. Need to file amended returns or file on a fiscal year basis

   b. Are low- or moderate-income filers

   c. Are filing returns for the first time

66. Mandatory e-filing is *not* required for a:

   a. Foreign corporation having assets of at least $10 million that files 300 returns

   b. Corporation having assets of less than $10 million

   c. Domestic corporation having assets of at least $10 million that files 250 returns

67. Certain exempt organizations may submit Form 990-N, the e-postcard, if the organizations have annual gross receipts of less than:

   a. $50,000

   b. $100,000

   c. $250,000

68. A partnership must e-file Form 1065 or 1065 B, as well as Schedules K-1, if over the course of the partnership's tax year, the partnership has more than:

   a. 50 partners
   b. 100 partners
   c. 250 partners

69. A specified tax return preparer is subject to mandatory e-filing if he or she reasonably expects to file at least _____ individual returns for the 2011 calendar year and at least _____ individual returns in subsequent years.

   a. 50; 2
   b. 75; 5
   c. 100; 11

70. The Electronic Tax Administration Advisory Committee (ETAAC) reported that one key to continued growth in individual e-filing is:

   a. Mandated e-filing requirement for preparers of individual returns
   b. Use of the AGI/PIN signature
   c. Mandating taxpayers who prepare tax returns using a computers to e-file their returns

Quizzer Questions: Module 3

71. Self-assessed taxes are those:

  a. Based on amounts reported on the taxpayer's tax return
  b. Based on determination the IRS makes after examinations
  c. Determined by the U.S. Tax Court

72. The IRS usually will withdraw its Notice of Federal Tax Lien if:

  a. The other creditors have priority over the IRS's tax lien in the taxpayer's assets
  b. The taxpayer enters an installment agreement to pay the liability
  c. The taxpayer sells the property subject to the lien

73. A levy on wages is:

  a. Noncontinuous
  b. Made only in cases when the assessment is on intangible property
  c. In effect from the date of the levy until the date of release

74. Reasonable collection potential (RCP) is calculated for purposes of:

  a. An offer in compromise based on doubt as to liability
  b. An offer in compromise based on doubt as to collectibility
  c. Any case of individual or business taxpayers in which there are no available financial statements

75. Which of the following is **not** a general type of effective tax administration offer in compromise?

  a. Individual economic hardship
  b. Business economic hardship
  c. Equity or public policy

76. An in-business trust fund express agreement is a type of:

  a. Installment agreement
  b. Offer in compromise
  c. Settlement agreement

77. If a taxpayer having tax liabilities exceeding $25,000 wishes to enter an installment agreement, the only type available is:

    a. Guaranteed installment agreement
    b. Installment agreement requiring financial analysis
    c. Streamlined installment agreement

78. Which type of collection appeal allows the taxpayer to appeal its decision to the Tax Court?

    a. Collection due process hearing (CDP)
    b. Equivalent hearing
    c. Collection appeals program (CAP) appeal

79. The IRS's collection powers do **not** include gathering information about the taxpayer from third parties. **True or False?**

80. A release of levy for economic hardship applies only to individual taxpayers. **True or False?**

81. Which of the following was **not** part of the Obama Administration's health care reform legislation?

    a. *Public Health Service Act*
    b. *Health Care and Education Reconciliation Act*
    c. *Patient Protection and Affordable Care Act*

82. Under the Patient Protection Act, health insurance exchanges established for employers having fewer than 100 employees are set to become operational by:

    a. January 1, 2012
    b. January 1, 2014
    c. January 1, 2018

83. Under the Consumer Operated and Oriented Plan (CO-OP) program:

    a. Coverage will be offered to individuals directly from Health and Human Services on a national level
    b. Grants or loans will be made to qualified nonprofit health insurance issuers who are granted exempt status
    c. Existing health insurance issuers may apply for exempt status as qualified nonprofit health insurance issuers

84. Under Code Sec. 6033(m), qualified nonprofit health insurance issuers must include on their returns:

    a. The issuer's reserves on hand and reserves required by the state
    b. Details about the health insurance market reforms for the issuers' states that were required by the *Public Health Service Act*
    c. Proof that the issuer's state has selected that issuer rather than another to carry out the reinsurance program

85. Business leagues such as chambers of commerce and boards of trade should direct their activities to the:

    a. Performance of services for individual members
    b. Improvement of business conditions of lines of business
    c. Benefit of businesses operated on a cooperative basis

86. Code Sec. 501(c)(3) nonprofit hospitals are prohibited from billing gross charges (such as those generated by chargemaster software) to patients qualifying for financial assistance under requirements of the:

    a. *Health Care and Education Reconciliation Act*
    b. *Medicare Modernization Act*
    c. *Patient Protection and Affordable Care Act*

87. If a hospital organization fails to meet the community health needs assessment requirements of Code Sec. 501(r)(3), the IRS may impose an excise tax of _____ for any applicable tax year.

    a. $10,000
    b. $25,000
    c. $50,000

88. Organizations exempt from filing a version of Form 990 include all of the following *except:*

    a. State institutions exempt from income tax under Code Sec. 115
    b. Private foundations whose funding comes from a small group of private sources
    c. U.S. instrumentalities created by Congress under Code Sec. 501(a)(1) or 501(1)

89. For tax year 2010, exempt organizations at or above these limits had to file Form 990:

    a. Organizations with gross receipts of more than $200,000 and total assets of more than $500,000
    b. Organizations with gross receipts totaling more than $500,000 and total assets of more than $1 million
    c. Organizations with gross receipts of more than $750,000 and total assets of more than $5 million

90. The threshold of gross receipts below which exempt organizations are required to file returns electronically was raised in 2010 to:

    a. $10,000
    b. $25,000
    c. $50,000

91. Under Code Sec. 4958, an excise tax is payable by a disqualified person or organization manager who participates in an excess benefit transaction that benefits a private shareholder or individual. *True or False?*

92. Business leagues seeking tax-exempt status may not include in membership tradespeople, spouses of members of another league, or cooperatives. *True or False?*

93. All hospitals are assumed to be Code Sec. 501(c)(3) charitable organizations unless they are part of a multifacility chain of providers. *True or False?*

94. The IRS has found individual credit unions liable for unrelated business income tax (UBIT), although Congress has not acted to repeal Code Sec. 501(c)(14) rules for credit unions in general. *True or False?*

95. The IRS has been following a practice of revoking the tax-exempt status rather than simply imposing the excise tax on credit unions conducting prolonged unrelated business activities. *True or False?*

TOP FEDERAL TAX ISSUES FOR 2012 CPE COURSE   (0759-3)

Module 1: Answer Sheet

NAME _____

COMPANY NAME _____

STREET _____

CITY, STATE, & ZIP CODE _____

BUSINESS PHONE NUMBER _____

E-MAIL ADDRESS _____

DATE OF COMPLETION _____

CFP REGISTRANT ID (for Certified Financial Planners) _____

CRTP ID (for CTEC Credit only) _____ (CTEC Course # 1075-CE-9841)

On the next page, please answer the Multiple Choice questions by indicating the appropriate letter next to the corresponding number. Please answer the True/False questions by marking "T" or "F" next to the corresponding number.

A $84.00 processing fee wil be charged for each user submitting Module 2 for grading.

Please remove both pages of the Answer Sheet from this book and return them with your completed Evaluation Form to CCH at the address below. You may also fax your Answer Sheet to CCH at 773-866-3084.

You may also go to **www.CCHGroup.com/TestingCenter** to complete your Quizzer online.

METHOD OF PAYMENT:

☐ Check Enclosed   ☐ Visa   ☐ Master Card   ☐ AmEx

☐ Discover   ☐ CCH Account* _____

Card No. _____ Exp. Date _____

Signature _____

* Must provide CCH account number for this payment option

EXPRESS GRADING: Please fax my Course results to me by 5:00 p.m. the business day following your receipt of this Answer Sheet. By checking this box I authorize CCH to charge $19.00 for this service.

☐ Express Grading $19.00   Fax No. _____

CCH
a Wolters Kluwer business

Mail or fax to:
CCH Continuing Education Department
4025 W. Peterson Ave.
Chicago, IL 60646-6085
1-800-248-3248
Fax: 773-866-3084   PAGE 1 OF 2

TOP FEDERAL TAX ISSUES FOR 2012 CPE COURSE   (0759-3)

Module 1: Answer Sheet

Please answer the Multiple Choice questions by indicating the appropriate letter next to the corresponding number. Please answer the True/False questions by marking "T" or "F" next to the corresponding number.

1. ___	10. ___	19. ___	28. ___
2. ___	11. ___	20. ___	29. ___
3. ___	12. ___	21. ___	30. ___
4. ___	13. ___	22. ___	31. ___
5. ___	14. ___	23. ___	32. ___
6. ___	15. ___	24. ___	33. ___
7. ___	16. ___	25. ___	34. ___
8. ___	17. ___	26. ___	35. ___
9. ___	18. ___	27. ___	

Please complete the Evaluation Form (located after the Module 3 Answer Sheet) and return it with this Quizzer Answer Sheet to CCH at the address on the previous page. Thank you.

TOP FEDERAL TAX ISSUES FOR 2012 CPE COURSE   (0760-3)

Module 2: Answer Sheet

NAME _____

COMPANY NAME _____

STREET _____

CITY, STATE, & ZIP CODE _____

BUSINESS PHONE NUMBER _____

E-MAIL ADDRESS _____

DATE OF COMPLETION _____

CFP REGISTRANT ID (for Certified Financial Planners) _____

CRTP ID (for CTEC Credit only) _____ (CTEC Course # 1075-CE-9838)

On the next page, please answer the Multiple Choice questions by indicating the appropriate letter next to the corresponding number. Please answer the True/False questions by marking "T" or "F" next to the corresponding number.

A $84.00 processing fee wil be charged for each user submitting Module 2 for grading.

Please remove both pages of the Answer Sheet from this book and return them with your completed Evaluation Form to CCH at the address below. You may also fax your Answer Sheet to CCH at 773-866-3084.

You may also go to **www.CCHGroup.com/TestingCenter** to complete your Quizzer online.

METHOD OF PAYMENT:

☐ Check Enclosed   ☐ Visa   ☐ Master Card   ☐ AmEx

☐ Discover   ☐ CCH Account* _____

Card No. _____ Exp. Date _____

Signature _____

* Must provide CCH account number for this payment option

EXPRESS GRADING: Please fax my Course results to me by 5:00 p.m. the business day following your receipt of this Answer Sheet. By checking this box I authorize CCH to charge $19.00 for this service.

☐ Express Grading $19.00   Fax No. _____

●.CCH
®
a Wolters Kluwer business

Mail or fax to:
CCH Continuing Education Department
4025 W. Peterson Ave.
Chicago, IL 60646-6085
1-800-248-3248
Fax: 773-866-3084

TOP FEDERAL TAX ISSUES FOR 2012 CPE COURSE   (0760-3)

Module 2: Answer Sheet

Please answer the Multiple Choice questions by indicating the appropriate letter next to the corresponding number. Please answer the True/False questions by marking "T" or "F" next to the corresponding number.

36. ___	45. ___	54. ___	63. ___
37. ___	46. ___	55. ___	64. ___
38. ___	47. ___	56. ___	65. ___
39. ___	48. ___	57. ___	66. ___
40. ___	49. ___	58. ___	67. ___
41. ___	50. ___	59. ___	68. ___
42. ___	51. ___	60. ___	69. ___
43. ___	52. ___	61. ___	70. ___
44. ___	53. ___	62. ___	

Please complete the Evaluation Form (located after the Module 3 Answer Sheet) and return it with this Quizzer Answer Sheet to CCH at the address on the previous page. Thank you.

TOP FEDERAL TAX ISSUES FOR 2012 CPE COURSE   (0761-3)

Module 3: Answer Sheet

NAME _____

COMPANY NAME _____

STREET _____

CITY, STATE, & ZIP CODE _____

BUSINESS PHONE NUMBER _____

E-MAIL ADDRESS _____

DATE OF COMPLETION _____

CFP REGISTRANT ID (for Certified Financial Planners) _____

CRTP ID (for CTEC Credit only) _____ (CTEC Course # 1075-CE-9842)

On the next page, please answer the Multiple Choice questions by indicating the appropriate letter next to the corresponding number. Please answer the True/False questions by marking "T" or "F" next to the corresponding number.

A $60.00 processing fee wil be charged for each user submitting Module 2 for grading.

Please remove both pages of the Answer Sheet from this book and return them with your completed Evaluation Form to CCH at the address below. You may also fax your Answer Sheet to CCH at 773-866-3084.

You may also go to **www.CCHGroup.com/TestingCenter** to complete your Quizzer online.

METHOD OF PAYMENT:

☐ Check Enclosed   ☐ Visa   ☐ Master Card   ☐ AmEx

☐ Discover   ☐ CCH Account* _____

Card No. _____ Exp. Date _____

Signature _____

* Must provide CCH account number for this payment option

EXPRESS GRADING: Please fax my Course results to me by 5:00 p.m. the business day following your receipt of this Answer Sheet. By checking this box I authorize CCH to charge $19.00 for this service.

☐ Express Grading $19.00   Fax No. _____

.CCH
a Wolters Kluwer business

Mail or fax to:
CCH Continuing Education Department
4025 W. Peterson Ave.
Chicago, IL 60646-6085
1-800-248-3248
Fax: 773-866-3084

TOP FEDERAL TAX ISSUES FOR 2012 CPE COURSE   (0761-3)

Module 3: Answer Sheet

Please answer the Multiple Choice questions by indicating the appropriate letter next to the corresponding number. Please answer the True/False questions by marking "T" or "F" next to the corresponding number.

71. ____	78. ____	84. ____	90. ____
72. ____	79. ____	85. ____	91. ____
73. ____	80. ____	86. ____	92. ____
74. ____	81. ____	87. ____	93. ____
75. ____	82. ____	88. ____	94. ____
76. ____	83. ____	89. ____	95. ____
77. ____			

Please complete the Evaluation Form (located after the Module 3 Answer Sheet) and return it with this Quizzer Answer Sheet to CCH at the address on the previous page. Thank you.